THE PROFESSIONAL RISK MANAGERS' GUIDE TO FINANCIAL MARKETS

Other PRMIA Institute Books

The Professional Risk Managers' Guide to Finance Theory
Edited by Carol Alexander and Elizabeth Sheedy

The Professional Risk Managers' Guide to Financial Instruments
Edited by Carol Alexander and Elizabeth Sheedy

The Professional Risk Managers' Guide to Energy Markets
Edited by Peter C. Fusaro

THE PROFESSIONAL RISK MANAGERS' GUIDE TO FINANCIAL MARKETS

Edited by
CAROL ALEXANDER
and
ELIZABETH SHEEDY

McGraw-Hill

New York   Chicago   San Francisco
Lisbon   London   Madrid   Mexico City
Milan   New Delhi   San Juan   Seoul
Singapore   Sydney   Toronto

1 2 3 4 5 6 7 8 9 0   FGR/FGR   0 9 8 7

ISBN: 978-0-07-154648-5
MHID: 0-07-154648-0

This publication is designed to provide accurate and authoritative information in regard to the subject matter covered. It is sold with the understanding that neither the author nor the publisher is engaged in rendering legal, accounting, futures/securities trading, or other professional service. If legal advice or other expert assistance is required, the services of a competent professional person should be sought.
—From a Declaration of Principles jointly adopted by a Committee
of the American Bar Association and a Committee of Publishers

McGraw-Hill books are available at special quantity discounts to use as premiums and sales promotions, or for use in corporate training programs. For more information, please write to the Director of Special Sales, Professional Publishing, McGraw-Hill, Two Penn Plaza, New York, NY 10121-2298. Or contact your local bookstore.

This book is printed on acid-free paper.

CONTENTS

ABOUT THE CONTRIBUTORS   ix

Chapter 1

The Structure of Financial Markets   1

Introduction   1
Global Markets and Their Terminology   2
Drivers of Liquidity   9
Liquidity and Financial Risk Management   13
Exchanges versus OTC Markets   15
Technological Change   17
Post-Trade Processing   21
Retail and Wholesale Brokerage   23
New Financial Markets   25
Conclusions   28
References   30
Notes   30

Chapter 2

The Money Markets   31

Introduction   31
Characteristics of Money Market Instruments   32
Deposits and Loans   33
Money Market Securities   40
Conclusions   45
Reference   46
Notes   46

Chapter 3

Bond Markets   49

Introduction   49
The Players   51
Bonds by Issuers   53

The Markets   63
Credit Risk   69
Conclusions   73
References   73
Notes   73

Chapter 4

The Foreign Exchange Market   75

Introduction   75
Exchange-Rate Quotations   77
Determinants of Foreign Exchange Rates   82
Spot and Forward Markets   86
Structure of a Foreign Exchange Operation   92
Conclusions   95
Reference   96
Notes   96

Chapter 5

The Stock Market   99

Introduction   99
The Characteristics of Common Stock   101
Stock Markets and their Participants   108
The Primary Market—IPOs and Private Placements   111
The Secondary Market—the Exchange versus OTC Market   113
Trading Costs   115
Buying on Margin   117
Short Sales and Stock Borrowing Costs   119
Exchange-Traded Derivatives on Stocks   121
Conclusions   123
References and Bibliography   123

Chapter 6

The Futures Markets   125

Introduction   125
History of Forward-Based Derivatives and Futures Markets   126
Futures Contracts and Markets   128

Options on Futures   142
Futures Exchanges and Clearing Houses   149
Market Participants—Hedgers   155
Market Participants—Speculators   160
Market Participants—Managed Futures Investors   163
Conclusions   164
References   166
Notes   166

Chapter 7

The Structure of Commodities Markets   167

Introduction   167
The Commodity Universe and Anatomy of Markets   168
Spot–Forward Pricing Relationships   177
Short Squeezes, Corners, and Regulation   184
Risk Management at the Commodity Trading Desk   187
The Distribution of Commodity Returns   196
Conclusions   197
References   199
Notes   199

Chapter 8

The Energy Markets   203

Introduction   203
Market Overview   204
Energy Futures Markets   208
OTC Energy Derivative Markets   222
Emerging Energy Markets   229
The Future of Energy Trading   236
Conclusions   239
References   240
Notes   240

INDEX   241

Canadian Securities Institute, Toronto, Canada

Moorad Choudhry is Head of Treasury at KBC Financial Products in London and is a Visiting Professor, Department of Economics, Finance and International Business, London Metropolitan University, UK.

Peter C. Fusaro is Chairman of Global Change Associates Inc, an energy and environmental advisory in New York (www.global-change.com).

Colin Lawrence, Ph.D., is based in Beijing where he is Financial Risk Management and Compliance Leader, IBM Global Business Services, Greater China Group and Asia Pacific. He is also Visiting Professor, Cass Business School, City University, London, UK.

Lionel Martellini, Ph.D., is a Professor of Finance at EDHEC Graduate School of Business, and the Scientific Director of EDHEC Risk and Asset Management Research Center (www.edhec-risk.com), Nice, France.

Alistair Milne, Ph.D., is Senior Lecturer, Faculty of Finance, Cass Business School, London, UK

Philippe Priaulet, Ph.D., is the Head of Relative Value at Natixis (Paris), and an Associate Professor in the Department of Mathematics of the University of Evry, France

Andrew Street, Ph.D., is the Managing Director, Value Consultants Limited, London, UK

CHAPTER 1

The Structure of Financial Markets

Colin Lawrence and Alistair Milne

INTRODUCTION

This chapter provides a general overview of the global markets for financial securities and derivatives, examining the different ways they are organized and operated, and the arrangements that support them. Subsequent chapters (2–7) will examine in greater detail the markets for: money, bonds, foreign exchange, stocks, futures, commodities, and energy.

Market structure is important to risk managers primarily through its impact on liquidity. A successful market, whether or not it exists in a physical location, brings together many buyers and sellers and is able to reduce search and transaction costs. Such a market provides the best possible conditions for financial risk management. Institutional arrangements for trading are crucial in achieving large volumes, good liquidity, and thus promoting effective risk management.

Risk managers should concern themselves with market structure because it can also affect other aspects of risk, including credit risk, business risks, operational risk and basis risk. For example, trades on over-the-counter markets often have greater credit risk than those transacted on exchanges, but, because they can be tailored to individual requirements, they have less basis risk. An example of business risk is the capture of trading by electronic communications networks, reducing the order volumes and revenues of NASDAQ dealer-brokers.

The next section defines some important terms for market structure and provides an overview of the most important markets worldwide. The following two sections discuss the main theme of this chapter, liquidity. They examine the key drivers of liquidity and the importance of liquidity for risk management, respectively. The next section analyzes the differences between trading on and off an exchange, while the following section examines the impact of new technology on markets. The link between operational risk and market structure is made in the next section, which discusses post-trade processing. The final two sections, prior to the Conclusions, deal with the intermediary role of brokers in markets and new markets.

GLOBAL MARKETS AND THEIR TERMINOLOGY

Trading of financial securities, derivatives, and other financial contracts takes place in two settings: formal financial exchanges and more loosely organized over-the-counter (OTC) markets.

Financial exchanges are formalized trading institutions. Rights to trade are limited to members, and there are detailed and explicit rules governing the conduct of trade and the contracts or securities that are traded. Exchanges also collect and disseminate pricing information, and facilitate post-trade risk management and final trade settlement. OTC refers to any financial market transaction that does not take place on a formal exchange. The attraction of an OTC trade is that the buyer and seller are free to negotiate all the contractual details. But participants do not have the protection of exchange procedures and rules.

Most equity trading takes place through exchanges. The principle that liquidity is linked to market volumes can be illustrated in equity markets. Table 1.1 presents statistics on the major equity markets. The bulk of equity trading, worldwide, is concentrated in a few major markets, mostly equity exchanges such as the NYSE, NASDAQ and the London Stock Exchange. The five leading markets account for more than sixty percent of equity market capitalization and equity trading.

Recently there has been a trend towards consolidation of these major exchanges. NYSE has merged with EuroNext, the London Stock Exchange is in the process of acquiring Borsa Italia, and other mergers have been mooted. These mergers are not yet having a major impact on the conduct

T A B L E   1.1

Key statistics for the principal global equity markets

2006	Market Cap (End Year), $US Trillion	Average Daily Turnover, $US Billion	Average Transaction Value, $US Thousand
NYSE	15.4	86.8	17.2
Tokyo	4.6	23.5	n/a
NASDAQ	3.9	47.0	9.0
London Stock Exchange	3.8	30.0	79.9
Euronext	3.7	15.1	36.6
Hong-Kong Exchanges	1.7	3.4	18.5
TSX group (Toronto)	1.7	5.1	13.9
Deutsche Börse	1.6	10.8	25.1
Other N. America	0.6	2.8	
Other European	5.5	27.7	
Emerging markets	14.1	56.5	
Total	50.6	278.3	

Source: World Federation of Exchanges and authors' calculations

of equity trading. There are substantial barriers, notably regulation and clearing and settlement, that force these merged entities to continue operating on a separate basis. However, if these barriers are overcome, technological merger of activities will then be possible and we will see truly global equity exchanges.

We will now look at other major financial markets for debt, foreign exchange, and derivatives, and examine how these activities are split between exchanges and OTC markets. Early markets for foreign exchange were the prototype for OTC arrangements. A market was established at a location where buyers and sellers of currency could approach established dealers and search for the best available exchange rate. Modern OTC markets rely on telephone and screen to link buyers and sellers with the market dealers, but the basics of the market remain the same. Dealers quote both bid and ask prices to prospective buyers and sellers. Dealers make a profit from order flow, both directly from the bid–ask spread, and also by anticipating short-term price movements using their privileged access to information on orders. But the dealer is also exposed to market risk from its holding of an inventory of currencies.

In such OTC markets a key role in the transfer of risk is often played by the "inter-dealer broker," perhaps better referred to as the dealer's broker—specialized firms where dealers may offload or purchase inventory. They, together with the continuous process of search by buyers and sellers, are the mechanism linking the market together.

Market makers also operate in exchanges, notably the "specialists" in the New York Stock Exchange, but, as we will discuss later, almost all security exchanges have found it more efficient to replace dealer market making with electronic order books.

Table 1.2 shows statistics on the size of global debt markets. These are values of the issued principal, not market values, and therefore not strictly comparable with equity market capitalizations shown in Table 1.1. Nevertheless they indicate that, taking account of government and financial institution debt (including the issue by banks of many kinds of asset-backed securities), the stock of debt on the market is considerably larger than that of equity.

Table 1.3 shows the market capitalization of bonds listed on principal exchanges. This is only a fraction of total market debt, with a large

T A B L E   1.2

Stock of international and domestic market debt, par values at end of December 2006 (US$ trillion)

	All Maturities			Remaining Maturity < 12 months		
	Domestic	International	Total	Domestic	International	Total
Government	24.0	2.2	26.2	6.2	0.2	6.4
Financial institutions	20.5	14.4	34.9	6.1	2.4	8.5
Corporate sector	5.7	1.9	7.6	0.8	0.2	1.0
Total	50.3	18.4	68.7	13.1	2.8	15.9

Source: Bank for International Settlements Quarterly Review, June 2007, Tables 12, 16, 17

T A B L E   1.3

Market capitalization of bonds listed on principal exchanges
(US$ trillion)

	Luxembourg	Osaka	Tokyo	London	Italy
Domestic public sector	0.0	4.8	4.7	0.8	1.1
Domestic private sector	0.2	0.1	0.0	1.4	0.1
Foreign	7.3	0.0	0.0	1.3	0.0
Total	7.5	4.8	4.7	3.5	1.2

Source: World Federation of Exchanges

concentration of issuance on the Luxembourg exchange, reflecting the importance of this listing for international bonds traded in Europe. Much debt, notably most corporate and financial institution debt issued in the USA, is not exchange listed (all that is required in this market is satisfaction of relevant SEC regulations).

With the exception of some government bonds, debt is traded on OTC markets rather than on exchanges. This is the case even when, as is usual in Europe, bonds are listed on an exchange. Issuers find it worthwhile to have a listing, demonstrating that they have satisfied certain exchange rules about accounting and other disclosure standards, even when trading itself still takes place outside of the exchange.

Table 1.4 shows trading volume statistics on another major OTC market, that for foreign exchange. These figures are for daily turnover,

T A B L E   1.4

Daily foreign exchange turnover, April 2007 (US$ billion)

Spot	1,005
Forward	362
Foreign exchange swaps	1,714
Total	3,081

Source: BIS triennial survey, 2007, Preliminary Gobal Results, Table 2, reporting gaps omitted

during the month of April 2004, for spot transactions, forward transactions and foreign exchange swaps (the combination of spot and offsetting forward position treated as a single transaction). This is an example of a very liquid market; the value of total foreign exchange trading of these three types of contract is approximately 10 times the combined value of trading on the world's equity markets.

Table 1.5 shows nominal and gross market values for OTC derivatives. Some, but not all, derivatives (including interest-rate swaps and the new market for credit derivatives) are OTC traded. Nominal contract values can be extremely large, notably for interest-rate swaps with notional outstanding principal of over US$90 trillion. Gross market values (the sum of the absolute market value of contracts) are a better indication of the size and importance of these markets; the gross market value of interest-rate swaps, for example, is still small compared to the nearly $50bn of outstanding market debt shown in Table 1.2.

Tables 1.6a–6c show the number of contracts traded on the principal derivative exchanges. These tables illustrate the tendency for trading of

TABLE 1.5

Major OTC derivatives, December 2006

	Notional Amounts, $US trillion	Gross Market Values, $US billion
Interest-rate swaps	229.8	4,116
Interest-rate options	43.5	636
Forward rate agreements	18.7	31
Currency forwards and foreign exchange swaps	19.8	467
Currency swaps	10.8	599
Currency options	9.6	196
Equity derivatives	7.5	851
Commodity derivatives	6.9	667
Single name credit default swaps	18.9	289
Multiple name credit default swaps	10.0	181
Other (including CDOs)	39.8	1,610
Total	169.7	4,029

Source: BIS quarterly review, June 2007, Table 19

T A B L E   1.6a

Principal exchanges for equity derivatives

	Individual Equity	Equity Index	
Millions of contracts traded: 2006	Options	Options	Futures
American Stock Exchange	187.0	10.0	–
Boston Options Exchange	92.3	–	–
Chicago Board Options Exchange	390.7	279.0	28.7
Chicago Mercantile Exchange	–	27.3	470.2
International Securities Exchange	583.7	8.2	–
EUREX	272.5	217.2	270.1
Euronext	155.5	50.3	72.1
Pacific Stock Exchange	196.6	–	–
Philadelphia Stock Exchange	265.4	7.6	–
Sao Paolo Stock Exchange	285.7	1.8	–
Korean Stock Exchange	1.2	2,414.4	46.7
Worldwide	2,070	3,282.3	531.3

Source: World Federation of Exchanges.

T A B L E   1.6b

Principal exchanges for fixed-income derivatives

	Government Debt		Interest Rate	
Millions of contracts traded: 2006	Options	Futures	Options	Futures
Australian Stock Exchange	3.1	45.1	–	22.9
Chicago Board of Trade	95.7	512.2	9.4	17.8
Chicago Mercantile Exchange	–	–	269.0	503.7
EUREX	76.3	654.1	–	–
Euronext	–	23.2	93.0	296.0
Korean Futures Exchange	–	10.3	–	–
Tokyo Financial Exchange	2.1	–	4.0	31.5
BM&F (Brazil)	–	–	10.5	180.8
Worldwide	177.2	1,271.4	386.8	1,349.7

Source: World Federation of Exchanges.
Figures of less than 1 million omitted from tabulation.

T A B L E 1.6c

Principal exchanges for currency/commodity derivatives

Millions of contracts traded: 2002	Currency		Commodity	
	Options	Futures	Options	Futures
BM&F (Brazil)	10.5	–	–	–
Budapest	–	10.0	–	–
Chicago Board of Trade	–	–	21.9	118.7
Chicago Mercantile Exchange	3.3	110.3	–	17.4
Dalian Commodity Exchange	–	–	–	117.7
ICE Futures	–	–	–	92.6
London Metal Exchange	–	–	8.4	78.5
Mercado a Término de Buenos Aires	–	–	–	11.9
	–			
MexDer (Mexico)	–	6.1	–	–
NY Board of Trade	–	3.7	11.7	28.2
NY Mercantile Exchange	–	–	54.4	178.9
Rofex (Argentina)	–	17.9	–	–
Shanghai Futures Exchange	–	–	–	58.1
Tel-Aviv Stock Exchange	7.4	–	–	–
Tokyo Grain Exchange	–	–	–	19.1
Zhengzhou Commodity Exchange	–	–	–	46.3
Worldwide	23.2	158.4	102.9	794.1

Source: World Federation of Exchanges.

Figures of less than 3 million (10 million for commodity futures) are omitted from tabulation.

particular contracts to concentrate on a small subset of exchanges. Thus equity index options are mostly traded on the Chicago Board Options Exchange, EUREX, and Euronext (Table 1.6a). Government debt contracts are mostly traded on EUREX and the Chicago Board of Trade, while interest-rate contracts are mostly traded on EUREX and the Chicago Mercantile Exchange (Table 1.6b).

This feature, the concentration of trading in particular trading arenas, is also apparent when comparing OTC and exchange-traded derivatives. Prominent OTC derivatives such as interest-rate swaps are traded in a few centers (concentrated in London and New York), while there is no equivalent exchange-traded contract. The vast majority of currency derivatives are traded OTC (currency forwards dwarf currency futures).

DRIVERS OF LIQUIDITY

The previous section shows that trading activity tends to concentrate in particular markets. Why is this so?

Historically, financial markets have developed in particular locations, for example, in the coffee shops and alleyways of Venice, London, and Amsterdam. Many of the earliest financial markets were for exchange of coin. Early markets for government bonds and shares operated in a similar fashion. The best prices and most reliable contracting, for both buyers and sellers, could be found in the established trading locations with greatest trading volumes. Liquidity—the promise of the best pricing with the least search effort—attracts more buyers and sellers. The presence of many buyers and sellers generates higher trading volumes which further narrows the gap between the prices for buying and selling (the "bid–ask spread"). This virtuous circle of liquidity/trading volumes has been a driving force for the development of financial markets, both historically and in the recent past.

As we discuss in this chapter there is a considerable variety in the way that markets are organized, from formalized exchanges to informal OTC markets (see below). There is also great variety in the mechanics of trading: in some markets computer technology matches buyers and sellers; while in others human beings still bring together market participants (see the section on technological change). But, although the technology of financial markets is often very different today from in the past, liquidity continues to be the primary driver of market development. Thus, while there is a general trend towards greater use of information technology to lower costs, a variety of different market arrangements can still succeed in capturing liquidity.

Automated trading systems are now common in both securities and derivatives trading (see below and Chapter 6). Outside of the USA the great majority of equity trading has now shifted from dealer-based market making onto electronic order books, such as the London Stock Exchange SETS system. We describe the operation of such systems in the section on technological change. Although these automated matching systems operate very differently from dealer markets, they still result in the same kind of trade-off between pricing and liquidity as in dealer markets. The amount of order flow placed on the order book is the key factor in determining liquidity, just as normal market size predicts liquidity in a dealer market. The greater the order flow, the more likely it is that large trades can be transacted without adverse price impact. Also, for illiquid stocks with relatively little order flow, the gap between limit-sell and limit-buy prices is usually comparatively large.

Occasionally one marketplace can succeed in capturing liquidity from another. The best-known recent example is when the Swiss-German derivatives exchange EUREX, taking advantage of its lower-cost automated trading system, captured the trade in German government bond futures contracts from the London LIFFE derivatives exchange (see the section on technological change for more detail on this episode). Subsequently, even when LIFFE adopted automated trading technologies as efficient as those of EUREX, it was unable to recapture the liquidity in this market. The shift in market liquidity was permanent.

Differences in liquidity can be especially pronounced when comparing individual securities. Table 1.7 compares two measures of liquidity for two dealer-traded shares, normal market size (NMS) and the bid–ask spread. Normal market size is the maximum size of transaction at which a dealer is prepared to transact at the stated bid (buying) and ask (selling) prices.

While these figures are not for actual stocks, they are representative of highly liquid and illiquid stocks traded in the major trading centers. They illustrate the marked difference in transaction costs (as represented by the final column, the bid–ask spread as a percentage of the mid-price) between the two groups. The liquid stocks generally have larger market capitalization and also have larger normal market size for transactions (although these are a relatively small proportion of total market capitalization).

Liquidity risk is also linked with perceived credit risk on individual securities. Compare markets for otherwise similar securities with different degrees of credit risk, for example BBB corporate bonds and AA corporate bonds. Credit risk is difficult to assess and so securities with lower

T A B L E   1.7

An example of dealer-traded liquid and illiquid stocks

Stock	Market Cap US $ million	NMS US $ thousand	Bid	Ask	Spread %
A—liquid	10,000	200.0	9.43	9.45	0.21
B—illiquid	1	0.1	2.50	3.50	33.00

credit risk are seen as more homogeneous and can be bought and sold more easily and in larger quantities without a substantial price impact.

This relative lack of liquidity is reflected in "credit" spreads over risk-free government bonds. Credit spreads on BBB bonds are much higher than those on AA bonds, a difference that cannot be fully explained by the higher historical rates of default on BBB bonds. This difference in liquidity was particularly evident during the "flight to quality" in 1998 following the Russian default, when spreads on liquid exposures (AAA and AA bonds) narrowed while at the same time spreads on BBB bonds substantially widened. This divergence underscores the importance of liquidity risk to a risk manager and of understanding how the organization of markets can affect liquidity risks.

There is also a close link between funding and liquidity, which has the tendency of pushing trading activity and price formation from cash onto derivatives markets. This is apparent, for example, in the much greater depth and liquidity of the interest-rate swap market compared to government bond markets. Taking a position in interest-rate swaps involves no exchange of principal, and hence no funding beyond any initial margin. Taking an equivalent position in the cash markets would require a large amount of capital funding. Hence market participants taking short-term positions almost always prefer to transact on the derivative rather than the cash market, and so trading and liquidity and best pricing all migrate onto the derivative interest-rate swap market (and other exchange-traded fixed-income derivative markets). A similar phenomenon can be observed in the greater liquidity of many credit derivatives, relative to underlying corporate or sovereign securities. This liquidity advantage is the reason for transacting on theoretically redundant derivative markets. Cash and derivative markets have a symbiotic relationship, with prices moving closely together and any remaining discrepancy in pricing reflecting differences in liquidity and transactions costs.

Repo Markets

Liquidity can also be created through the removal of credit (counterparty) risk, most notably in money markets through the use of the "sale and repurchase agreement" or repo. The repo is a short-term contract in which one party agrees to sell a security (most often a high-quality bond such as a government bond or AAA corporate bond) to another party (the lender) and then repurchase it subsequently at a higher price. Any coupon or dividend payments are still paid to the original owner, not the temporary purchaser of the security. (For a more detailed descriptions of repo trans-actions than we are able to give here, see Steiner (1997) and Choudhry (2002).)

To take a simple example, a creditor might agree with a bank to sell a quantity of government bonds for $100 and to repurchase them three months later for $101. This is effectively a loan of $100 with a quarterly interest payment of $1 (equivalent to an annual interest rate of just over 4%). The advantage of borrowing via a repo instead of using a conven-tional loan is that, provided the borrower has acceptable securities to pledge, they can borrow at close to a risk-free rate of interest (risk is almost entirely removed by requiring that the market value of the bonds used as collateral be substantially above the amount borrowed, thus the bonds might have a market value of $110 for this loan of $100, a "hair cut" of 10%).

In developed money markets repos can be conducted over the whole range of maturities, from overnight to many months. Because they signif-icantly reduce counterparty exposure, repos are the preferred form of transaction for many money market participants. They are used by central banks to conduct their short-term borrowing and lending so as to make monetary policy effective (market operations). The reduction of counter-party risk and consequent interest-rate reduction makes repo the preferred transaction for corporate borrowers; only if they are unable to pledge high-quality securities for repo borrowing will they take up other forms of borrowing such as issue of commercial paper, the drawdown of bank lines of credit, or (in the case of financial institutions) interbank borrowing. Furthermore, there are a variety of repo and reverse repo transactions which vary with time, duration and the specific collateral that is pledged (including stocks, bonds, and commodities). Repo financing offers an efficient vehicle for fund managers to finance their securities, thus enabling leverage.

Repos are also used for the "shorting" of securities (since every repo involves as its counterpart a security loan). The way this is done is through a "reverse repo," that is, acting on the other side of a repo contract, accept-ing the loan of a particular security, and then immediately selling that security.

Thus, for example, to short $1m of bonds issued by Daimler-Chrysler for a period of 1 month, from April 1 to April 30, a market par-ticipant would first lend, say, $975,000 to some counterparty in return for a pledge of the $1m worth of Daimler-Chrysler bonds. The Daimler-Chrysler bonds would then immediately be sold for $1m. In order to unwind the repo contract a month later, the bonds would have to be repurchased at the end-of-month market price. The overall deal will make a profit or a loss, depending upon how much Daimler-Chrysler bonds have fallen or risen in price over the month. If the bonds have fallen a lot in value then it will cost relatively little to repurchase at the end of the month and the shorting position will make an overall profit.

The development of repo contracts has added to the liquidity of money markets and, by making it easier to "short-sell" securities, has also encouraged the closer integration of cash and derivatives markets. Indeed, repos play a crucial role in the pricing of all fixed-income derivatives. For example, in pricing a total return swap or credit default swap, traders or dealers will have to hedge these positions. Financing of these hedges invariably involves repos. For example, if a dealer sells a credit default swap, a hedge could involve the shorting of the corporate bond which would be financed through a reverse repo. Futures prices on fixed-income securities depend critically on repos.[1] The repo is hence a valuable tool for the risk manager and, through increasing liquidity, has also had a beneficial impact on financial markets as a whole.

LIQUIDITY AND FINANCIAL RISK MANAGEMENT

This section discusses the management of liquidity risks in different markets. Before doing this it is helpful to think more carefully about the nature of liquidity. There are many definitions—we all know what liquidity is, yet find it surprisingly hard to define it. Perhaps the best definition comes from Nobel prizewinner James Tobin. Liquidity is defined by the ability to sell or buy a commodity or service at "fair market" value. If you are selling your house, then it might take months for you to sell at "fair market" value if there is a lack of buyers. If you sell it instantly, you might have to sacrifice the price at which you sell. This adverse price impact results from the illiquidity of the housing market.

In technical jargon, a liquid market exists when the seller (buyer) faces a perfectly elastic demand curve. This means that an unlimited quantity can be sold (bought) at the market price. In financial markets, this clearly is not the case. In reviewing broker screens, one can note bid–offer spreads (or limit orders on an order-driven system) and one is forced to ask: "How much can I sell or buy at the quoted price?" We can define the "implicit" amount that an intermediary will transact as the normal market size. For example, the normal market size in $/€ might well be around $100m. What happens if a dealer has to sell, say, $1bn? Quite clearly the screen's bid–offer spread will no longer be relevant since other wholesale buyers will be unwilling to carry such a large inventory—they would have to line up buyers on the other side of the trade to whom they can sell on the dollars.

For a risk manager a major concern is the possibility of a sharp drop in the volume of order flow and hence in market liquidity. Unfortunately, such a dislocation in liquidity often results when unexpected information reaches the market and coincides with an increase in the volatility of market prices. For the risk manager this has important consequences for hedging. In addition, traditional value-at-risk estimates may understate the true risk of loss, especially in cases where large inventories (relative to normal market size) are held. (See Chapter 2 for a discussion of value-at-risk models.)

One way of addressing this issue is to calculate the "liquidity adjusted" value-at-risk, a measure that formally accounts for the impact of reduced liquidity (see Lawrence and Robinson, 1997). Liquidity-adjusted value-at-risk assumes that liquidity is "endogenous." That is, liquidity is affected by the actions of the trader himself. We consider briefly how to model this aspect of liquidity risk.

In assessing liquidity-adjusted value-at-risk, this model examines the optimal speed with which to close a position. The inventory liquidator is faced with a trade-off: if he tries to unwind rapidly, he will be forced to pay a sizeable transaction cost due to the market impact and increased bid–ask spread associated with a large transaction. On the other hand, if he holds his position and liquidates slowly he will be exposed to adverse market movements for longer, leading to ongoing hedging costs and capital requirements to support the risk position. The model identifies the optimal pace of liquidation which occurs when the transaction costs (associated with that pace of liquidation) are just equal to the marginal cost of hedging plus the additional capital charge for holding on to the inventory. Simple value-at-risk models which implicitly assume that financial assets can be bought or sold at infinite elasticities can underestimate the value-at-risk dramatically, especially in more exotic markets.

This model of liquidity-adjusted value-at-risk suggests some practical conclusions about the relationship between liquidity and risk in different financial markets. Exposure to risk will depend upon the aggregate position held in a particular security or contract, and how this compares to typical trading levels. Liquidity risk can arise in even deep and liquid markets if the aggregate position is large enough so as to be difficult to unwind. Under stressed volatile conditions dealers may be less willing to deal and the "normal market size" can itself fall, further exacerbating exposure to risk.

Finally, risk managers need to be aware that the ability to buy and sell at a fair market price can sometimes almost entirely disappear; because of the intimate links between cash and derivatives markets, this can have widespread impacts across financial markets. During the crises of both 1987 and 1998, it became difficult or even impossible to transact on many key markets. In 1987 both trading capacity and systems for posting margins in equity future markets were overwhelmed by the dramatic fall of equity prices, resulting in the effective closure of the derivative market and a consequent massive loss of liquidity on the cash equity market. In 1998 the massive positions taken by LTCM, and by other traders imitating their strategies, became totally illiquid as credit and liquidity spreads widened in the wake of the Russian default. The result was a collapse of liquidity in all but the most standardized products.

EXCHANGES VERSUS OTC MARKETS

Why are some contracts traded on exchanges and others in less formal OTC markets? Financial exchanges offer their members a bundle of related services:[2]

1. Setting standards for traded financial products
2. Providing price information
3. Protecting against the risk of an agreement not being fulfilled (counterparty risk)
4. Facilitating the matching of buyers with sellers at agreed prices

We now discuss the first three of these services and how they are also supplied in OTC markets. We leave discussion of the matching of buyers with sellers until the following section on technological change.

In order for a company to list on a security exchange such as the New York Stock Exchange, the London Stock Exchange, or the Deutsche Börse, it must satisfy additional requirements over and above those of general company law. Accounts must be prepared according to specified standards and released at specified frequency (for larger companies quarterly statements are now usually required). Companies are also required to publicly release any significant price information. All this gives greater confidence, to the purchaser of a listed equity, that the characteristics of the share are well understood and that there will be a ready market should there be a need to sell the share. Exchange rules also govern the market for corporate acquisition, imposing rules for the announcement of bids and the conduct of a contested acquisition.

The provision of price information is a major source of exchange revenues. A live feed of the current trading prices is a valued trading resource; hence, financial institutions and independent traders are prepared to pay substantial charges for live price feeds. Delayed feeds—of 15 minutes or so—are of little value to traders and can be obtained for free from websites and other sources. Trading prices are also needed, for example, by asset managers or hedge funds as a check that they are obtaining best execution from their brokers.

Price information on OTC markets emerges from the process of comparing quotes from several competing dealers. Provided the market is liquid, it is not difficult to obtain this information. Foreign exchange markets provide a good illustration, where there is such a high level of competition that quotes from different dealers differ by only very small amounts and a single market price emerges. The market for interest-rate swaps is similarly highly liquid. Indeed, so liquid is this market that the interest-rate yield curve emerging from swap transactions is regarded as a much more accurate measure of market interest rates than the relatively illiquid government bond curve. Government bonds are usually only traded actively fairly close to the time of issue. Hence the interest-rate swap market, where all maturities are traded actively all the time, has become the benchmark for interest-rate measurement.

Protection against counterparty risk is of particular importance in derivative contracts, which can be in force for several months or even years before they are finally settled. In contrast, the contract for the sale of a security is typically settled within three days. Derivative exchanges deal with this through the device of the clearing house, which becomes the counterparty to all derivative trades on the exchange, and imposes margin requirements on participants based on their net position vis-à-vis the clearing house. The question then arises, when will market participants choose to transact on an exchange and when will they choose an OTC market? In order to attract participation the major OTC markets have to have their own arrangements to deal with counterparty risk. They are open to highest-quality credits; only well-known financial institutions with credit ratings of AA or better are accepted. As a result, trade is possible without there being the same degree of netting or margining as is applied to exchange-traded derivatives.

This is well illustrated in forward foreign exchange where there are sufficient high credit quality participants that the OTC market has no difficulty providing the same control of counterparty risk and much greater liquidity than the competing exchange-traded contracts. As a result, the quantity of trade in OTC currency forwards dwarfs the liquidity of exchange-traded currency futures. The quality of entrants and size of transactions is different. There is no need for the same level of margining or other techniques to control counterparty risk, since the barrier to entry (the required credit standing) acts in place of "margining."

OTC markets have developed their own procedures for obtaining contractual certainty and reducing counterparty risk. The International Swaps and Derivatives Association (ISDA) has developed a number of "master contracts" covering the range of OTC derivatives. These master contracts allow for greater flexibility than anything traded on a derivatives exchange; buyers and sellers are free to alter specific aspects of the contract, to meet their own requirements. ISDA master agreements also support bilateral netting arrangements that act to reduce counterparty exposures.

Another key issue in the choice between exchange and OTC market is the trade-off between tailor-made solutions and basis risk. Exchanges provide liquidity in a few standardized contracts, but such contracts may not be appropriate for hedging purposes because small differences in maturity or other contractual details can lead to an unacceptable mismatch between the hedge and the position being hedged (basis risk). Much of the demand for interest-rate swaps arises from the fact that they can be tailored exactly to the hedging requirements of the participant, for example when replicating a structured interest-rate product. This explains why interest-rate swaps are an OTC rather than an exchange-traded product.

TECHNOLOGICAL CHANGE

Changing technology is closing the gap between exchange and OTC trading. This section will review the impact of new technology on the process of matching buyers and sellers in both exchange and OTC trading.

We then discuss how this is eroding the contrast between the two forms of market organization (for an in-depth discussion, see Allen *et al.,* 2001).

Exchanges are well placed to take advantage of new technology to lower trading costs. They can invest, on behalf of members, in screen-based computerized systems for matching buyers and sellers. These so-called electronic order books replace the traditional floor-based, "open outcry" trading mechanisms. An example is the SETS system used for share trading on the London Stock Exchange. Until the mid-1990s, share trades in London and elsewhere were executed on the floor of the exchange; members of the exchange had to physically go onto the floor and find a matching buyer or seller. This matching was facilitated by identified locations for trade in specific shares. Dealers would congregate in the relevant location to perform their market-making function.

By moving to screen-based trading, SETS has achieved considerable reductions in the human resources involved in matching buyers and sellers, while also facilitating price comparisons. In order book systems of this kind, buyers and sellers enter an order onto the system for a given share, indicating both an amount and a price at which they are willing to buy or sell. For example, an order might be placed to buy 1,000 Vodafone shares at £10.00 or less per share. If there is already an order in the system to sell 1,000 Vodafone shares at £9.95 then an immediate match can be made for a trade of 1,000 shares and the deal is executed at £9.95. If there is no matching order then the new order is placed in the system until one can be found.

Exchange members can view the SETS screen and choose to "hit" available orders. They can see the whole range of orders, buy and sell, for a particular stock and the difference between the lowest offered sell price and the highest offered buy price. The major European exchanges, including Deutsche Börse and Euronext, operate using similar order book systems.

While the balance of advantage nowadays seems to lie with the electronic order-driven system for the matching of most trades there are important exceptions. For smaller less-liquid equities there may be insufficient orders on the book. For this reason the London Stock Exchange also offers an alternative order-driven matching system for smaller, less-liquid shares, known as SETSmm. This is a cross between a dealer quote-driven and automated order-driven system, with dealers providing regular buy and sell orders to maintain liquidity. The liquidity argument is also used to justify the continued use of a dealer quotes as the basis for much of the trading on the New York Stock Exchange, where "specialists" are allocated by the exchange to act as dealers in specified stocks with responsibility for maintaining liquid pricing. While their primary responsibility is to maintain liquidity, these specialists themselves nowadays operate electronic order books and for more liquid stocks their quoted prices may in fact reflect limit orders placed on these electronic order books.

Another dramatic illustration of the impact of technology in reducing trading costs is in the field of exchange-traded derivatives. For over a hundred years, since the creation of commodity derivative exchanges in the late nineteenth century, the technique used to match buyers and sellers of derivatives has been "open outcry," with buyers and sellers congregating in a restricted location, the trading pit, in order to buy and sell futures and options. Within the major exchanges there were separate pits for each category of derivative (e.g. a pit for Eurodollar interest-rate options, a pit for dollar-sterling currency futures, etc.). Orders had to be taken into the pit by specialized runners who would then search amongst dealers in the pit to obtain the best price.

The advantage of low-cost computer technology is dramatically illustrated by the success of the Swiss-German-owned EUREX exchange in capturing trade in the major German government debt derivative contracts from the London-based LIFFE exchange. EUREX was able to offer much lower trading costs than LIFFE through the use of a computerized trading system instead of open outcry. While it took time to establish EUREX as a serious competitor, within a few months from mid-1997 to mid-1998, EUREX captured the liquidity in the major government bond future contracts (like the Bund contract) and this trading moved out of LIFFE onto EUREX. Subsequently open outcry trading was abandoned in LIFFE (now part of the Euronext group).

Some open outcry trading still takes place in the major US derivative exchanges: the Chicago Board of Trade and the Chicago Mercantile Exchange, but is subject to challenge. In a period of only four years, the IESE electronic exchange has succeeded in capturing much of the liquidity in equity options (see Weber, 2003). EUREX has now established itself in Chicago as EUREX US, offering contracts that compete with some of the major contracts on the established Chicago exchanges. It is seeking, once again, to use a more efficient trading technology to capture market liquidity (see Young, 2004). The Chicago exchanges are responding with improvements in their own trading efficiency and a gradual switch to their own computerized systems.

Information technology is also having a major impact on OTC markets. Here the traditional telephone based comparison of prices amongst dealers is increasingly supplanted by electronic based systems, both electronic communication networks (or ECNs) that allow prices to be posted publicly and crossing systems that automatically match buying and selling orders. OTC markets such as NASDAQ cannot co-ordinate technological change in the same way as organized exchanges. But participants will still employ systems which facilitate price comparison and look for and take advantage of better pricing (narrower bid–ask spreads) than is available from dealers. This explains, for example, why a large part of the volume of NASDAQ trading now passes through the electronic communication system or ECN Inet (formed from the 2002 acquisition of the Island by Instinet).

Crossing networks are independent matching systems, working in a similar fashion to the electronic order books used on the European securities exchanges. As a result, much of the standard smaller size trade has migrated onto these electronic systems. A large proportion of NASDAQ orders are now fulfilled electronically, with only the larger deals, which have price impact, being fulfilled by NASDAQ dealers. As a result, there has been an effective convergence of the organization of NASDAQ—the OTC securities market—with other exchange-based securities markets using electronic order books. In exchanges in Europe such as London and the Deutsche Börse, while orders of less than normal market size can be easily accommodated on the SETS system, larger orders can only be fulfilled by a process of negotiation. That is, the larger orders which have price impact are also routed away from automated electronic markets and directed to a phone- and screen-based dealer network. This convergence may have some way to go. It can, for example, be argued that the abolition of exchanges and their replacement by OTC arrangements supported by ECNs could substantially reduce trading costs, in Europe and elsewhere (Domowitz and Steil, 2002).

Similar convergence can be observed between the markets for OTC and exchange-traded derivatives. Here new netting and margining services are being created for OTC derivatives, by, for example, London Clearing House-Clearnet with its SwapClear service. This service provides multilateral netting and margining for interest-rate swap contracts. Developments such as these allow OTC markets to provide as high a level of counterparty protection as exchanges.

It is sometimes argued that a switch from order matching by people (in pits or dealer markets) to electronic matching by machines can lead to a loss of liquidity and so increase both trading costs and risks. This kind of argument is made most often by floor-based traders defending themselves from the threat of technological change, but is voiced also by other more disinterested parties. As we have already seen, it is the case that purely electronic matching systems have difficulty in providing liquidity for larger trades. But it is a mistake to view such systems in isolation; in practice they are always accompanied by a range of alternative mechanisms for the execution of larger trades, including parallel dealer markets and wholesale brokerage. There is little evidence that electronic trading arrangements have difficulty in providing market liquidity on a day-to-day basis; indeed, the success of EUREX and IESE in capturing trading volumes and liquidity suggests the opposite. It is possible that in a severe market crisis, such as that of 1987, a market organized around an electronic trading system might suffer an (even) greater price decline than a pure dealer-based system. But this is a rather theoretical argument. In practice, commercial logic seems to be forcing all systems to adopt electronic systems. Management and regulators must simply focus on how to make these systems work as well as possible in stressed situations.

POST-TRADE PROCESSING

After a trade is "executed" further steps are required to complete the transaction. Nowadays, with increasing competition in trading spaces and consequent reduction in "bid–ask" spreads, it is often such post-trade processing that creates the largest part of the cost of trading.

We can begin with the example of a securities trade, such as a bond or stock. After a deal is struck, three further steps are then undertaken:

- *Comparison and confirmation.* Before the trade can be further processed it is necessary to conduct both comparison (does the information recorded by both sides of the trade agree?) and confirmation (is this what the investor really intended?). Following the trade, buyer and seller exchange messages confirming both their agreement to trade and all the details of the trade (security or contract, quantity, price, arrangements for settlement, etc.); and a broker needs to obtain positive confirmation from the investor (sometimes referred to as affirmation) that the trade complies with the original order.

- *Netting.* A considerable reduction in the value and volume of securities trades for settlement can be achieved by netting offsetting cash and security flows. This is usually undertaken through a central counterparty (discussed further below). Netting allows a party's commitments to be reduced to a single daily payment and single net figure for the acquisition of each security.

- *Settlement.* The positioning of securities and the arrangement of payment occur prior to settlement. Settlement involves the final transfer of ownership of securities (delivery) in exchange for corresponding payments.

These steps take place sequentially. In most major financial centres most securities trades are processed on a "T+3" basis, with matching and netting of trades completed by the end of T+1 (i.e. one day after the date of trade), preparation for settlement during T+2, and final settlement on T+3. Nowadays in all leading centres settlement is delivery versus payment (known as "DVP"), removing any risk of the loss of principal through counterparty default.

A number of institutions are involved in post-trade activities. Where netting takes place, it is usually on a multilateral basis and organized through a central counterparty or clearing house, such as London Clearing House-Clearnet (in the UK, France, and a number of other European countries), EUREX Clearing (in Germany), Depository Trust & Clearing Corporation or DTCC (in the USA). As we have already discussed, these central counterparties are extending their netting and risk management services into new markets.

Security settlement can be undertaken either through a central security depository (such as Euroclear-Crest, DTCC, or Clearstream) or by a competing custodian bank. In order for a securities trade to settle it is necessary for the security to pass from one "security account" to another and for there to be a corresponding payment from one bank account to another. Securities accounts can be offered either by the central depositories where securities are located or by custodian banks that hold securities on behalf of final investors. While DTCC offers a single post-trade processing solution for US transactions, post-trade processing elsewhere remains fragmented. As a result trading, especially cross-border trades, continues to be both costlier and riskier in Europe than in the USA.

Operational problems in trading are often associated with post-trade processing. Trading failures are much more common when manual processing is required, with the attendant risk of human error. Fortunately, such operational events tend to occur independently. Failures in post-trade processing may be higher than desired, but there is a good deal of diversification over time, average losses are predictable, and with improvements in procedures and reporting the level of losses can be reduced.

The goal nowadays for many back-office processes is to achieve "straight-through" processing, that is, for all the details of post-trade processing to be input in standard form (referred to as "standard settlement instructions") at the time the trade takes place; and then for all subsequent post-trade processing to take place without manual intervention. The great advantage of straight-through processing is the major reduction in operational risks and the high costs of manual processing.

The industry still remains some way from full straight-through processing for many trades, especially those that are cross-border or nonstandard. As a result, there continue to be considerable costs and high levels of operational risk in post-trade processing. Operational risks are especially high for cross-border trading, a major issue for the development of European financial markets where post-trade arrangements continue to be highly fragmented, and also for investors in emerging markets.

Both central securities depositories and custodians also offer a number of other commercial services. They assist clients (securities brokers, asset managers) with their cash and collateral management, ensuring that they have sufficient securities and cash on account to settle all trades. They also lend securities (see the section on Repo Markets, above, for discussion of the reverse repo), so providing liquidity to the post-trade process and to derivative markets. Services to securities holders include tax payment and reporting, administering corporate actions, and marking of portfolios to market.

RETAIL AND WHOLESALE BROKERAGE

Not everyone can deal directly on financial markets. Exchange trading is limited to members—always established professional firms. OTC markets have their own limits on participation: only well-rated firms are accepted as counterparties, only certain minimum sizes of deal are acceptable, and only regular participants who have established their identities with dealers and know the specific trading conventions for that market are able to trade freely.

Effectively this means that smaller deals, "retail trades," cannot be handled directly on the market. Someone—the broker—has to collect together a number of retail orders and be responsible for passing them through onto the exchange or to an OTC dealer.

Financial firms with direct access to the financial markets can therefore make additional revenue by acting as brokers, that is, taking and executing orders on behalf of customers who cannot themselves deal directly on the market. (In fields such as insurance brokerage is also used to refer to the matching of buyers with sellers, but the mechanism is the same—in this case there are sellers who do not deal directly with small clients, and so a broker is needed to bring them together.) Brokerage has in the past been a highly profitable activity for investment banks and other financial institutions, using their privileged membership of exchanges or their established position in OTC markets to turn a substantial profit. Profit margins were exceptionally large for retail customers. They can still be high for customers who are naive enough to walk into a high-street bank to make a modest trade in a share or bond, and are charged a considerably greater fee than is imposed by the exchange where the deal takes place. But over recent years falling costs of information technology have allowed many newcomers to act as brokers, and margins have fallen dramatically.

What we have described so far is the low-risk activity of "retail brokerage," handling orders that are too small, or come from insufficiently creditworthy customers, to be placed directly onto the market. Many of our comments about operational risks and operational costs in post-trade processing apply also to retail brokerage. In the past there have been high levels of operational costs, such as repudiated orders, but such costs have been fairly predictable and the application of information technology is greatly reducing such problems.

There is another important and distinct brokerage activity known as "wholesale" broking, which means handling orders that are too large to be placed directly on the market and breaking them up and splitting them between buyers. Wholesale broking of this kind is carried out both by investment banks and by a number of small specialized wholesale brokerage firms. These firms take little direct credit risk, but potentially huge operational risks due to the large value of deals that they handle on behalf of clients.

The line between brokerage and dealing is a fuzzy one. Brokers attract orders to both buy and sell. Once they have a sufficient order flow they can cut costs, both by matching trades on their own books without ever going to the market (so-called "internalization") and by meeting orders out of their own inventory. Regulators and audit firms therefore pay close attention, to ensure that customers are still offered at least the best market price ("best execution") even when the order is not fulfiled on the market.

Nowadays, a large proportion of securities and derivatives trading is driven by hedge funds. The bigger hedge funds are often in the position of placing orders that are too large to be placed directly onto the market.

Therefore, for these funds a critical relationship is with their prime broker who will handle all aspects of trade execution, passing on orders and dividing them amongst different brokers for execution, as well as providing the entire range of post-trade reporting and analysis services. The prime broker is also a major secured lender to the hedge fund (making use of the repo contract described earlier). The prime broker to a hedge fund is always one of the major investment banks.

Prime brokerage has grown to be one of the more lucrative investment banking activities. It offers large margins and also the opportunity to observe hedge fund activities and make profitable proprietary trades based on knowledge of the client hedge funds' positions.

NEW FINANCIAL MARKETS

This chapter has compared the activities on the principal securities and derivative markets. An analysis of the structure of financial markets would, however, be incomplete, without a discussion of the rapid development of new markets, especially for structured products, of the past decade.

Much of the trading of interest-rate swaps is related to their use for the creation of structured notes and in structured finance. Structured notes are OTC interest products customized to client specifications. Structured notes are extraordinarily flexible; they can be created with virtually any conceivable interest-rate profile, based on both floating and fixed rates, domestic and foreign currency. One well-known example is the inverse floating-rate note, where the return varies in the opposite direction to LIBOR interest rates. If LIBOR increases by 100 basis points, the interest paid on this product declines by 100 basis points.

Structured notes provide great flexibility in meeting client needs. They can be tailored precisely to match anticipated interest and currency exposures, that is to say, they are very effective hedging tools. They also can be used to get around regulatory restrictions (institutions barred, for example, from investing in emerging markets can still obtain the benefits of exposure to the higher returns available in emerging market products by purchasing a structured note from an OECD financial institution with returns linked to one or a basket of emerging markets). They are also very effective for tax purposes; for example, a structured note may be issued by a vehicle situated in a country with a double-taxation treaty with the country of the purchaser, allowing the reclaim of withholding tax, even though the financial returns are related to the interest rates in a country with no double-taxation treaty.

Another important structured financial product is the asset-backed security, backed either by mortgages (the MBS) or other bank loan assets (the ABS), a product discussed in more detail in Alexander and Sheedy (2008b), Chapter 6. This instrument was pioneered in the USA in the 1980s, with the development of tranched mortgage backed securities. In these products a trust or special purpose vehicle (SPV) is set up to hold mortgages transferred off a bank's balance sheet. The SPV issues debt obligations referred to as tranches, ranging from the most senior tranches—which have first claim on the cash-flows from the underlying assets—to the most junior. The volume of asset-backed security issuance is now very large in the USA and growing rapidly in Europe (Table 1.8).

The most recent development in the field of structured finance, which has used many of the techniques of asset backed securitization, is the explosive growth of collateralized debt obligations or CDOs (Table 1.8). This is a broad term used to refer to a wide range of new structured financial products, other than the traditional ABS or MBS. CDOs have allowed corporate loans or bond obligations to be securitized, either by directly securitizing corporate loans or bonds (the cash-flow CDO) or using credit default swaps to create a security which synthetically replicates these cash flows (the synthetic CDO). CDOs are also issued using ABS or MBS as collateral.

A major reason for the rapid growth of CDO issuance is their appeal to institutional investors such as pension funds and insurance companies.

T A B L E   1.8

Structured financial product volumes (US$ billion)

	2004	2005	2006	2007 1st half
US MBS issuance	1,779.1	1,966.3	2,002.6	1,137.6 (est)
US ABS amount outstanding	1,827.8	1,955.2	2,130.4	
European MBS and ABS issuance	243.5	327.0	458.9	
Global CDO issuance	157.4	271.8	549.3	313.6

Source: Thomson Financial, taken from www.sifma.org

The senior tranches of the CDO can achieve a AAA or better rating (so called "super senior" tranches) while offering a yield uplift relative to AAA corporate bonds. There is a huge investor appetite for such highly rated debt securities. The riskier tranches can also offer very attractive yields relative to equivalently rated corporate bonds. This advantage however comes with a catch. As yet there has been relatively little experience with the rating of CDOs and it is unclear whether the ratings of CDO tranches are as reliable or stable as those of corporate bonds. Recent events have caused concern. In the first half of 2007, the emergence of credit problems in the sub-prime sector of the US mortgage lending market was followed by the downgrading to speculative status of the tranches of a number of CDOs backed—directly or indirectly—by sub-prime mortgage assets. This directly affected only one part of the much wider CDO market, but there are signs that this experience is causing investors to have doubts about the credit quality of CDOs unrelated to sub-prime mortgages, and as a result it is becoming much more difficult to sell these tranches to investors.

Another growth area has been the secondary loan trading market, which again has grown significantly. It enables those banks unable to participate in syndications to buy loan assets, allowing banks that are over-concentrated to reduce their exposure (see the website of the loan syndication and trading association www.lsta.org for statistics on the growth of this market). Another important driver of this new market has been the introduction of the euro, which supports a sufficiently large and liquid market in euro-denominated credits, which could not have been supported in, say, Deutschemarks or French francs alone, and the syndicated loan market has grown especially rapidly in Europe.

The syndicated loan and CDO markets have together provided much of the funding for the recent boom in private equity buyouts. Typically the first funding for a buyout is in the form of a syndicated leveraged loan. Subsequently, a leveraged buyout can be refinanced through CDO issuance. However, recent concerns about the losses in US sub-prime have raised some doubts about whether the same volume of financing for private equity deals will continue to be available in the future.

The major impact of securitization, together with secondary loan trading, is quite revolutionary. Traditionally the business model of the commercial bank was to take deposits and to lend and hold both these assets and liabilities on balance sheet. But today we are in a very different environment, with the huge growth of securitizations (including CDOs) enabling banks to package their loans and sell them as securities. Retail lending has for some time been transferred off-balance sheet, with the biggest market for asset-backed securities that for US mortgage-backed securities (backed by Ginnae Mae and Freddie Mac), which is bigger and often more liquid than the US government treasury market. Now the corporate loans are also no longer a long-dated "buy and hold" instrument; as the CDO and secondary loan markets expand, corporate lending is becoming an increasingly liquid asset.

A third closely related development has been the growth of the credit derivative market, including credit default swaps enabling banks to "insure" against defaults. A critical feature of the credit default swap, unlike a credit insurance contract, is that there is no requirement that the purchaser of protection hold the underlying insured assets. In the even of default "event" the default swaps can be settled either by transfer of the physical asset or by payment of a cash difference, based on a post-default market price of the insured asset. The rapid growth of the credit derivatives market has, however, concerned regulators, especially the concentration risk of protection; with a few major institutions selling most of the protection; and continuing problems with the both the clearing and settlement of CDS trades.

These new markets create both opportunities and risks. We can expect the development of these new liquid markets for credit to improve the ability of risk managers to control and respond to credit risk, and to reduce the overall costs of intermediation between savers and borrowers. But at the same time, because these markets are very new, there must be concerns about how well participants understand the risks they are taking on. The possibility of mispricing and of dramatic loss of liquidity in the event of crisis cannot be dismissed.

CONCLUSIONS

This chapter has surveyed the structure of financial markets. We have compared activity in securities markets (equities and bonds), foreign exchange and derivatives, and discussed key organizational and structural features of modern markets.

We emphasize the association between the organization of markets and the availability of liquidity, that is, the opportunity to buy or sell without affecting prices. We noted the "virtuous circle" of liquidity, the tendency for market activity to concentrate on a single trading platform so as to obtain the best pricing. We also observed the increasing liquidity of derivative markets, the "symbiotic" relationship between cash and derivatives pricing, and the tendency for trading activity to migrate from cash to derivatives.

One lesson is that effective management of liquidity risk requires an appreciation of how markets are organized and how they interact. Where contracts are homogeneous, markets are effectively linked together, and positions are small, liquidity problems are relatively unlikely to arise; but where products are diverse, markets are fragmented, and positions are large then liquidity is a serious potential problem.

We have compared over-the-counter markets and exchanges, noting that the development of new trading technologies and the spread of central counterparty services is leading to a convergence of these two forms of market organization. Standard trades are now often matched through automated systems—whether on exchanges or OTC—and in both cases dealers or brokers are often taking responsibility for matching larger orders.

While there are a few markets—notably the NYSE—where matching of buyers and sellers is still undertaken through dealer quotation, automated trade matching is now standard practice for standard size trades. Automation is significantly reducing trading costs, but liquidity for large trades still depends upon the intervention of brokers to match buyers and sellers. A brokerage service is also still used for small retail trades, but here competition and new technology have dramatically reduced both costs and profit margins.

We have briefly described post-trade securities processing, including both the netting of credit risks through central counterparties and the final transfer of ownership against payment. We have noted the potential for high levels of operational costs and risk wherever there is manual intervention. The use of information technology to standardize procedures "straight-through processing") is reducing these operational costs but is still limited for many cross-border transactions.

The final section concluded with a review of some of the newest financial products, including structured securities and credit products such as loan trading and credit derivatives. These products, like previous financial innovations, promise to improve liquidity and reduce the overall costs of financial intermediation between savers and investors. But because they are so new these products are not always well understood, and the possibility of losses from mispricing or a systemic crisis cannot be ignored.

REFERENCES

Alexander, C and Sheedy, E (2008b) *The Professional Risk Managers' Guide to Financial Instruments* (New York: McGraw Hill).

Allen, H, Hawkins, J, and Sato, S (2001) Electronic trading and its implications for financial systems. In S Sato and J Hawkins (eds), BIS Papers No. 7 – Electronic Finance: A New Perspective and Challenges (available via http://www.bis.org).

Choudhry, M (2002) *The Repo Handbook* (Oxford: Butterworth Heinemann).

Domowitz, I and Steil, B (2002) Innovation in equity trading systems: the impact on trading costs and the cost of equity capital. In B Steil, DG Victor, and RR Nelson (eds), *Technological Innovation and Economic Performance* (Princeton, NJ: Princeton University Press).

Lawrence, C and Robinson, G (1997) Liquidity, dynamic hedging derivatives and value at risk. In *Risk Management for Financial Institutions: Advances in Measurement and Control* (London: Risk Books, pp. 63–72).

Lee, R (1998) *What is an Exchange?* (Oxford: Oxford University Press).

Steiner, R (1997) *Mastering Repo Markets* (London: FT Pitman).

Tavakoli, JM (2003) *Collateralized Debt Obligations and Structured Finance* (New York: Wiley).

Weber, B (2003) Adoption of electronic options trading at the IESE. *IT Pro*, July (available via http://www.london.edu/sim/Working_Papers /SIM22.pdf).

Young, PL (2004) The Battle of Chicago: Chicago after Eurex US. In *The Handbook of World Stock, Derivative and Commodity Exchanges 2004* (available via http:// www.exchange-handbook.co.uk).

NOTES

1. See for example, Choudhry, pp. 331–408 for an extensive analysis of the implied repo rate.
2. See Lee (1998) for a detailed survey of the function and governance of exchanges.

CHAPTER 2

The Money Markets

Canadian Securities Institute

INTRODUCTION

The interest-rate market is the market in which individuals and businesses lend cash to other individuals and businesses and in return receive compensation in the form of interest. Most lending and borrowing occurs through some sort of intermediary, including deposit-taking institutions such as banks, trust companies, or credit unions, and investment banks and dealers who underwrite interest-rate securities on behalf of borrowers, including corporations, governments, and supranational institutions such as the World Bank.

The interest-rate market is not a market with a single physical location. It is made up of several thousand financial institutions and several million customers who interact face-to-face, by telephone, over the Internet, or on private computer networks every business day around the globe. Lenders constantly seek out the highest interest rates, while borrowers continuously search for the cheapest source of funds.

When a lender makes a loan to a borrower, an interest-rate asset is created for the lender and an interest-rate liability is created for the borrower. This chapter examines the various instruments that are available in the interest-rate market, broken down into the market for deposits and loans and the market for securities.

CHARACTERISTICS OF MONEY MARKET INSTRUMENTS

The cash market for interest-rate assets and liabilities can be thought of as two distinct but related markets: the market for *deposits and loans* and the market for *securities*. The wide variety of instruments in these two categories, which are known collectively as *fixed-income instruments*, may have any or all of the following six characteristics:

- *Term*. The term of a fixed-income instrument is the length of time that the borrower borrows the money. The day that marks the end of the term is sometimes referred to as the maturity date. Terms can range from as short as one day to an infinite amount of time.[1] Most terms, however, are between one day and 30 years. Some instruments, known as revolving loans, do not have a specific maturity date; the borrower may pay off a revolving loan at any time.

- *Principal*. The principal is the amount that the borrower agrees to repay to the lender on the maturity date. The principal has many synonyms in the interest-rate market, including face value, par value, and deposit or loan—although technically the last two terms describe a type of instrument, rather than the amount lent. Some instruments require the borrower to repay the entire principal on the maturity date, while others require the borrower to repay the principal in instalments over the life of the loan. The principal is usually the same as the amount lent, although in some instances it may be more.

- *Interest rate*. This is the amount that the borrower agrees to pay the lender for the use of the money, usually expressed as an annual percentage of the principal. Interest payments may be paid in regular instalments over the term of the instrument, or in a lump sum at the maturity date. For example, an interest rate of 6% per annum means either that the borrower must pay the lender interest of 6% on the value of the principal every year, or that the borrower must pay a proportion of 6% if interest payments are made more frequently, or that the borrower must pay the equivalent of 6% in annual interest at maturity when the principal is repaid. For interest-rate securities such as bonds that pay interest at regular intervals, the interest rate is also known as the coupon rate. The interest rate can be fixed over the term of the loan, or can vary, or float, according to market interest rates. When the interest rate varies, there may be a limit placed on how high or low the interest rate can go.

- *Marketability.* If ownership of the interest-rate asset or liability can be readily transferred to a third party, the instrument is said to be marketable. Most interest-rate securities are marketable instruments.

- *Security.* Fixed-income instruments can be either secured, or collateralized, by specific assets, or unsecured. If an instrument is secured, the lender has the right to take ownership of the specified assets if the borrower does not fulfil his or her obligation to repay the principal. If an instrument is unsecured, the lender has no specific claim to any of the borrower's assets if the borrower does not repay the principal. In this case, the lender is an unsecured creditor who relies on the borrower's general ability to meet financial obligations.

- *Call or put features.* Some instruments have a provision that allows the borrower to repay the principal (a call feature) or the lender to demand repayment of the principal (a put feature) before the maturity date.

DEPOSITS AND LOANS

Banks, credit unions and trust companies (which as a group will be referred to as just "banks") and large investment dealers are the dominant players in the domestic markets for deposits and loans to individuals and businesses.

Deposits

Banks accept deposits from businesses in three basic forms.

1. *Demand deposits*, more commonly known as checking accounts, can be withdrawn by the depositor at any time, without giving any notice to the bank. Most banks pay little or no interest on demand deposits.

2. *Notice deposits*, which consist primarily of savings accounts, require the depositor to give the bank advance notice before withdrawing the funds, although this requirement is rarely, if ever, enforced. Notice deposits are floating-rate deposits.

The rates offered by most banks are usually quite low, and they change infrequently.

3. *Fixed-term deposits* have fixed terms and must be repaid, with interest, to the depositor on the maturity date. Fixed-term deposits are also known as term deposits or time deposits. Some fixed-term deposits, however, have a provision that allows the depositor to withdraw the deposit before the maturity date. There may or may not be a penalty for doing so.

Banks offer fixed-term deposits with both fixed and floating rates of interest. The interest rate on floating-rate term deposits is usually tied to a benchmark interest rate, also called a reference rate. These rates include administered rates, which are set by various institutions or policy makers, such as a bank's prime rate, or a market rate, which is determined by the trading activity in a certain market, such as the 90-day Treasury bill rate.

Loans

Banks lend money to businesses in many different forms. Loans to medium-sized and large corporations are usually structured as *credit facilities*, also called *credit lines*. A credit facility is a flexible, customized arrangement in which the corporation has a variety of ways to borrow from the bank. Banking is a competitive industry, and individual banks try to win new business and retain their current clients by offering a wide menu of choices. Typically, credit facilities allow corporations to borrow through fixed-rate term loans, floating-rate loans, or bankers' acceptances, which are discussed in detail in the section on Money Market Securities. Except for the most creditworthy corporations, most bank lending is secured by the corporation's physical assets or receivables.

Credit facilities are tailored to suit the needs of the borrower. At any given time, a borrower does not usually require all the funds that the bank makes available in different forms as part of the facility, but has access to the money whenever it is needed. To compensate the banks for being ready and willing to lend the entire amount of the credit facility, the corporation usually pays a standby or commitment fee on the facility's unused portion. The fee is expressed as a percentage of the unused portion, and is usually quite small.

Banks also make one-off floating-rate loans to corporations based on the bank's prime rate plus a spread. So-called prime-based lending is more expensive for corporations than, for example, bankers' acceptance issues, because a bank's prime rate is always higher than its bankers' acceptance rate.

The largest banks also participate in syndicated lending to very large, mostly publicly traded financial and nonfinancial corporations. In syndicated lending, a group of banks lend money on common terms to a single borrower. The loans can be structured as credit facilities, with a range of options for the borrower, or as one-time loans with fixed- or floating-rate terms. The total amount lent is usually quite large, and many of these loans exceed $1 billion. By sharing the loan among several lenders, banks lessen their exposure to a given borrower.

Repurchase Agreements

A repurchase agreement, or *repo*, is a loan in which a borrower sells a security to a lender at one price with an agreement to buy the security back on a future date at a higher price. Although it is simply the other side of the same agreement, the lender's position in the agreement is generally referred to as a reverse repurchase agreement, or *reverse repo*.

An *overnight repo* is a repo with a term of one day. Term repos are repos with any term longer than one day. The higher price at which the security will be repurchased is determined by the repo rate. The security sold to the lender acts as collateral for the loan. If the borrower cannot repay the funds on the maturity date of the repo, the lender gets to keep the securities.

The repo rate for a particular repurchase agreement depends on several factors, including the quality of the collateral and the term of the agreement. The quality of the collateral affects the credit risk and liquidity of the security. The effect of the repo's term on the repo rate depends on the general level of interest rates in the market for different terms to maturity.

Investment dealers make extensive use of repurchase agreements to finance their inventories of equity and interest-rate securities. They pay interest according to the standard formula for computing the interest on a short-term loan:

$$\text{Interest paid} = \text{principal} \times \text{interest rate} \times (\text{DTM/ADC}). \qquad (2.1)$$

where
DTM = the number of days until maturity,
ADC = the denominator of the relevant day-count convention.[2]

Example 2.1

Suppose ABC Securities has just bought $5 million worth of a Government of Canada bonds from National Securities. The bonds will be held in inventory for resale to ABC's clients. ABC expects to sell the bonds within a week. To pay for the bonds, ABC can use its own funds or it can borrow the money in the repo market.

To finance the purchase, ABC enters into a seven-day term repo with CIBC. ABC agrees to deliver to CIBC the $5 million worth of bonds in return for $4,995,205.48 today. ABC will then use the proceeds from this loan to pay National Securities for the bonds.

At the end of the repo agreement, CIBC will return the bonds to ABC and ABC will give $5 million to CIBC. The difference between the two payments, $4,794.52, represents the interest on the loan. This was calculated based on a repo rate of 5%. Then, using (2.1) the interest paid is

$$\$5 \text{ million} \times 0.05 \times \frac{7}{365} = \$4,794.52.$$

If ABC succeeds in selling the bonds to its clients by the end of the week, it will have the funds it needs to repay CIBC and will get the bonds back so that they can be delivered to the clients who purchased them.

International Markets

The international market for deposits and loans is known as the *Eurocurrency market*. This is the market for term deposits and loans in a currency other than the local currency of the bank branch that is accepting the deposit or extending the loan.

The Eurocurrency market, which is most active in London, UK, grew rapidly in the 1980s, largely in response to regulatory restrictions placed on financial institutions within their domestic markets. Although some of these regulations have since been relaxed, many still exist, making the Eurocurrency market a vital source of relatively low-cost, short-term funding for large multinational corporations and internationally active financial institutions. The largest segment of the Eurocurrency market is by far the *Eurodollar market*. This is the market for US dollar time deposits and loans. Let us examine how a Eurodollar deposit is created.

Example 2.2

Suppose that ABC Corp, a Canadian company, owns a maturing time deposit of US$10 million with Citibank, which is based in New York City. ABC will not require the funds for another three months, so the company's treasurer solicits two quotes on a new three-month time deposit: one from Citibank in New York and one from the London branch of Deutsche Bank. Deutsche Bank offers ABC a slightly higher interest rate than Citibank, so the treasurer decides to deposit the money with Deutsche Bank in London.

When the original term deposit matures, ABC owns a US$10 million demand deposit (i.e. a checking account) with Citibank in New York. The treasurer of ABC instructs Citibank to transfer the demand deposit to Deutsche Bank's account with Citibank in New York.[3] Once this is complete, the Eurodollar deposit has been created. Table 2.1 shows how the scenario looks using T-accounts.[4]

Note that Citibank is simply transferring ownership of the demand deposit to Deutsche Bank. The demand deposit, and the actual funds backing it, remain in New York. In other words, there is no US$10 million sitting in Deutsche Bank's vaults in London.

But the scenario does not end here. Deutsche Bank now owns a US$10 million demand deposit and has promised to pay interest to ABC Corp. on its three-month Eurodollar time deposit. Deutsche Bank needs to put that demand deposit to work in a manner that will generate enough interest not only to cover its interest payment to ABC, but also to turn a small profit. If it cannot quickly find a customer who needs to borrow US$10 million, Deutsche Bank will lend the money to another bank in

T A B L E   2.1

Creation of a Eurodollar time deposit

United States	London	
Citibank	Deutsche Bank	
$10 million demand deposit due to Deutsche Bank	$10 million demand deposit in Citibank	$10 million Eurodollar time deposit due to ABC Corp.

the Eurodollar interbank market. This process may continue for several more stages, with several banks borrowing the money and then relending it to other banks, until the demand deposit in New York is finally transferred to a borrower who actually needs the US$10 million.

Suppose that Deutsche Bank buys a three-month Eurodollar time deposit from Royal Bank in London. Deutsche Bank will instruct Citibank in New York to transfer ownership of the demand deposit, this time to Royal Bank.[5] To entice Deutsche Bank to make the Eurodollar deposit with it, Royal Bank will offer Deutsche Bank a slightly higher rate than Deutsche Bank has promised to pay ABC Corp.

Now suppose that Royal Bank does have a customer, XYZ Inc., that needs a US$10 million loan, which Royal Bank is able to provide thanks to its newly acquired ownership of a US$10 million demand deposit with Citibank. To complete the cycle, Royal Bank instructs Citibank to transfer ownership of the US$10 million demand deposit to XYZ Inc.[6] Table 2.2 presents the new scenario.

In the above example we used a three-month deposit to illustrate how Eurocurrencies are created, but banks in the Eurocurrency market regularly accept deposits (and extend loans) with a range of terms, from

T A B L E   2.2

A second Eurodollar time deposit and the final borrowing

United States		London	
Citibank		**Deutsche Bank**	
	$10 million demand deposit due to XYZ Inc.	$10 million Eurodollar time deposit in Royal Bank	$10 million Eurodollar time deposit due to ABC Corp
		Royal Bank	
		$10 million loan to XYZ Corp.	$10 million Eurodollar time deposit due to Deutsche Bank
		XYZ Inc.	
		$10 million demand deposit in Citibank	$10 million due to Royal Bank

one day up to one year. The most popular terms are one day, one week, one month, three months, and six months.

The type of interest that the banks pay on Eurocurrency deposits is known as *add-on interest*. That is, interest is added to the deposit amount and paid when the deposit matures. The actual amount of interest is calculated on a money market yield basis using (2.1) with an actual/360 day-count convention.

Example 2.3

In the Eurodollar market, if a corporation puts US$1 million into a three-month time deposit on March 1 with an interest rate of 6% per annum, the number of days for which the borrower will pay interest at maturity is 92, calculated as follows.

March 2 to March 31	30	days
April 1 to April 30	30	days
May 1 to May 31	31	days
June 1	1	day
	92	days

Note that the day count begins the day after the deposit is made and ends with the maturity date.

Using (2.1), the total interest received by the depositor at maturity for the 92 days is:

$$\$1 \text{ million} \times 0.06 \times \frac{92}{360} = \$15,333.$$

At maturity, the deposit will be worth the US$1 million principal plus US$15,333 interest.

The London Interbank Offered Rate (LIBOR)

On each business day in London, banks in the Eurocurrency interbank market constantly lend and borrow Eurocurrency deposits to and from each other. The most popular currencies represented include the US dollar, the Japanese yen, the Swiss franc, the Canadian dollar, the Australian dollar, and the euro. The rates the banks bid for deposits and offer for loans in each of these currencies are regularly posted on quotation and automated trading systems such as Reuters, Bridge Telerate, and Bloomberg.

At 11:00 a.m. London time each day, the British Bankers' Association (BBA) surveys the rates offered by at least eight banks chosen for their "reputation, scale of activity in the London market, and perceived expertise in the currency, concerned," and giving due consideration to credit standing.[7] It ranks the quotes from highest to lowest, drops the highest and lowest 25%, and takes the average of the remaining 50%.[8] The result is the official BBA *London Interbank Offered Rate* (LIBOR) for the specific currency and maturity.

Why is BBA LIBOR important? For the US dollar in particular, LIBOR has become the primary benchmark interest rate for many short-term US dollar loans to corporations, including those made in the US domestic market. The interest rate on these loans is quoted as a spread above or below LIBOR, such as "three-month LIBOR − 0.25%"or "six-month LIBOR + 2.25%." The size of the spread depends primarily on the credit quality of the customer borrowing the money. While most corporations can only borrow at a spread above LIBOR, some of the most credit-worthy customers can obtain loans at rates below LIBOR.

US-dollar LIBOR is also the basis for settling many interest-rate futures contracts, including the most liquid contract of all, the three-month Eurodollar contract that trades on the Chicago Mercantile Exchange, as well as most over-the-counter interest-rate derivatives.

MONEY MARKET SECURITIES

Money market securities are loans that have been structured so that they can be traded among investors in the secondary market with a wide variety of structures and characteristics. Money market securities are initially issued with terms of one year or less. They allow investors to place their excess cash in short-term instruments that, all else being equal, are less risky than securities with longer terms. They also allow investors to get a higher rate of return than they would from money sitting in a traditional bank account, while at the same time providing the issuers of money market securities with a relatively low-cost source of short-term funding.

While it is true that money market securities have lower risk than longer-dated bonds, market participants are exposed to risk at a number of levels, namely:

- *Interest-rate risk*. The risk that interest rates will rise (fall) and the price of the security will accordingly fall (rise). See Alexander and Sheedy (2008b), Chapter 2 for further discussion of the inverse relationship between interest rates and prices of securities.

- *Credit risk*. The risk that the issuer of the security will default on its obligations to repay interest, principal, or both.
- *Liquidity risk*. The risk that an investor wishing to sell a security is not able to do so quickly without sacrificing price.

Money market securities often trade in denominations that are too large for individual investors. *Cash management trusts* or *money market mutual funds* have become popular vehicles that enable the small investor to participate in these markets. Such funds pool the resources of many investors and can trade in money market securities on their behalf, managing the risks in accordance with the fund's trust deed.

Treasury Bills

Treasury bills (also known as *T-bills*) are short-term securities issued by governments, normally national governments, often using auction mechanisms, as part of their liquidity management operations. Credit risk is very low or effectively non-existent, depending on the credit standing of the issuing government. Investors can purchase T-bills on either the primary or the secondary market; that is, either at auction or from a securities dealer. Liquidity is excellent in the secondary market.

T-bills do not explicitly pay interest. Instead, they are sold to investors for less than their face value; when they mature, they are repaid at their face value. The difference between the issue price and the face value represents the return on the investment for the purchaser. Securities that pay interest in this fashion are known as discount instruments because they are issued and traded at a discount (that is, a lower price) to their face value.

Because of different market conventions, the quoted yield on some government T-bills is not directly comparable to the quoted yield on others. For example, Canadian T-bill yields are known as *bond equivalent* or *money market* yields, while US T-bill yields are known as *bank discount* yields.

The following equation is used to calculate the (bond equivalent) yield of a T-bill from its price:

$$Y = \frac{FV - P}{P} \times \frac{ADC}{DTM},$$
(2.2)

Where

Y = the yield

FV = the face value of the T-bill

P = the price of the T-bill

DTM = the number of days until maturity

ADC = the denominator of the relevant day count convention.

Alternatively, if we know the yield we can calculate its price. Rearranging (2.2) we have:

$$P = \frac{FV}{1 + \left(Y \times \dfrac{DTM}{ADC} \right)}.$$

(2.3)

Example 2.4

If a 90-day Government of Canada Treasury bill with a face value of $1 million is offered for a price of $990,000, the yield on the T-bill is:

$$\frac{\$1 \text{ million} - \$990,000}{\$990,000} \times \frac{365}{90} = 0.040965 = 4.0965\%.$$

Hence a 90-day Canadian T-bill with a face value of $1 million offered at a yield of 4.0965% has a price calculated as:

$$P = \frac{\$1 \text{ million}}{1 + \left(0.040965 \times \frac{90}{365} \right)} = \$990,000.$$

Commercial Paper

Corporations in need of short-term financing usually borrow money from one or more banks. For large corporations with good credit ratings, an alternative to bank lending is the commercial paper market. Commercial paper is similar to T-bills. It does not pay explicit interest: it is issued at a discount to its face value and it matures at face value. Commercial paper is often backed by the liquidity of a bank line of credit. The existence of the line of credit, however, does not mean a guarantee of repayment to the investor. The yields on commercial paper (and other money market securities) will generally be higher than those on T-bills because of the relatively greater credit risk and liquidity risk.

Promissory notes are very similar to commercial paper. They are bills issued by a borrower without the credit support of a financial institution (see the following discussion of bankers' acceptances for comparison).

Bankers' Acceptances

A banker's acceptance (BA) is short-term debt that is issued by a corporation and guaranteed by a bank. BAs may be used to facilitate the purchase and sale of goods, either domestically or internationally, or to borrow money for any purpose. BAs trade on the credit quality of the accepting bank, not that of the originating corporation. We show by example how a banker's acceptance is created.

Example 2.5

Suppose that Joe's Furniture Emporium (JFE) has a credit facility with Scotiabank that includes the option of issuing $10 million of BAs at an interest rate equal to Scotiabank's 3-month BA rate plus 150 basis points. (One hundred basis points equals one percentage point.) BAs are marketable securities, and Scotiabank's BA rate represents the rate at which Scotiabank is willing to buy BAs in the marketplace.

JFE decides that it needs $10 million in financing for three months and so it informs Scotiabank that it will draw down on its BA facility. If Scotiabank's three-month BA rate is currently 5%, JFE will issue what is, in effect, a marketable IOU to Scotiabank to pay it $10 million in three months' time. The IOU is then accepted by the bank, hence the name.

Once Scotiabank accepts the IOU from JFE, a banker's acceptance is created. Scotiabank will lend JFE the discounted value of $10 million based on Scotiabank's BA rate of 5%, and at maturity JFE will pay the face value to Scotiabank. The actual amount that JFE borrows from Scotiabank is calculated using equation (2.3), based on Scotiabank's BA rate and the number of days in the three-month period. If there are 91 days in the three-month period, JFE will receive

$$P = \frac{\$10 \text{ million}}{1 + \left(0.05 \times \frac{91}{365}\right)} = \frac{\$10 \text{ million}}{1.012465753} = \$9,876,877.$$

The extra 150 basis points that JFE pays to Scotiabank represents the stamping fee, which is Scotiabank's compensation for effectively guaranteeing JFE's debt. JFE must pay the stamping fee to Scotiabank in advance. If we substitute the face value for the principal and the stamping fee (in decimal terms) for the interest rate, equation (2.1) can be used to calculate the stamping fee on a Canadian BA. So, JFE will immediately pay Scotiabank a stamping fee of

$$\$10 \text{ million} \times 0.015 \times \frac{91}{365} = \$37,397.$$

The net effect is that JFE has borrowed \$9,839,480 (\$9,876,877 −\$37,397) and will repay \$10 million at maturity.[9]

Using (2.1) to calculate the dollar value of the stamping fee results in an effective borrowing cost (on a bond-equivalent basis) that is slightly higher than if we simply added the stamping fee to Scotiabank's BA rate. This is because the value of the stamping fee is based on the face value of the BA rather than the amount lent. To calculate JFE's effective borrowing cost, use (2.2), substituting the amount borrowed for the "price":

$$\frac{\$10 \text{ million} - \$9,839,480}{\$9,839,480} \times \frac{365}{91} = 0.06543 = 6.54\%.$$

The payment of the stamping fee has the effect of increasing JFE's cost of funds to 6.54% on a bond equivalent basis.

At this point, Scotiabank owns the BA. It may choose to hold it as part of its securities portfolio, or sell it to another market participant, such as a pension fund, mutual fund, or another bank that wants to invest in a liquid, short-term money market security. When the BA matures, 91 days after it is issued, Scotiabank will pay the holder of the BA its \$10 million face value, which Scotiabank will in turn receive from JFE.

Certificates of Deposit

A certificate of deposit is a time deposit with a bank which can be traded. They generally have maturity of less than three months. They can be thought of as bank bills where the issuer is the bank. Not surprisingly, they pay the same yield as BAs. They are often used by banks for the purpose of asset/liability management.

CONCLUSIONS

Money markets provide lenders and borrowers with a great deal of flexibility in terms of borrowing and deposits. As a result, they tend to be very active markets as well. Below are some key points to remember:

- The key characteristics of money market instruments are their term, principal, interest rate, marketability, security, and call or put features.
- Deposits come in three basic forms: demand deposits, notice deposits, and fixed-term deposits.
- Demand deposits are basically chequing accounts and generally do not pay interest.
- Notice deposits are savings accounts that generally pay a low, floating rate of interest that changes infrequently.
- Very large corporations can borrow large sums of money from a syndicate of banks. The loans can be structured as credit facilities, or may be one-off fixed- or floating-rate loans.
- A repurchase agreement, or repo, is a loan in which a borrower sells a security to a lender at one price and agrees to buy back the security on a future date at a higher price. The loan is collateralized by the security itself.
- The Eurocurrency market is the largest segment of the international market for deposits and loans. It is the market for fixed-rate term deposits and loans in a currency other than the local currency of the bank branch that is accepting the deposit or extending the loan.
- LIBOR stands for the London Interbank Offered Rate and represents an average rate on Eurocurrency deposits offered by eight large banks in the London market.

- LIBOR serves as an important benchmark for lending rates, both in the domestic market and the international market. LIBOR is also used as a reference rate for many interest-rate derivatives.

- Money market securities are initially issued with terms of one year or less. They generally do not pay interest, but trade in the secondary market at a price that is less than their face value. At maturity the issuer repays the face value, and the difference between the face value and the issue or purchase price is the interest on the loan.

- Treasury bills are issued by governments, primarily national governments.

- Commercial paper is issued by large corporations.

- Corporations issue bankers' acceptances (BAs) through a bank that guarantees the issue. BAs trade on the credit quality of the guarantor bank rather than the originating corporation. The guarantor bank charges the corporation a stamping fee to provide this guarantee.

REFERENCE

Alexander, C and Sheedy, E (2008b) *The Professional Rish Managers' Guide to Financial Instruments* (New York: McGraw-Hill).

NOTES

1. In the 1980s some companies issued debt known as perpetuities, which had no stated maturity date. The perpetuities called for the issuing companies to pay interest for ever. Almost all of the perpetuities, however, included a provision to allow the issuer to redeem them after a certain number of years.
2. A day-count convention is a method of calculating interest for periods of less than one year. The different segments of the interest-rate market use different day-count conventions, including actual/actual (or actual/365), actual/360, and 30/360, which assumes that each month is 30 days long and therefore a year has only 360 days. See Chapter 3 for further details.
3. This assumes, of course, the Deutsche Bank has an account with Citibank in New York.
4. A T-account is an accounting tool used to keep track of two-sided transactions. In our example, assets (deposits in other banks or loans to other parties) are on the left-hand side and liabilities (deposits due to other parties) are on the right-hand side.
5. Again, we assume that Royal Bank's London branch has an account with Citibank in New York.

6. Once again, we assume that XYZ has an account with Citibank in New York. If none of these Citibank-account assumptions were true, the demand deposit would be transferred between each party's New York-based bank.

7. From "The BBA LIBOR Fixing–Definition" on the British Bankers' Association website, www.bba.org.uk.

8. For example, if there are eight banks surveyed on a particular day, the two highest rates and the two lowest rates are dropped, and the average of the remaining four becomes the official LIBOR rate. If sixteen banks are surveyed, the four highest rates and the four lowest rates are dropped, and the average of the remaining eight becomes the official LIBOR rate.

9. Sometimes the bank that stamps the BA is different from the bank that actually lends the money to the corporation.

CHAPTER 3

Bond Markets

Moorad Choudhry, Lionel Martellini and Philippe Priaulet

This chapter describes the operation of bond markets. The focus is on market participants, the characteristics of bonds according to the type of issuer, the conventions and practices of bond markets (and the role of credit risk in bond markets). We also discuss some important trends that have impacted the bond market.

INTRODUCTION

In most countries government expenditure exceeds the level of government income received through taxation. This shortfall is met by government borrowing, and bonds are issued to finance the government's debt. The core of any domestic capital market is usually the government bond market, which also forms the benchmark for all other borrowing. Government agencies also issue bonds, as do local governments or municipalities. Often (but not always) these bonds are virtually as secure as government bonds. Corporate borrowers issue bonds both to raise finance for major projects and also to cover ongoing and operational expenses. Corporate finance is a mixture of debt and equity, and a specific capital project will often be financed by a mixture of both.

The debt capital markets exist because of the financing requirements of governments and corporates. The source of capital is varied, but the total supply of funds in a market is made up of personal or household savings, business savings, and increases in the overall money supply. However, the requirements of savers and borrowers differ significantly, in that savers have a short-term investment horizon while borrowers prefer to take a longer-term view. The "constitutional weakness" of what would otherwise be unintermediated financial markets led, from an early stage, to the development of financial intermediaries.

The world bond market has increased in size more than 15 times in the last thirty years. Table 3.1 shows that the United States constitutes one third of the world's bond market.

The origin of the spectacular increase in the size of global financial markets was the rise in oil prices in the early 1970s. Higher oil prices stimulated the development of a sophisticated international banking system, as they resulted in large capital inflows to developed country banks from the oil-producing countries. A significant proportion of these capital flows were placed in *Eurodollar* deposits in major banks. The growing trade deficit and level of public borrowing in the United States also contributed. The last twenty years have seen tremendous growth in capital markets' volumes and trading. As capital controls were eased and exchange rates moved from fixed to floating, domestic capital markets became internationalized. Growth was assisted by the rapid advance in

T A B L E   3.1

Gross external debt securities, 2007 Q1

Country	Nominal Value ($ millions)	Percentage of World Market
United States	6,352,147	33.01%
Germany	1,957,424	10.17%
United Kingdom	1,844,791	9.59%
France	1,682,003	8.74%
Netherlands	843,563	4.38%
Japan	542,184	2.82%
Australia	494,336	2.57%
Canada	374,306	1.95%
Denmark	201,996	1.05%
Switzerland	73,953	0.38%
Total	19,241,646	

Source: Joint BIS-IMF-OECD-WB Statistics on External Debt.

information technology and the widespread use of financial engineering techniques. Today we would think nothing of dealing in virtually any liquid currency bond in financial centres around the world, often at the touch of a button. Global bond issues, underwritten by the subsidiaries of the same banks, are commonplace. The ease with which transactions can be undertaken has also contributed to a very competitive market in liquid currency assets.

THE PLAYERS

A wide range of participants are involved in the bond markets. We can group them broadly into borrowers and investors, plus the institutions and individuals who are part of the business of bond trading. Borrowers access the bond markets as part of their financing requirements; hence, borrowers can include sovereign governments, local authorities, public sector organizations, and corporations. Virtually all businesses operate with a financing structure that is a mixture of debt and equity finance, and debt finance almost invariably contains a form of bond finance.

Intermediaries and Banks

In its simplest form a financial intermediary is a broker or agent. Today we would classify the broker as someone who acts on behalf of the borrower or lender, buying or selling a bond as instructed. However, intermediaries originally acted between borrowers and lenders in placing funds as required. A broker would not simply on-lend funds that had been placed with it, but would accept deposits and make loans as required by its customers. This resulted in the first banks.

A *retail bank* deals mainly with the personal financial sector and small businesses, and in addition to loans and deposits also provides cash transmission services. A retail bank is required to maintain a minimum cash reserve, to meet potential withdrawals, but the remainder of its deposit base can be used to make loans. This does not mean that the total size of its loan book is restricted to what it has taken in deposits: loans can also be funded in the wholesale market.

An *investment bank* will deal with governments, corporates, and institutional investors. Investment banks perform an agency role for their customers and are the primary vehicle through which a corporate will borrow funds in the bond markets. This is part of the bank's corporate

finance function. It will also act as wholesaler in the bond markets, a function known as *market making*. The bond issuing function of an investment
bank, by which the bank will issue bonds on behalf of a customer and
pass the funds raised to this customer, is known as *origination*. Investment
banks will also carry out a range of other functions for institutional
customers, including export finance, corporate advisory services
and fund management. Other financial intermediaries will trade not on
behalf of clients but for their own book. These include arbitrageurs and
speculators. Usually such market participants form part of investment
banks.

Institutional Investors

We can group the main types of institutional investors according to the
time horizon of their investment activity:

- *Short-term institutional investors.* These include banks and
  building societies, money market fund managers, central banks,
  and the treasury desks of some types of corporates. Such bodies
  are driven by short-term investment views, often subject to close
  guidelines. Banks will have an additional requirement to
  maintain liquidity, often in fulfilment of regulatory authority
  rules, by holding a proportion of their assets in the form of
  short-term instruments that are easy to trade.
- *Long-term institutional investors.* Typically these types of
  investors include pension funds and life assurance companies.
  Their investment horizon is long-term, reflecting the nature of
  their liabilities. Often they will seek to match these liabilities by
  holding long-dated bonds.
- *Mixed horizon institutional investors.* This is possibly the largest
  category of investors and will include general insurance
  companies and most corporate bodies. Like banks and financial
  sector companies, they are also very active in the primary
  market, issuing bonds to finance their operations.

Market Professionals

These players include the banks and specialist financial intermediaries
mentioned above, firms that one would not automatically classify as

"investors" although they will also have an investment objective. Their time horizon will range from one day to the very long term. They include:

- proprietary trading desks of investment banks;
- bond market makers in securities houses and banks providing a service to their customers;
- inter-dealer brokers that provide an anonymous broking facility.

Proprietary traders will actively position themselves in the market in order to gain trading profit, for example in response to their view on where they think interest rate levels are headed. These participants will trade direct with other market professionals and investors, or via brokers.

Market makers or "traders" (also called "dealers" in the United States) are wholesalers in the bond markets; they make two-way prices in selected bonds. Firms will not necessarily be active market makers in all types of bonds; smaller firms often specialize in certain sectors. In a two-way quote the *bid price* is the price at which the market maker will buy stock, so it is the price the investor will receive when selling stock. The *offer price* or ask price is the price at which investors can buy stock from the market maker. As one might expect, the bid price is always lower than the offer price, and it is this spread that represents the theoretical profit to the market maker. The bid–offer spread set by the market maker is determined by several factors, including supply and demand, and liquidity considerations for that particular stock, the trader's view on market direction and volatility, as well as that of the stock itself, and the presence of any market intelligence. A large bid–offer spread reflects low liquidity in the stock, as well as low demand.

To facilitate a liquid market there also exist *inter-dealer brokers* (IDBs). These provide an anonymous broking facility so that market makers can trade in size at the keenest prices. Generally, IDBs will post prices on their screens that have been provided by market makers on a no-names basis. The screens are available to other market makers (and in some markets to other participants as well). At any time IDB screen prices represent the latest market price and bid–offer spread. IDBs exist in government, agency, corporate, and Eurobond markets.

BONDS BY ISSUERS

This section describes the main classes of bonds by type of borrower. On the public side we distinguish between *sovereign bonds* issued by national governments, *agency bonds* issued by public bodies, and *municipal bonds* issued by local governments. On the private side we have the *corporate bonds* issued by corporations, and we further distinguish between *domestic* and *foreign bonds*, and *international bonds*, the latter constituting the large class of *Eurobonds*. Here we discuss the special characteristics of each of these types of bond.

Government Bonds

The four major government bond issuers in the world are the euro-area countries, Japan, the United States, and, to a lesser extent, the United Kingdom. Table 3.2 gives a country percentage breakdown of the JP

T A B L E   3.2

JP Morgan Global Government Bond Index (July 2007)

Market	$US Value	Weight in Index	Daily Yield	Macaulay Duration	Remaining Maturity
Global Index	**369.935**	**100%**	**3.78**	**6.26**	**8.33**
United States	389.739	23.42%	4.83	5.26	7.2
United Kingdom	488.691	6.43%	4.79	9.38	15.31
Sweden	526.647	0.76%	4.26	5.11	6.1
Spain	572.243	3.43%	4.44	6.37	8.85
Netherlands	342.837	2.23%	4.42	6.17	8.26
Japan	223.882	29.07%	1.74	6.18	6.9
Italy	642.861	9.50%	4.72	7.03	10.07
Germany	320.949	10.34%	4.36	6	8.17
France	426.760	8.81%	4.41	6.35	8.89
Denmark	460.351	0.82%	4.36	5.31	6.57
Canada	496.038	2.05%	4.5	7.53	11.34
Belgium	397.249	2.74%	4.45	6.15	8.22
Australia	585.723	0.40%	6.1	4.81	5.96
New Zealand	231.735		6.98	4.68	5.76
Ireland	515.968		4.42	6.28	7.64
Finland	280.376		4.35	4.69	5.36
Portugal	257.300		4.53	6.29	8.2
South Africa	609.478		8.58	5.32	8.37

Morgan Global Government Bond Index, which is a benchmark index for developed government debt markets.

Table 3.3 compares the features of the world's most important government bond markets. Note the minor variations in market practice with regard to the frequency of coupons, the day-count basis, benchmark bonds, etc. Most government bonds are issued by a standard auction process, where the price is gradually reduced until it meets a bid. The sale price varies for each successful bidder, depending on the bid price. Others use the so-called Dutch auction system. Under this system the securities are allocated to bidders starting with the highest bid. The price at which the final allocation is made becomes the price at which *all* securities are sold.

Table 3.4 shows the country yield curves at the time of writing, and a subset of them are graphed in Figure 3.1. Note the variability in yield

F I G U R E   3.1

Bloomberg screen IYC showing yield curves for US, UK, French, and German government bond markets, July 23, 2007

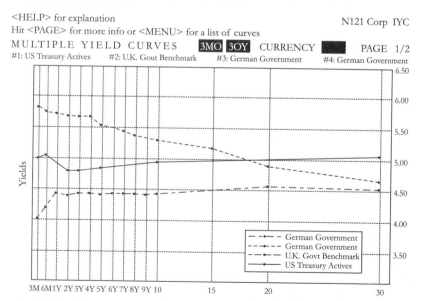

TABLE 3.3

Government bond markets: characteristics of selected countries

	Credit Rating	Maturity Range	Dealing	Benchmark Bonds	Issuance	Coupon and Day-Count Basis
Australia	AAA	2–15 years	OTC Dealer network	5, 10 years	Auction	Semi-annual, actual/actual
Canada	AAA	2–30 years	OTC Dealer network	3, 5, 10 years	Auction, subscription	Semi-annual, actual/actual
France	AAA	BTAN: 1–7 years OAT: 10–30 years	OTC Dealer network. Bonds listed on Paris Stock Exchange	BTAN: 2 and 5 year OAT: 10 and 30 years	Dutch auction	BTAN: Semi-annual, actual/actual OAT: Annual, actual/actual
Germany	AAA	OBL: 2, 5 years BUND: 10, 30 years	OTC Dealer network. Listed on Stock Exchange	The most recent issue	Combination of Dutch auction and proportion of each issue allocated on fixed basis to institutions	Annual, actual/actual
South Africa	A	2–30 years	OTC Dealer network. Listed on Johannesburg SE	2, 7, 10, 20 years	Auction	Semi-annual, actual/365
Singapore	AAA	2–20 years	OTC Dealer network	1, 5, 10, 20 years	Auction	Semi-annual, actual/actual
Taiwan	AA–	2–30 years	OTC Dealer network	2, 5, 10, 20, 30 years	Auction	Annual, actual/actual
United Kingdom	AAA	2–50 years	OTC Dealer network	5, 10, 30 years	Auction, subsequent issue by "tap" subscription	Semi-annual, actual/actual
United States	AAA	2–30 years	OTC Dealer network	2, 5, 10, 30 years	Auction	Semi-annual, actual/actual

Source: Choudhry (2004)

TABLE 3.4

Country yield curves (as at July 23, 2007)

Term (years)	Australia	Canada	France	Germany	South Africa	Singapore	Taiwan	United Kingdom	United States
1	6.2774	4.7260	4.3931	4.4222	9.7810	2.3570		5.7023	
2	6.3251	4.6256	4.4529	4.3980	9.3730	2.4503	2.4877	5.6706	4.7877
3	6.3188	4.6137	4.5929	4.4212	9.0520			5.6688	4.7981
4	6.2859	4.5939	4.4560	4.4336				5.6741	
5	6.2611	4.5844	4.4672	4.4138		2.6298	2.6457	5.5345	4.8455
7		4.5669	4.4570	4.4264	8.4990	2.8715		5.4512	
10	6.0940	4.5543	4.4880	4.4190	8.3710	2.9446	2.6078	5.2966	4.9519
15	6.0939	4.5636	4.5920		8.3190	3.1331	2.5859	5.1829	
20		4.5571	4.5870	4.5726	8.2180	3.3301	2.5608	4.8957	
30		4.4970	4.6100	4.5275	7.9217		2.6591	4.6554	5.0570

Yield source: Bloomberg L. P.

curves between countries reflecting their varying economic conditions and risk profiles. While most have an upward-sloping (or normal) yield curve, two of the yield curves (UK and Australia) are quite flat. Discussion of the various theories explaining the shape of the yield curve can be found in Alexander and Sheedy (2008a), Chapter 6.

In the US case, government securities are issued by the US Department of the Treasury and backed by the full faith and credit of the US government. These are called "Treasury securities." The Treasury market is the most active market in the world, thanks to the large volume of total debt and the large size of any single issue. The amount of outstanding marketable US Treasury securities is huge, with a value over $4 trillion as of December 2006. The Treasury market is the most liquid debt market, that is, the one where pricing and trading are most efficient. The bid–offer spread is far lower than in the rest of the bond market. Recently issued Treasury securities are referred to as *on-the-run* securities, as opposed to *off-the-run* securities, which are old issued securities. Special mention must be made of benchmark securities, which are recognized as market indicators. There typically exists one such security on each of the following yield curve points: 2 years, 5 years, 10 years, and 30 years. As they are over-liquid they trade richer than all of their direct neighbours.

Example 3.1

On December 7, 2001, the five-year US Treasury benchmark bond had a coupon of 3.5% and a maturity date of November 15, 2006. It had been issued on of November 15, 2001. In contrast, a five-year off-the-run US T-bond had a coupon of 7% and a maturity date of July 15, 2006. Its issuance date was of July 15, 1996. Note the difference of coupon level between the two. There are two reasons for that: first, the five-year off-the-run T-bond was originally a 10-year T-bond. Its coupon reflected the level of 10-year yields at that time. Second, the level of the US government yield curve on July 15, 1996 was at least 200 basis points over the level of the US government yield curve on November 15, 2001. Furthermore, on December 7, 2001, the yield of the off-the-run bond was 4.48% as opposed to 4.45% for the benchmark bond, which illustrates the relative richness of the latter. Government bonds are traded on major exchanges as well as *over the counter*.[1] The New York Stock Exchange had over 660 government issues listed on it at the end of 2003, with a total par value of $3.1 billion.

US Agency Bonds

These are issued by different organizations, seven of which dominate the US market in terms of outstanding debt: the Federal National Mortgage Association (Fannie Mae), the Federal Home Loan Bank System (FHLBS), the Federal Home Loan Mortgage Corporation (Freddie Mac), the Farm Credit System (FCS), the Student Loan Marketing Association (Sallie Mae), the Resolution Funding Corporation (RefCorp), and the Tennessee Valley Authority (TVA). Agencies have at least two common features:

- *They were created to fulfil a public purpose.* For example in the USA, Fannie Mae and Freddie Mac aim to provide liquidity for the residential mortgage market. The FCS aims to support agricultural and rural lending. RefCorp aims to provide financing to resolve thrift crisis.
- *The debt is not necessarily guaranteed by the government.* Hence it contains a credit premium. In fact in the USA, there are a few federally related institution securities, such as the Government National Mortgage Association (GNMA), and these *are* generally backed by the full faith and credit of the US government. There is no credit risk, but since they are relatively small issues they contain a liquidity premium.

Agencies are differently organized. For instance, Fannie Mae, Freddie Mac, and Sallie Mae are owned by private-sector shareholders, the FCS and the FHLBS are cooperatives owned by the members and borrowers. One sizeable agency, the Tennessee Valley Authority, is owned by the US government.

Municipal Bonds

Municipal securities constitute the municipal market, that is, the market where state and local governments—counties, special districts, cities, and towns—raise funds in order to finance projects for the public good such as schools, highways, hospitals, bridges and airports. Typically, bonds issued in this sector are exempt from federal income taxes, so this sector is referred to as the *tax-exempt sector*. There are two generic types of municipal bonds: *general obligation bonds* and *revenue bonds*. The former have principal and interest secured by the full faith and credit of the issuer and are usually supported by either the issuer's unlimited or limited taxing power. The latter have principal and interest secured by the revenues generated by the operating projects financed with the proceeds of the bond issue. Many of these bonds are issued by special authorities created for the purpose.

Corporate Bonds

Corporate bonds are issued by entities belonging to the private sector. They represent what market participants call the credit market. In the corporate markets, bond issues usually have a stated term to maturity, although the term is often not fixed because of the addition of call or put features. The convention is for most corporate issues to be medium- or long-dated, and rarely to have a term greater than 20 years. In the US market prior to the Second World War it was once common for companies to issue bonds with maturities of 100 years or more, but this is now quite rare. Only the highest-rated companies find it possible to issue bonds with terms to maturity greater than 30 years; during the 1990s such companies included Coca-Cola, Disney, and British Gas.

Investors prefer to hold bonds with relatively short maturities because of the greater price volatility experienced in the markets since the 1970s, when high inflation and high interest rates were common. A shorter-dated bond has lower interest-rate risk and price volatility than a longer-dated bond. There is thus a conflict between investors, whose wish is to hold bonds of shorter maturities, and borrowers, who would like to fix their borrowing for as long a period as possible. Although certain institutional investors such as pension fund managers have an interest in holding 30-year bonds, it would be difficult for all but the largest, best-rated companies, to issue debt with a maturity greater than this. Highly rated corporate borrowers are often able to issue bonds without indicating specifically how they will be redeemed. By implication, maturity proceeds will be financed out of the company's general operations or by the issue of another bond. However, borrowers with low ratings may make specific provisions for paying off a bond issue on its maturity date, to make their debt issue more palatable to investors. For instance, a ring-fenced sum of cash (called the *sinking fund*) may be put aside to form the proceeds used in the repayment of a fixed-term bond. A proportion of a bond issue is redeemed every year until the final year when the remaining outstanding amount is repaid. In most cases the issuer will pass the correct cash proceeds to the bond's trustee, who will use a lottery method to recall bonds representing the proportion of the total nominal value outstanding that is being repaid. The trustee usually publishes the serial numbers of bonds that are being recalled in a newspaper such as the *Wall Street Journal* or the *Financial Times*. The price at which bonds are redeemed by a sinking fund is usually par. If a bond has been issued above par, the sinking fund may retire the bonds at the issue price and gradually decrease this each year until it reaches par.[2] Sinking funds reduce the credit risk applying to a bond issue, because they indicate to investors that provision has been made to repay the debt. However, there is a risk associated with them, in that at the time bonds are paid off they may be trading above par due to a decline in market interest rates. In this case investors will suffer a loss if it is their holding that is redeemed.

Bonds that are secured through a charge on fixed assets such as property or plant often have certain clauses in their offer documents that state that the issuer cannot dispose of the assets without making provision for redemption of the bonds, as this would weaken the collateral backing for the bond. These clauses are known as *release-of-property* and *substitution-of-property* clauses. Under these clauses, if property or plant is disposed, the issuer must use the proceeds (or part of the proceeds) to redeem bonds that are secured by the disposed assets. The price at which the bonds are retired under this provision is usually par, although a special redemption price other than par may be specified in the repayment clause.

A large number of corporate bonds, especially in the US market, have a *call provision*. Borrowers prefer this as it enables them to refinance debt at cheaper rates when market interest rates have fallen significantly below their level at the time of the bond issue. A call provision is a negative feature for investors, as bonds are only paid off if their price has risen above par. Although a call feature indicates an issuer's interest in paying off the bond, because they are not attractive for investors, callable bonds pay a higher yield than non-callable bonds of the same credit quality.

In general, callable bonds are not callable for the first 5–10 years of their life, a feature that grants an element of protection for investors. Thereafter a bond is usually callable on set dates up to the final maturity date. In the US market another restriction is that of refunding redemption. This prohibits repayment of bonds within a set period after issue with funds obtained at a lower interest rate or through issue of bonds that rank with or ahead of the bond being redeemed. A bond with refunding protection during the first 5–10 years of its life is not as attractive as a bond with absolute call protection. Bonds that are called are usually called at par, although it is common also for bonds to have a call schedule that states that they are redeemable at specified prices above par during the call period.

Corporate bonds are traded on exchanges and OTC. Outstanding volume as at the end of 2003 was $8.1 trillion (see Choudhry, 2004). The corporate bond market varies in liquidity, depending on the currency and type of issuer of any particular bond. As in the case of sovereign bonds, liquidity is greater for recent issues. But corporate bonds in general are far less liquid than government bonds: they bear higher bid–ask spreads.

Example 3.2

On July 31, 2007, the bid–ask price spread for the T-bond 4% November 2012 amounted to 7 cents, whereas for the Ford corporate bond 7.8% June 2012 it amounted to 50 cents. The pricing source that is used is the Bloomberg Generic Value, that is, the average of the prices of the most active contributors. It is a market consensus price.

Eurobonds (International Bonds)

The Eurobord is one of the most liquid corporate bond types. It is an international bond issued and traded across national boundaries.

In any market there is a primary distinction between *domestic* bonds and other bonds. Domestic bonds are issued by borrowers domiciled in the country of issue, and in the currency of the country of issue. Generally they trade only in their original market. A *Eurobond* is issued across national boundaries and can be in any currency, which is why they are also sometimes called *international* bonds. In fact, it is now more common for Eurobonds to be referred to as international bonds, to avoid confusion with "euro bonds," which are bonds denominated in *euros*, the currency of 13 countries of the European Union (EU). As an issue of international bonds is not restricted in terms of currency or country, the borrower is not restricted as to its nationality either. There are also *foreign* bonds, which are domestic bonds issued by foreign borrowers. An example of a foreign bond is a *Bulldog*, which is a sterling bond issued for trading in the UK market by a foreign borrower. The equivalent foreign bonds in other countries include *Yankee* bonds (USA), *Samurai* bonds (Japan), *Alpine* bonds

(Switzerland), and *Matador* bonds (Spain). There are detailed differences between these bonds, for example in the frequency of interest payments that each one makes and the way the interest payment is calculated. Some bonds, such as domestic bonds, pay their interest *net*, which means net of a withholding tax such as income tax. Other bonds, including Eurobonds, make *gross* interest payments.

Nowhere has the increasing integration and globalization of the world's capital markets been more evident than in the Eurobond market. It is an important source of funds for many banks and corporates, not to mention central governments. The Eurobond market continues to develop new structures in response to the varying demands and requirements of specific groups of investors. Often the Eurobond market is the only opening for certain types of government and corporate finance. Investors also look to the Eurobond market due to constraints in their domestic market, and Euro securities have been designed to reproduce the features of instruments that certain investors may be prohibited from investing in domestically. Other instruments are designed for investors in order to provide tax advantages. The traditional image of the Eurobond investor, the so-called "Belgian dentist," has changed and the investor base is both varied and geographically dispersed.

THE MARKETS

A distinction is made between financial instruments of up to one year's maturity and instruments of over one year's maturity. Short-term instruments make up the *money market* while all other instruments are deemed to be part of the *capital market*. There is also a distinction made between the *primary market* and the *secondary market*. A new issue of bonds made by an investment bank on behalf of its client is made in the primary market. Such an issue can be a *public offer*, in which anyone can apply to buy the bonds, or a *private offer*, where the customers of the investment bank are offered the stock. The secondary market is the market in which existing bonds are subsequently traded.

Bond markets are regulated as part of the overall financial system. In most countries there is an independent regulator responsible for overseeing both the structure of the market and the bona fides of market participants. For instance, the US market regulator is the Securities and Exchange Commission (SEC). The UK regulator, the Financial Services Authority (FSA), is responsible for regulating both wholesale and retail markets;

for example, it reviews the capital requirements for commercial and investment banks, and it is also responsible for regulating the retail mortgage market. Money markets are usually overseen by the country's central bank—for example, the Federal Reserve manages the daily money supply in the USA, while the Bank of England provides liquidity to the market by means of its daily money market repo operation.

The Government Bond Market

Government bonds are traded on the following four markets: in addition to the primary and secondary markets, we have the *when-issued market* and the *repo market*.

- The primary market: newly issued securities are first sold through an auction, which is conducted on a competitive bid basis. The auction process happens between the government and primary/non-primary dealers according to regular cycles for securities with specific maturities.[3]

- The secondary market: here a group of government securities dealers offer continuous bid and ask prices on specific outstanding government bonds. This is an OTC market.

- The when-issued market: here securities are traded on a *forward* basis before they are issued by the government.

- The repo market: in this market securities are used as collateral for loans. A distinction must be made between the *general-collateral* repo rate (GC) and the *special* repo rate. The GC repo rate applies to the major part of government securities. Special repo rates are specific repo rates. They typically concern on-the-run and cheapest-to-deliver securities, which are very expensive. This is the reason why special repo rates are at a level below the GC repo rate. Indeed, as these securities are very much in demand, the borrowers of these securities on the repo market receive a relatively lower repo rate compared to normal government securities

The bonds issued by regional governments and certain public sector bodies, such as national power and telecommunications utilities, are usually included as "government" debt, as they are almost always covered by an explicit or implicit government guarantee. All other categories of borrower are therefore deemed to be "corporate" borrowers. Generally the term "corporate markets" is used to cover bonds issued by nongovernment borrowers.

The Corporate Bond Market

In the context of a historically low level of interest rates, linked to a decreasing trend in inflation as well as in budget deficits, the corporate bond market is rapidly developing and growing. This strong tendency affects both the supply and the demand. While corporate supply is expanding, in relation to bank disintermediation, corporate demand is rising as more and more investors accustomed to dealing with only government bonds are including corporate bonds in their portfolios so as to capture spread and generate performance.

The Market by Country and Sector

Within the four major bond markets in the world, the US dollar (USD) corporate market is the most mature, followed by the sterling (GBP) market and the euro (EUR) market. The Japanese yen (JPY) market differentiates itself from the others, because of the credit crunch situation and economic difficulties it has been facing since the Asian crisis. The USD corporate bond market is the largest and most diversified: it is for instance more than twice as big as the euro market, and low investment-grade ratings are much more represented (being over 80% of the index).

The corporate bond market can be divided into three main sectors: financial, industrial, utility. Apart from the USD market, the financial sector is over-represented. It is another proof of the maturity of the USD market, where the industrial sector massively uses the market channel in order to finance investment projects. It is also worth noting that the sector composition in the USD market is far more homogeneous than in the other markets. For example, the banking sector is systematically predominant in the GBP, EUR, and JPY financial markets, while the telecommunication sector exceeds one third of the euro industrial market. As a result, local credit portfolio diversification can be better achieved in the USD market than in the others.

Underwriting a New Issue

The issue of corporate debt in the capital markets requires a primary market mechanism. The first requirement is a collection of merchant banks or investment banks that possess the necessary expertise. Investment banks provide advisory services on corporate finance as well as underwriting services, which is a guarantee to place an entire bond issue into the market in return for a fee. As part of the underwriting process the investment bank will either guarantee a minimum price for the bonds, or aim to place the paper at the best price available. The major underwriting institutions in emerging economies are often branch offices of the major integrated global investment banks.

Small size bond issues may be underwritten by a single bank. It is common, however, for larger issues, or issues that are aimed at a cross-border investor base, to be underwritten by a syndicate of investment banks. This is a group of banks that collectively underwrite a bond issue, with each syndicate member being responsible for placing a proportion of the issue. The bank that originally won the mandate to place the paper invites other banks to join the syndicate. This bank is known as the *lead underwriter, lead manager,* or *book-runner.* An issue is brought to the market simultaneously by all syndicate members, usually via the *fixed price re-offer* mechanism.[4] This is designed to guard against some syndicate members in an offering selling stock at a discount in the *gray market*, to attract investors.[5] This would force the lead manager to buy the bonds back if it wished to support the price. Under the fixed price re-offer method, price undercutting is not possible as all banks are obliged not to sell their bonds below the initial offer price that has been set for the issue. The fixed price usually is in place up to the first settlement date, after which the bond is free to trade in the secondary market.

The Eurobond Market

The key feature of a Eurobond is the way it is issued, internationally across borders and by an international underwriting syndicate. The method of issuing Eurobonds reflects the cross-border nature of the transaction and, unlike government markets where the auction is the primary issue method, Eurobonds are typically issued under a fixed price re-offer method (see above) or a *bought deal.*[6]

The range of borrowers in the Euromarkets is very diverse. From virtually the inception of the market, borrowers representing corporates, sovereign and local governments, nationalized corporations, supranational institutions, and financial institutions have raised finance in the international markets. The majority of borrowing has been by national governments, regional governments, and public agencies of developed countries, although the Eurobond market is increasingly a source of finance for developing country governments and corporates.

Governments and institutions access the Euromarkets for a number of reasons. Under certain circumstances it is more advantageous for a borrower to raise funds outside its domestic market, due to the effects of tax or regulatory rules.[7] The international markets are very competitive in terms of using intermediaries, so a borrower may well be able to raise cheaper funds in the international markets.

Other reasons why borrowers access Eurobond markets include:

- A desire to diversify sources of long-term funding. A bond issue is often placed with a wide range of institutional and private investors, rather than the more restricted investor base that may prevail in a domestic market. This gives the borrower access to a wider range of lenders, and for corporate borrowers this also enhances the international profile of the company.
- For both corporates and emerging country governments, the prestige associated with an issue of bonds in the international market.
- The flexibility of a Eurobond issue compared to a domestic bond issue or bank loan, illustrated by the different types of Eurobond instruments available.

Against this are balanced the potential downsides of a Eurobond issue, which include the following:

- For all but the largest and most creditworthy of borrowers, the rigid nature of the issue procedure becomes significant during times of interest-rate and exchange-rate volatility, reducing the funds available for borrowers.
- Issuing debt in currencies other than those in which a company holds matching assets, or in which there are no prospects of earnings, exposes the issuer to foreign exchange risk.

Table 3.5 shows some of the outstanding issues in the Eurobond market in 2005. The market remains an efficient and attractive market in which a company can raise finance for a wide range of maturities. The institutional investors include insurance companies, pension funds,

TABLE 3.5

Selected euro-denominated Eurobond issues in 2005

Issuer	Moodys/S&P Rating	Coupon	Maturity	Issue Size	Launch spread to benchmark (bps)
Daimler Chrysler NA	A3/BBB	4.875%	June 15, 2010	USD 1,000 million	130
Development Bank of Japan	Aaa/AAA	4.25%	June 9, 2015	USD 700 million	38.8
Federal Home Loan Bank	AAA	3.625%	June 20, 2007	USD 4,000 million	17
GE Capital	Aaa/AAA	4.75%	June 15, 2011	GBP 250 million	52
General Electric Capital Corp	Aaa/AAA	4.00%	June 15, 2009	USD 500 million	48
If Skadeforsakring AB	Baa2/BBB	4.943%	Perpetual/callable	EUR 150 million	179.8; fixed coupon to June 2015, thereafter 3-month Euribor + 265
ING Group N.V.	A2/A–	4.176%	Perpetual/callable	EUR 500 million	95.3; fixed coupon to June 2015, thereafter 3-month Euribor + 180
Kingdom of Belgium	Aa1/AA+	3.000%	March 28, 2010	EUR 6,145 million	9
Korea Exchange Bank	Baa3/BB+	5.00%	June 10, 2015	USD 300 million	151
Lambay Capital Securities	Baa1	FRN	Perpetual	GBP 300 million	3-month LIBOR + 166. Coupon step-up after 2015
LB Baden-Wuerttemberg	Aaa/AAA	6.50%	November 26, 2007	NZD 50 million	23
Legal & General Group	A2/A	4.00%	June 8, 2025	EUR 600 million	85.1
Portugal Telecom	A3/A–	4.50%	June 16, 2025	EUR 500 million	137
Republic of El Salvador	Baa3/BB+	7.65%	June 15, 2035	USD 375 million	345
Republic of Turkey	B1/BB–	7.00%	June 15, 2020	USD 1,250 million	332.4
Zurich Finance (USA) Inc	Baa2/BBB+	4.50%	June 15, 2025	EUR 500 million	135.00 to June 2015; thereafter 3-month Euribor + 220

Source: Bloomberg L.P.

investment trusts, commercial banks, and corporations—just as in domestic corporate bond markets. Other investors include central banks and government agencies; for example, the Kuwait Investment Office and the Saudi Arabian Monetary Agency both have large Eurobond holdings. In the UK, banks and securities houses are keen holders of Eurobonds issued by other financial institutions.

Market Conventions

A particular market will apply one of five different methods to calculate accrued interest:

actual/365	Accrued = coupon days/365
actual/360	Accrued = coupon days/360
actual/actual	Accrued = coupon days/actual number of days in the interest period
30/360	See below
30E/360	See below

When determining the number of days in between two dates, include the first date but not the second; thus, under the actual/365 convention, there are 37 days between August 4 and September 10. The last two conventions assume 30 days in each month, so for example there are 30 days between February 10 and March 10. Under the 30/360 convention, if the first date falls on the 31st, it is changed to the 30th of the month, and if the second date falls on the 31st and the first date is on the 30th or 31st, the second date is changed to the 30th. The difference under the 30E/360 method is that if the second date falls on the 31st of the month it is automatically changed to the 30th. The day-count basis, together with the coupon frequency, of selected major government bond markets around the world is given in Table 3.6.

CREDIT RISK

As is the case for government and municipal bonds, the issuer of a corporate bond has the obligation to honour his commitments to the bondholder. A failure to pay back interests or principal according to the terms of the agreement constitutes what is known as *default*. Basically, there are two sources of default. First, the shareholders of a corporation can decide to break the debt contract. This comes from their limited liability status: they

T A B L E   3.6

Selected bond market conventions

Market	Coupon Frequency	Day Count Basis	Ex-Dividend Period
Australia	Semi-annual	actual/actual	Yes
Austria	Annual	actual/actual	No
Belgium	Annual	actual/actual	No
Canada	Semi-annual	actual/actual	No
Denmark	Annual	actual/actual	Yes
Eurobonds	Annual	30/360	No
France	Annual	actual/actual	No
Germany	Annual	actual/actual	No
Ireland	Annual	actual/actual	No
Italy	Annual	actual/actual	No
New Zealand	Semi-annual	actual/actual	Yes
Norway	Annual	actual/365	Yes
Spain	Annual	actual/actual	No
Sweden	Annual	30E/360	Yes
Switzerland	Annual	30E/360	No
United Kingdom	Semi-annual	actual/actual	Yes
United States	Semi-annual	actual/actual	No

Source: Choudhry (2004)

are liable for the corporation's losses only up to their investment in it. They do not have to pay back their creditors when it affects their personal wealth. Second, creditors can prompt bankruptcy when specific debt protective clauses, known as covenants, are infringed.

In case of default, there are typically three eventualities:

- First, default can lead to immediate bankruptcy. Depending on the seniority and face value of their debt securities, creditors are fully, partially, or not paid back thanks to the sale of the firm's assets. The percentage of the interests and principal they receive, according to seniority, is called the *recovery rate*.

- Second, default can result in a reorganization of the firm within a formal legal framework. For example, under Chapter 11 of the American law, corporations that are in default are granted a deadline so as to overcome their financial difficulties. This depends on the country's legislation.

- Third, default can lead to an informal negotiation between shareholders and creditors. This results in an exchange offer through which shareholders propose to creditors the exchange of their old debt securities for a package of cash and newly issued securities.

A corporate debt issue is priced over the same currency government bond yield curve. A liquid benchmark yield curve therefore is required to facilitate pricing. The extent of a corporate bond's yield spread over the government yield curve is a function of the market's view of the credit risk of the issuer (for which formal credit ratings are usually used) and the perception of the liquidity of the issue. The pricing of corporate bonds is sometimes expressed as a spread over the equivalent maturity government bond, rather than as an explicit stated yield, or sometimes as a spread over another market reference index such as LIBOR. Figure 3.2 illustrates some typical yield spreads for different ratings and maturities of corporate bonds.

Corporate bonds are much affected by credit risk. Their yields normally contain a default premium over government bonds, accounting for

FIGURE   3.2

Yield spread by rating and maturity

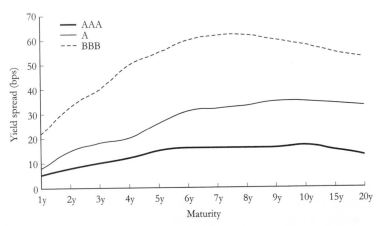

total default or credit risk, as well as over swaps. Swap spread, that is, the difference between the swap yield and the government yield with same maturity, is regarded as a systematic credit premium. In the four main bond markets swap yields reflect bank risk with rating AA, that is, the first rating grade below AAA, the normal rating for government bonds, accounting for specific default or credit risk.

Formal credit ratings are important in the corporate markets. Investors usually use both a domestic rating agency in conjunction with the established international agency such as Moody's or Standard & Poor's. As formal ratings are viewed as important by investors, it is in the interest of issuing companies to seek a rating from an established agency, especially if it is seeking to issue foreign currency and/or place its debt across national boundaries. Generally Eurobond issuers are investment-grade rated, and only a very small number are not rated at all.

Treasury securities are considered to have no credit risk. The interest rates they bear are the key interest rates in the US as well as in international capital markets. Agency securities' debt is high-quality debt. As a matter of fact, all rated agency senior debt issues are triple-A rated by Moody's and Standard & Poor's. This rating most often reflects healthy financial fundamentals and sound management, but also and above all the agencies' relationship to the US government. Among the numerous legal characteristics of the government agencies' debt, one can find that:

- agencies' directors are appointed by the President of the United States;
- issuance is only upon approval by the US Treasury;
- securities are issuable and payable through the Federal Reserve System;
- securities are eligible collateral for Federal Reserve Bank advances and discounts;
- securities are eligible for open market purchases.

Municipal debt issues, when rated, carry ratings ranging from triple-A, for the best ones, to C or D, for the worst ones. Four basic criteria are used by rating agencies to assess municipal bond ratings:

- the issuer's debt structure;
- the issuer's ability and political discipline for maintaining sound budgetary operations;

- the local tax and intergovernmental revenue sources of the issuer;
- the issuer's overall socio-economic environment.

CONCLUSIONS

In this chapter we have described the structure of the bond markets and the nature of the main market participants. These are comprised of issuers, investors and intermediaries.

- *Issuers* are those who have a requirement to raise capital, and can be sovereign governments, government agencies, multilateral agencies, and corporates. Bonds are rated in terms of their credit quality, which reflects the quality of the issuer. Certain sovereign issuers such as the USA, the UK, Germany, and Japan are viewed as triple-A or risk-free credit quality. Credit quality ranges from triple-A to D, meaning the issuer is in default.
- *Investors* are fund managers, insurance companies, corporates, and agencies. Bond markets are essentially over-the-counter markets, although a large number of them are listed on stock exchanges, such as the NYSE, Irish Stock Exchange, and Luxembourg Stock Exchange. This listing enables institutional investors to hold them, who might otherwise be prevented from holding unlisted products.
- *Intermediaries* include commercial and investment banks, who act as underwriters to bond issuances, as well as brokers and advisors. Note that banks also act as issuers and investors.

REFERENCES

Alexander, C and Sheedy, E (2008a) *The Professional Risk Managers' Guide to Finance Theory* (New York: McGraw-Hill).

Choudhry, M (2004) *Fixed Income Markets: Instruments, Applications, Mathematics* (Singapore: Wiley).

Martellini, L, Priaulet, S, and Priaulet, P (2003) *Fixed-Income Securities: Valuation, Risk Management and Portfolio Strategies* (Chichester: Wiley).

NOTES

1. Generally OTC refers to trades that are not carried out on an exchange but directly between the counterparties.

2. Another method by which bonds are repaid is that the issuer will purchase the required nominal value of the bonds in the open market; these are then delivered to the trustee, who cancels them.

3. The US auction cycles are as follows: two-year notes are auctioned every month and settle on the 15th. Five-year notes are auctioned quarterly, in February, May, August, and November of each year, and settle at the end of the month. Ten-year notes are auctioned quarterly, in February, May, August, and November of each year, and settle on the 15th of the month. Thirty-year bonds are auctioned semi-annually: in February and August of each year, and settle on the 15th of the month. Auctions are announced by the Treasury one week in advance, the issuing date being set one to five days after the auction.

4. In a fixed price re-offer scheme the lead manager will form the syndicate, which will agree on a fixed issue price, a fixed commission and the distribution amongst themselves of the quantity of bonds they will take as part of the syndicate. The banks then re-offer the bonds that they have been allotted to the market, at the agreed price. This technique gives the lead manager greater control over an issue. It sets the price at which other underwriters in the syndicate can initially sell the bonds to investors. The fixed price re-offer mechanism is designed to prevent underwriters from selling the bonds back to the lead manager at a discount to the original issue price, that is, "dumping" the bonds.

5. The gray market is a term used to describe trading in the bonds before they officially come to the market, mainly market makers selling the bond short to other market players or investors. Activity in the gray market serves as useful market intelligence to the lead manager, who can gauge the level of demand that exists in the market for the issue.

   A final decision on the offer price is of course not made until the actual issue date.

6. In a bought deal, a lead manager or a managing group approaches the issuer with a firm bid, specifying issue price, amount, coupon, and yield. Only a few hours are allowed for the borrower to accept or reject the terms. If the bid is accepted, the lead manager purchases the entire bond issue from the borrower. The lead manager then has the option of selling part of the issue to other banks for distribution to investors, or doing so itself. In a volatile market the lead manager will probably parcel some of the issue to other banks for placement. However, it is at this time that the risk of banks dumping bonds on the secondary market is highest; in this respect lead managers will usually pre-place the bonds with institutional investors before the bid is made. The bought deal is focused primarily on institutional rather than private investors. As the syndicate process is not used, the bought deal requires a lead manager with sufficient capital and placement power to enable the entire issue to be placed.

7. There is no formal regualtion of the Eurobond market as such, but each market participant will be subject to the regualtion of its country regulator

The Foreign Exchange Market

Canadian Securities Institute

INTRODUCTION

The foreign exchange (or forex) market encompasses all the places in which one nation's currency is exchanged for another at a specific exchange rate. An *exchange rate* is the price of one currency in terms of another. For example, a Canadian dollar exchange rate of US$0.63 means that it costs 63 US cents to buy one Canadian dollar.

In 2004, the BIS's Triennial Survey[1] showed that the global average daily turnover in the interbank foreign exchange market was US$1,880 billion. This is a 36% increase from the BIS's previous survey in 2001, measured at constant exchange rates. The BIS cited four factors for the increase in activity:

- investor interest in foreign exchange as an asset class;
- greater activity by asset managers;
- the growing importance of hedge funds.

The Survey further revealed that US dollar/euro is by far the most traded currency pair with 28% of global turnover, followed by dollar/yen with 17% and dollar/sterling with 14%. The United Kingdom continued to be the most active trading centre, accounting for 31% of total turnover, followed by the United States (19%), and Japan (8%).

The broadest definition of the forex market includes foreign currency purchases by individuals at bank branches for vacations or other personal reasons, as well as the large volumes exchanged between businesses and corporations and their respective banks. The largest component of the forex market, however, is the *interbank* market. The interbank market is an over-the-counter (OTC) market dominated by large financial institutions that buy and sell currencies among themselves. According to the 2004 BIS Survey, banks reported that 53% of foreign exchange market turnover was with other reporting banks and a further 33% with other financial institutions including hedge funds, leaving only 14% of turnover with nonfinancial customers.

In the next section we examine the interbank market in more detail. Then, in the following section, we describe different types of exchange-rate quotations. We also explain how participants in the interbank market get quotes from one another, the role of the US dollar and how currencies are quoted relative to the US dollar, and how cross rates are calculated. Next we provide a discussion of the different factors that affect foreign exchange rates. We then outline the differences between the spot and forward markets. After that an overview of a typical foreign exchange operation is provided, before the Conclusion.

The Interbank Market

The interbank foreign exchange market has been described as a "decentralized, continuous, open bid, double-auction" market. Let us look at these terms one by one.

- *Decentralized.* The interbank market is an OTC market without a single location. It operates globally, through telephone and computer systems that link banks and other currency traders. Most trading activity, however, occurs in three major financial centres: London, New York, and Tokyo. Smaller but important interbank centres exist in Frankfurt, Paris, Singapore, and Toronto. This decentralization makes it extremely difficult to regulate the market. There is no true "regulator" of foreign exchange markets, although the Bank for International Settlements (BIS) collects data on foreign exchange market activity. Forex markets are self-regulating, with associations such as the International Swaps and Derivatives Association playing an important role in fostering high standards of commercial conduct and promoting sound risk management practices. In addition, the capital adequacy requirements which apply to all financial institutions help to ensure that the risk of bank failure is minimized.

- *Continuous.* Price quotes in the interbank foreign exchange market vary continuously. Banks call each other and ask for the current market price for a particular currency trade. They are quoted a bid/offer price that is stated as the price of one currency in terms of the other. The bid/offer price can change from moment to moment, reflecting changes in market sentiment as well as demand and supply conditions.

- *Open bid.* Those who request a bid/offer price do not have to specify the amount they wish to exchange, or even whether they intend to buy or sell the currency. This is what is meant by an open bid: the bank that provides the quotation is open to buy or sell. The amount of the transaction is also left open, although conventional limits exist on what can be exchanged at the quoted rates. Typical price quotations are for trades worth US$5–10 million or equivalent.

- *Double auction.* Banks that receive calls for quotations also call other banks and ask for their market, that is, their buy (bid) and sell (ask) rates. The obligation to be both a price "maker" and a price "taker" is what is meant by a "double auction."

EXCHANGE-RATE QUOTATIONS

An exchange rate can be expressed relative to either of the two currencies involved. A *direct terms* quote is based on a single unit of the domestic currency unit.[2] An exchange rate of C$1.5873 per US dollar is a direct terms quote from the perspective of an American. From a Canadian perspective, however, it is an indirect terms quote, meaning the number of *domestic* currency units that can be purchased with one foreign currency unit. An indirect terms quote expresses how much a single unit of the foreign currency is worth in terms of the domestic currency—it is simply the opposite or "reciprocal" of a direct terms quote. That is,

$$P_{B/A} = (P_{A/B})^{-1} = 1/P_{A/B}$$

where $P_{A/B}$ is the price of currency A in terms of currency B and $P_{B/A}$ is the price of currency B in terms of currency A.

Interbank participants may deal directly with one another or indirectly through a system of foreign exchange brokers or electronic brokering systems.

Direct Dealing

Direct dealing is the common practice by which a trader at one bank telephones a trader at another bank to get a quote on a certain currency. One of the advantages of this type of dealing is that a professional business relationship between the two traders develops over time, which could prove valuable in certain market situations. For example, if a certain currency is experiencing a temporary or even prolonged bout of illiquidity, an established relationship with another bank that deals in that currency may help a trader complete a deal at a reasonable price.

Banks control the amount of trading that they do with each other by placing limits on the amount of business that they will do with any other bank. The setting of these limits is a credit decision, made by senior risk managers. Banks limit their exposure to any given counterparty in order to minimize default risk, which is the risk that the other party to a trade cannot meet its contractual obligations on any given trade.

Foreign Exchange Brokers

Given the large number of banks participating in the global interbank market, or even within North America, Europe, or Asia, one can imagine the intricate network of contacts and technology required to maintain relationships with as many other banks as possible. The use of inter-dealer brokers allows a bank to economize on its contacts with other market participants in one location. A foreign exchange broker acts as a middleman, bringing together two banks that have expressed an interest in buying or selling a currency at a specific price. For this service, brokers charge both the buyer and the seller a commission based on the size of the deal. Commission rates are generally very similar across the board, but in certain cases discounts may be provided to banks that do very large trades.

Most brokers work in the large financial trading centers of London, New York, and Tokyo, although some work in the smaller trading centers. Banks submit bids and offers for pairs of currencies to the brokers and the brokers are expected to disseminate or "work" the orders to their respective networks. They do this by broadcasting the best bids and offers in various currencies over speakers that are physically located at a bank's trading desk. When a trader wants to execute a deal based on the prices that are being broadcast, they will shout back to the broker via an open, direct telephone line, "mine" (that is, I want to buy the currency) or "yours" (I want to sell the currency).

Brokers will not reveal which banks are behind the prices until a deal is actually approved by both parties, assuming that both banks are able to deal with the other based on the limits they have imposed on their dealings. Brokers try to avoid matching banks that do not or cannot deal with each other. This is known as being aware of "who will take which names" and which banks are "full" on a given name.

The use of a broker guarantees anonymity to the buyer and seller. This is important to the trading process, because traders usually prefer not to reveal their position or market view to others in the market. Once a deal is concluded and both parties agree on the details, the deal is processed and confirmed by the respective back offices of the parties involved, including the broker. Brokers try to remain neutral in their dealings with banks and are not allowed to take positions the way banks can.

Electronic Brokering Systems

Until recently, "physical" brokering—the process just described—was a key source of quotes and counterparties. However, due to the rapid evolution of technology and computing power, the physical brokering business is rapidly being supplanted by electronic brokering systems. Electronic brokering is similar to physical brokering, except that orders are placed into a computer system rather than with a person. The system automatically matches bids and offers as the price of a currency fluctuates and "market" orders are matched with open orders.

The major providers of electronic brokering systems are EBS and Reuters. Other technology innovators have a smaller presence but are constantly trying to expand their share of the market as electronic brokering increases in importance.

The Role of the US Dollar

The US dollar has been the world's primary vehicle currency for almost a century. This means that it is the accepted benchmark currency against which most other currencies are valued, because most global trade transactions take place in US dollars. In addition, it is readily accepted as legal tender in some countries, and can be easily exchanged into the domestic currency in most others. Most currency trading in the interbank market therefore involves the US dollar on one side of the transaction—the BIS 2004 Survey showed that the US dollar is involved in 89% of all reported transactions.

Most currencies are quoted in direct terms from the US perspective. For example, a 120.92 quote for Japanese yen (JPY) means that one US dollar is worth ¥120.92, or that it takes ¥120.92 to buy one US dollar. A JPY quote of 120.92 translates into a value of US$0.00827 for one Japanese yen. If a currency is quoted in the former manner, a rising quote signifies a strengthening of the US dollar relative to the other currency or a weakening of the currency relative to the US dollar.

Some currencies, however, are quoted indirectly from the US perspective, including the British pound sterling (GBP), the euro (EUR), the Australian dollar (AUD) and the New Zealand dollar (NZD). This type of quote indicates the value of a single unit of the relevant currency in terms of US dollars. For example, a 1.6234 quote for GBP means that one British pound is worth US$1.6234, or that it takes US$1.6234 to buy one British pound. A GBP quote of 1.6234 translates into a value of £0.6160 for one US dollar. If a currency is quoted in the former way, a rising quote signifies strength in the other currency relative to the US dollar (and weakness in the US dollar versus the currency).

Market and Quoting Conventions

Traders have special ways of quoting bid and offer prices for foreign currencies. For example, a trader at bank A may call a trader at bank B and ask for B's market on the Canadian dollar (CAD) versus USD. B shows a market price of 1.5599–1.5604. Normally the trader at B would not waste his and the caller's time by saying "one fifty-five ninety-nine" and "one fifty-six-oh-four" but would rather quote only the last two decimal places, or points, as in "ninety-nine" and "oh-four". Traders are always aware of what this means and will always know what the initial numbers are (often referred to as the "big figure").

This quote means that the trader at B is willing to buy USD at C$1.5599 and is willing to sell USD at C$1.5604. In other words, A can either sell USD to B and receive C$1.5599 or buy USD from B and pay C$1.5604. These quotes are usually valid for amounts between US$5 million and US$10 million. The exact amounts are usually set up in advance. If a bank needs to trade a larger amount of money, the trader at bank A will specify this before the trader at bank B provides the quote. If A buys USD at 1.5604 from B then it is paying or taking the offer. The bank A trader may simply say "mine," which is interbank shorthand for "the US dollars are mine at your offer price." If the trader at A wants to sell US dollars to B he or she will say "yours," meaning the US dollars are yours at your bid price.

Table 4.1 provides a typical list of quotes on several currencies relative to the USD. The bid–offer spread for most large, relatively liquid foreign currencies is usually 3–10 "points." In times of extreme illiquidity, however, the spread can be significantly larger.

Sometimes a trader may quote a "choice" market, meaning the bid/offer price is the same and the interested party has the choice of buying or selling at this price. A choice market suggests extremely high liquidity in the market.

Cross Trades and Cross Rates

Most foreign currencies are not traded or quoted directly against one another. For example, if a corporation wants to sell Mexican pesos (MXN) in exchange for Hong Kong dollars (HKD), the transaction would take place as a cross trade that involves selling MXN for USD and then selling USD for HKD. The quote that is supplied for this trade would be derived from the two currencies' quotes versus the US dollar. This quote is known as a cross rate.

T A B L E   4.1

Typical foreign exchange quotes

Currency	Bid	Offer
CAD	1.5599	1.5604
GBP	1.5370	1.5375
EUR	0.9835	0.9839
JPY	117.50	117.60
CHF	1.4909	1.4915
AUD	0.5440	0.5449

Example 4.1: Cross Rates

Suppose a bank is willing to buy and sell foreign currencies to and from its largest corporate customers at the exchange rates shown in Table 4.1. If one of these customers wants a quote to buy CAD for JPY, the bank will arrive at a bid–offer spread for its cross rate as follows. The customer will sell CAD for USD at 1.5604. In other words, one Canadian dollar yields US$0.6409. The customer will buy JPY for USD at 117.50. In other words, one Japanese yen costs US$0.00851. Overall, one Canadian dollar will buy 0.6409/0.00851 = ¥75.30.

If a customer wants to sell JPY for CAD, the cross rate would be calculated as follows. The customer will sell JPY for USD at 117.60. In other words, one Japanese yen yields US$0.0085. The customer will buy CAD for USD at 1.5599. In other words, one Canadian dollar costs US$0.6411. Overall, one Canadian dollar will cost 0.6411/0.0085 = ¥75.40.

Altogether, the bank's bid–offer spread for the CAD in terms of JPY is 75.30–75.40. In other words, the bank is willing to buy Canadian dollars at ¥75.30 or sell Canadian dollars for ¥75.40.

DETERMINANTS OF FOREIGN EXCHANGE RATES

This section will give only a brief overview of the determinants of the value of a currency. Whole books have been written on how and why currency values change. Ask a forex trading professional why a currency is appreciating and sometimes, half-jokingly, he or she will say that there is more demand than supply. In fast-changing markets, when it is not immediately evident what is influencing currency value changes, this short answer is true, but it is not the whole story.

The Fundamental Approach

Foreign exchange rates have strong, long-term relationships with a country's identifiable economic fundamentals. These include: gross domestic product (GDP); rate of inflation; productivity; interest rates; employment levels; balance of payments; and current account balance. The performance of a national economy is generally measured by changes in its GDP. From quarter to quarter, and from year to year, various statistical agencies report on this measure. If the economy of one country is performing well relative to that of another country, the country with the stronger economic performance will usually have a stronger currency. Comparisons of the economic strength of countries are most often conducted relative to the United States.

Currencies are affected not only by what has happened in the past but also by expectations and forecasts of future performance. Attempts to anticipate the future movement of a currency are also usually done relative to the US dollar, because most currencies trade directly against the dollar. It is difficult to anticipate where the Swedish krona will be relative to the Mexican peso, but both these currencies can be compared to the American dollar. From there it is possible to come up with a calculated or projected cross rate, but this rate will have a larger margin for error.

Real GDP is related to inflation levels. Higher levels of inflation will erode the domestic value of the currency, because it now takes more domestic currency to buy foreign goods. Higher levels of inflation also reduce the real level of interest rates. Foreign investors will have less incentive to invest in a country with high inflation.

The productivity of a country also affects the value of the currency. For instance, when productivity increases because of technological advances, this improvement translates into stable prices and low inflation. The currency market rewards countries with high levels of productivity, as it did the United States in the mid- to late-1990s. Many economic analysts believe that this was a key reason for the strong US dollar during the 1990s.

Real interest rates also help determine the value of a currency. For instance, if the Bank of Canada advocates a "tight" monetary policy by raising interest rates, then (all things being equal) this policy will attract more foreign investment in Canadian money assets. Conversely, if monetary policy is "loose," foreign investors may abandon the Canadian dollar in favor of higher-yielding currencies.

The level of employment in a nation also influences the value of a currency. When employment levels are high, consumer and general household consumption will be strong and the economy will benefit. During much of the 1990s, the US economy performed relatively well. Good employment opportunities and consumer purchases helped prevent the US economy from slowing down and bolstered the value of the US dollar.

A country's balance of payments helps determine the value of a currency. The larger the balance of payments, the stronger the currency value relative to other world currencies. A major component of the balance of payments equation is the current account balance. While the current account balance is derived from the value of a country's merchandise and service imports and exports, as well as the flow of interest and dividends to and from the country, it can also be related to the level of savings and investment in the country and the government's budget balance. In general, the greater the government's surplus, the greater the current account balance. When the current account balance is positive and the trend is positive, the domestic currency will be strong. It makes sense that as governments move from deficits to surpluses, the value of the currency will rise.

The above list is by no means exhaustive and other factors can influence the value of a currency. Globalization has increased the number of influences on the currency of each country. Forecasters must consider the effects of dozens of factors that may influence the value of a currency. This can be a difficult and tedious process with no guarantee of success or accuracy.

A Short-Term Approach

Many interested parties participate in the foreign exchange market, including both passive and active stakeholders. Foreign exchange professionals, including traders and account executives at banks, all watch the above factors to discern long-term trends in the value of a currency. However, foreign exchange traders tend to have a shorter-term view and work within certain limits. They have to meet profit targets that may be daily, weekly or monthly, so they react to events that influence a currency in the shorter term.

The forex market is fast-moving and volatile. On any given day, a currency may move a few points or several hundred points. Traders try to take advantage of these changes, large or small, to make a profit. Traders consult charts and use technical analysis to understand currencies the same way that equity analysts and traders try to understand the position and future of a particular company or industry. Charts show short-term patterns that may help a trader make a decision.

One factor that influences the value of a currency in the short term is the general level of liquidity. Markets usually exhibit a certain degree of fluidity, but at times liquidity dries up. During these times, currency values may be quite volatile. Speculators enter the market and try to push the currency in a certain direction to suit their position. Movements can be abrupt and exaggerated, and traders must take care not to get trapped in this environment with an unfavorable position. Fortunately, this situation is usually temporary.

The interplay between the futures and the cash markets can affect currency values. Usually, the cash market leads the futures market. However, at times this pattern is reversed for a very brief period. This reversal creates short-term disequilibrium and markets become very volatile until liquidity is restored. Temporary opportunities may open up, creating a trading frenzy for a short period.

Traders often try to manipulate or push the market to achieve a more favourable position. For example, a large institution, usually a bank, may hold a certain position in the foreign exchange OTC derivatives market. Suppose a bank is short a CAD/USD call option with a strike price of 1.5000 and a knock-out feature at 1.5800—meaning that the call option becomes void if during the life of the contract the spot price hits 1.5800. If the current spot market is at 1.5650, the bank's trader may try to push the market above 1.5800 to avoid the potential payout to the buyer of the option.

Unexpected political events or world crises can affect currency values. In a crisis, investors look for safe places to invest and certain currencies, such as the US dollar or the Swiss franc, are considered safe havens. Money will flow from weaker second-tier currencies to these safe havens. These market conditions are temporary and impossible to predict, but can have devastating long-term results for an individual market participant. In fast-changing markets, only the bravest or most foolhardy participants come out to play; most business is done on an as-needed basis.

Central Bank Intervention

Central banks (CBs) carry enormous clout in the foreign exchange markets but they usually exercise their power cautiously. However, from time to time, CBs intervene in the foreign exchange markets. Some CBs are more active than others and levels of transparency vary. Most CBs try to keep a variety of options available to ensure the greatest impact when they do intervene.

CBs generally let the market determine the level of a currency. Most CBs in industrialized countries work to foster sustainable economic prospects and keep prices stable, rather than dictating or managing the level of the home currency. From time to time, however, CBs do intervene in the foreign exchange market. The intervention can take the form of what is known as *moral suasion*, whereby a CB spokesperson may offer the markets the CB's views on the current value of the home currency. These views reveal the CB's preferred position for the currency. Usually, the market acts to adjust the currency value to the desired levels to prevent direct intervention from the CB. However, market participants occasionally take positions opposite to the CB's preference. This can be a dangerous game, as the consequence may be high for both the CB and these contrary market participants. The CB may lose face because its credibility is at stake. The contrary market participants risk big losses if the CB decides to intervene.

CBs intervene from time to time when markets get disorderly. Opinions may differ as to whether a market is behaving in a disorderly way, but CBs like the Bank of Canada employ professional forex personnel who can interpret market conditions so that intervention is accurate and effective and stability can be restored. Some interventions are focused on keeping a certain pair of currencies within a certain range. For instance, the Bank of Japan tends to state openly where it would like to see the value of the Japanese yen relative to the US dollar. Market participants know the Bank's biases and try to avoid provoking the Bank of Japan for fear that it will intervene directly. CBs also communicate with their counterparts in other countries to monitor conditions. They may ask their counterparts to intervene on their behalf if the situation is sufficiently serious.

In summary, CBs in industrialized nations intervene in the marketplace to influence the short-term movement of currencies. This intervention is different from the post World War II to 1971 Bretton Woods regime, under which intervention by a CB was an official proclamation of a structural change in the value of a currency. Today, the general philosophy is that the markets will ultimately dictate currency equilibrium.

SPOT AND FORWARD MARKETS

A currency can be bought or sold in either the spot market or the forward market.

The Spot Market

The interbank spot market consists of purchases and sales of currency for *immediate delivery*. For CAD and USD transactions, "immediate delivery" occurs on the next business day after the trade is completed. For most other currencies, including the major European and Asian currencies, "immediate delivery" occurs two business days after the trade date. Each currency transaction involves two sets of payments, one for each of the two currencies involved in the trade.

Suppose that on Monday a trader at Bank of Montreal (BMO) buys US$10 million spot from a trader at CIBC at a CAD exchange rate of 1.5604. To settle this transaction, CIBC will notify its correspondent bank in New York to debit its US dollar account by US$10 million and send the money to BMO's correspondent bank in New York for further credit to BMO.[3] The transfer of US dollars through the correspondent banks is done through the Clearing House Interbank Payments System (CHIPS), a central clearing house for USD transactions conducted by its member banks. The CHIPS transfer will settle the next business day, on Tuesday (assuming both Monday and Tuesday are US business days).

At the same time, BMO will send CIBC C$15,604,000 through the Large Value Transfer System (LVTS) operated by the Canadian Payments Association (CPA). BMO will use the Society for Worldwide Interbank Financial Telecommunications (SWIFT) system to transmit the instructions. At the end of the day, the LVTS balance for each CPA member is settled by a debit or credit to its account with the Bank of Canada. If this forex trade is the only transaction between CIBC and BMO on this day (an unrealistic assumption), then BMO's account with the Bank of Canada will be debited by C$15,604,000 and CIBC's would be credited for the same amount, all for settlement on Tuesday.

The Forward Market

The main thing that distinguishes the forward market from the spot market is the timing of delivery. Spot market transactions settle one or two business days after the trade date, but the settlement of forward market transactions can occur from one week after the trade date to as much as 10 years after the trade date. Because of this delayed settlement, forward prices are different from spot prices. In other words, not only is the time of delivery between a spot and forward transaction different, but usually the price is too. The principles of currency forward pricing are discussed in Alexander and Sheedy (2008b), Chapter 3.

Liquid forward markets exist in the major currencies for one-month, two-month, three-month, six-month and one-year delivery dates.[4] Longer delivery periods are possible for certain pairs of currencies (such as CAD/USD). All the pertinent details of the trade—the price (exchange rate), the size of the trade, and the settlement procedures—are agreed to at the time of the trade. This commitment to trade currencies at a previously agreed exchange rate is known as a forward contract.

The characteristics of trading in the spot interbank market also apply to trading in the forward interbank market. That is, the market is a decentralized, continuous, open-bid, double-auction market. Most currencies are quoted relative to the US dollar in either direct or indirect terms. Transactions are conducted either directly between bank traders, or through physical or electronic brokering systems. Forward transactions are settled just like spot transactions, and involve a transfer of currencies in two different countries.

Forward Discounts and Premiums

Apart from the delivery date, the other major difference between spot and forward transactions is the price at which forward trades occur. The absolute difference between the spot and forward price of a currency is called the *currency swap rate* or, simply, "swap points." The relative annualized difference is known as a *forward premium* or *forward discount*, depending on whether the forward price F_n is higher or lower than the spot price S:

$$\text{Swap rate or swap points} = F_n - S. \tag{4.1}$$

$$\text{Forward premium or forward discount} = \frac{F_n - S}{S} \times \frac{360}{n}. \tag{4.2}$$

Example 4.2: Currency Swap Rates and Forward Premiums

Suppose the CAD/USD spot price is 1.5870 and the one-month (30-day) CAD/USD forward price is 1.5884. Then the one-month CAD/USD swap rate is $1.5884 - 1.5870 = 0.0014$. Traders would call this a swap rate of 14 points.

The annualized one-month forward premium (or forward discount, if the forward price is less than the spot price) is:[5]

$$\frac{1.5884 - 1.5870}{1.5870} \times \frac{360}{30} = 0.010586 = 1.06\%.$$

Since the CAD/USD quote is the price of the US dollar in terms of Canadian dollars, we say the US dollar is trading at a one-month forward *premium* of 1.06% relative to the Canadian dollar. Conversely, we could say that the Canadian dollar must be trading at a one-month forward *discount* of approximately the same amount — "approximately," because the process of inverting currency quotes alters the exact value of the premium or discount. If the inversion is calculated to several decimal places, the difference will be small. If it is rounded to three or four decimal places, the difference will be larger.

For example, if we invert the spot and forward CAD/USD quotes above and round them to four decimal places, we get a spot value of 0.6301 and a forward value of 0.6296. Plugging these values into (4.2) gives

$$\frac{0.6296 - 0.6301}{0.6301} \times \frac{360}{30} = -0.00952 = -0.95\%$$

that is, a discount of 0.95%. Here the difference (1.06% compared to -0.95%) seems quite pronounced. But if we repeat this calculation using, say, eight decimal places, 0.63011972 and 0.62956434, the difference is negligible:

$$\frac{0.62956434 - 0.63011972}{0.63011972} \times \frac{360}{30} = -0.010577 = -1.06\%$$

Interest-Rate Parity

What determines the forward exchange rate—and hence the swap rate and the forward discount or premium? As with most other financial forward contracts, the forward price is derived from the spot price, based on the cost-of-carry model. If it is not, arbitrage can produce risk-free profits. The arbitrage transactions that keep forward exchange rates in line with spot exchange rates are known as covered interest arbitrage. In foreign exchange trading, the effect of covered interest arbitrage is known as interest-rate parity.

Interest-rate parity means that the currency of a country with a low interest rate should trade at a forward premium relative to the currency of a country with a high interest rate. Interest-rate parity effectively eliminates the interest-rate differential between countries after foreign exchange risk has been eliminated with a forward contract.

When interest-rate parity holds, the *covered interest differential*—that is, the difference between the interest rate in one country and the interest rate in another country, combined with a forward contract—is zero. Put another way, the interest-rate differential should be approximately equal to the forward discount or premium. If it is not, covered interest arbitrage by interbank and large institutional traders will quickly eliminate the interest-rate differential. Interbank and large institutional traders focus on Eurocurrency interest rates, because they can easily borrow and lend large amounts of money in this market.

Example 4.3: Covered Interest Arbitrage

Suppose that the spot CAD/USD exchange rate is 1.5870 and that three-month (91-day) interest rates in the Eurocurrency market are 3.5% for Canadian dollars and 3% for US dollars. Also, suppose that the three-month CAD/USD forward rate is 1.5870, the same as the spot price. Since the Eurocurrency rates for US dollars are lower than they are for Canadian dollars, the US dollar should be trading at a forward premium relative to the Canadian dollar. Since it is not, covered interest arbitrage will produce a risk-free profit. There are four steps in the covered interest arbitrage:

1. **Borrow US dollars.** If US$1 million is borrowed in the Eurodollar market at 3%, the amount that must be repaid at the end of three months is:

$$\$1 \text{ million} + \left(\$1 \text{ million} \times 0.03 \times \frac{91}{360} \right) = \$1,007,583.$$

2. **Sell US dollars and buy Canadian dollars spot.** Convert the US$1 million to Canadian dollars at the spot rate of 1.5870 for proceeds of C$1,587,000.

3. **Invest the Canadian dollars.** Invest the Canadian dollars in the Eurocurrency market for three months to earn 3.5%. After three months, the Canadian dollar investment will be worth:

$$C\$1,587,000 + \left(C\$1,587,000 \times 0.035 \times \frac{91}{360} \right) = \$1,601,040.$$

4. Sell Canadian dollars and buy US dollars forward. Sell C$1,601,040 forward at the three-month CAD/USD forward rate of 1.5870 for proceeds in three months' time of 1,601,040/1.5870 = US$1,008,847.

In the three months, the proceeds from the Canadian dollars investment can be used to satify the obligation of the forward contract and on return will produce US$1,008,847, of which US$1,008,583 must be used to repay the USD loan. After all the transaction have setteled, US$ 1264 is left as a risk-free profit.

In the example above, when other interbank and institutional traders realise that covered interest arbitrage offers a risk-free profit, they too will engage in these transactions. This will have the following effects: US dollar interest rates in the Eurocurrency market rise as traders borrow US dollars; the CAD/USD spot rate falls as traders sell US dollars spot; Canadian dollar interest rates fall as traders invest Canadian dollars; the CAD/USD forward rate rises as traders buy US dollars forward. Eventually, all four prices and rates will converge on values that reduce any chance of a risk-free profit when carrying out covered interest arbitrage.

The following equation can be used to determine the fair value forward exchange rate that eliminates risk-free profits from covered interest arbitrage, assuming equal borrowing and lending rates and no bid–ask spreads:

$$F_{X/Y} = S_{X/Y} \frac{1 + r_X n / 360}{1 + r_Y n / 360}, \tag{4.3}$$

where $F_{X/Y}$ is the n-day forward exchange rate for currency X in terms of currency Y, $S_{X/Y}$ is the spot exchange for currency X in terms of currency Y, r_X and r_Y are the interest rates on currencies X and Y respectively, stated as money market yields in decimal form, and n is the number of days covered by the two investments and the forward contract.

Example 4.4: Fair Value Forward Rates

Based on a spot CAD/USD exchange rate of 1.5870 and 91-day Eurocurrency rates of 3% for US dollars and 3.5% for Canadian dollars, the three-month forward rate should be:

$$1.5870 = S_{X/Y} \frac{1 + 0.035 \times 91 / 360}{1 + 0.03 \times 91 / 360} = 1.5870 \frac{1.008847222}{1.007583333} = 1.5890.$$

Returning to the covered interest arbitrage example above, if the forward rate had been 1.5890 rather than 1.5870, the proceeds from the forward contract in step 4 would have been 1,601,040/1.5890 = US$1,007,577. This is actually US$6 less than we need to repay our US dollar loan, which would remove the incentive to engage in these transactions in the first place.

Remember that when interest-rate parity holds, the annualized forward discount or premium should be approximately equal to the interest-rate differential. Based on a forward price of 1.5890, the annualized forward premium on the US dollar is equal to:

$$\frac{1.5890 - 1.5870}{1.5870} \times \frac{360}{91} = 0.004986 = 0.499\%.$$

This is almost exactly equal to the 0.5% differential between US dollar and Canadian dollar interest rates. In other words, the premium paid to lock in a forward purchase of US dollars will effectively eliminate the higher interest rates earned by investing in Canadian dollars.

Example 4.5: Hedging in the Forward Markets

A Canadian firm imports components for its manufacturing process from the United States. The company is expecting a large shipment three months from now, at which time a payment of US$3,000,000 will be required. Concerned about a possible appreciation in the USD, the CFO decides to hedge this short USD position.

Using the rates from the previous example, the CFO can buy US dollars at 1.5890 for delivery in three months. Once the forward contract is in place, the CFO knows with certainty that the shipment of components will cost C$4,767,000 (3,000,000 × 1.5890), regardless of exchange-rate movements in the forthcoming months.

STRUCTURE OF A FOREIGN EXCHANGE OPERATION

Trading rooms around the world are set up in a similar fashion. Although the number of employees and floor space may vary, a large trading operation in London, Tokyo, or New York will look very similar. Most foreign exchange operations have the following structure. A spot desk consists of several employees who trade various currencies on a spot basis in the interbank market. The domestic currency most likely is the focal point of the whole trading operation and a chief or senior trader is responsible for generating a certain profit figure for the trading operation. This proprietary trading uses the bank's capital and a certain return is expected on the capital employed. Depending on the risk profile, certain traders may be assigned to work with other currencies that represent the bank's interests or for which the bank has economies of scale. For example, many banks trade euros, yen, pounds sterling, and Swiss francs because of the depth and liquidity of these markets. Some banks employ traders to work with second- or third-tier currencies. These "exotics" are typically tied to customer transactions; although the trades are smaller, they can be very profitable.

The spot desk is complemented by a forward desk, staffed by employees who trade and manage the bank's forward currency positions. Depending on its scope of operation, the forward desk may also be involved in other banking operations, such as the money market or funding desk. A bank may try to fund its loan obligations by trading in currencies other than the domestic currency; this is where the forward desk plays a key role. The forward desk also manages the bank's cumulative forward position derived from the activities of the bank's corporate clients.

A chief trader usually manages the spot desk and the forward foreign exchange desk. These two desks are responsible for trading, as opposed to advisory services to clients. The compensation paid to trading professionals in this area is usually tied to the profits generated by their trades. A medium-sized or larger forex trading operation may also include a forex derivatives desk. This desk would be responsible for trading exchange-traded or OTC options and currency futures. Most banks have a section within the forex department known as *foreign exchange advisory services*, sometimes called a sales desk. The role of the advisory desk's account executives is to attract new forex business or clients to the bank, provide professional services to existing clients, and provide pricing for clients. Sales executives work closely with other officers of the bank, especially credit personnel, to ensure that deals with clients remain within prescribed credit limits. The sales desk can be broken down into three subcategories: institutional coverage to larger, more sophisticated accounts, such as governments or money managers; corporate or commercial accounts; and the retail business from the branch network.

All these desks together constitute the *front office*. A healthy conflict often exists between the trading and sales desks because of different objectives related to the pricing of forex products. Sales executives always want competitive rates for their existing clients or for prospecting opportunities, while the traders need to maximise profits.

All the dealing operations in the front office are supported by *back office* departments. The back office processes the transactions, including record keeping, applying checks and balances, ledger and sub-ledger activity accounting, reconciliations, deal confirmations, and deal settlements. In smaller operations, the back office may also be required to monitor the dealing limits of the foreign exchange traders to ensure compliance.

The increasing sophistication of financial products and some high-profile financial fiascos have led to the evolution of an area often referred to as the *middle office*. This group is essentially a risk management group mandated to ensure compliance within the trading room. The risk management group identifies, quantifies, monitors, and analyzes the risk–reward profile of a trading operation in terms of market, liquidity, credit, and operations.

Front office (i.e. trading and sales) and back office objectives are not the same. The former is profit-motivated, while the latter is focused on checks and balances. The personnel in these two different groups usually report to different senior officers of a bank to ensure that no conflict of interest arises.

Foreign exchange operations vary from firm to firm, with differences mostly in degree as opposed to kind. For instance, a smaller forex group may have some crossover in responsibility, whereby a spot trader also trades forex derivatives or a trader of secondary currency also trades the forward book. Some organizations employ a "corporate dealer" who carries out both trading and advisory functions.

It is important to distinguish the responsibilities of a forex trader from those of an account executive. The forex trader is paid to take positions in the marketplace, but the account executive is not. Although this distinction may vary from one firm to another, advisory personnel are generally not supposed to take positions either from the market directly or from clients. Although there is no specific academic requirement for the position of account executive, most account executives have some post-secondary education. In addition, management encourages account executives to enrol in industry courses to gain additional insight and knowledge of foreign exchange markets and other aspects of the business. Banks tend to be fairly generous in their financial support for employees. Compensation for foreign account executives and traders usually has a fixed component and a variable bonus, depending on how well the department performs over the budget year. Forex professionals in banks do not work on commission.

CONCLUSIONS

An exchange rate is the price of one currency in terms of another. The interbank foreign exchange market is known as a decentralized, continuous, open-bid, double-auction system because it operates through telephone and computer systems that link banks and other currency traders around the world; price quotes in the interbank foreign exchange market vary continuously during the trading day; the trader who requests a quote does not have to specify the amount he or she wishes to exchange, or even whether he or she intends to buy or sell the currency; and banks that receive calls for quotes also call other banks and ask for their market.

A direct terms quote is the number of foreign currency units that can be bought with one domestic currency unit, while an indirect terms quote is the number of domestic currency units that can be bought with one foreign currency unit.

Direct dealing describes the common practice by which a trader at one bank telephones a trader at another bank to get a quote on a certain currency. A foreign exchange broker acts as a middleman, bringing together two banks that have expressed an interest to buy or sell a currency at a specific price. In electronic brokering, orders are placed into a computer system rather than with an individual broker. The system automatically matches bids and offers as the price of a currency fluctuates and as "market" orders are entered.

Most currency trading in the interbank market involves the US dollar on one side of the transaction. If we take the US perspective, most currencies, including the Canadian dollar, are quoted indirectly against the US dollar. A few currencies, including the British pound and the euro, are quoted against the US dollar directly.

A cross rate is a quote for a foreign currency against another foreign currency, without reference to the US dollar. It is important to use the correct quote relative to US dollar when determining the bid and offer quote of a foreign currency relative to another foreign currency. If the party asking for the quote wants to buy currency A in exchange for currency B, the provider of the quote must use an offer quote on currency A and a bid quote on currency B. The actual quote may be stated in terms of either currency A or currency B.

Low levels of liquidity may exaggerate short-term movements in the currency in one direction or the other. The currency futures market can lead the cash market for brief periods of time. Traders can try to manipulate prices. Unexpected political events or world crises can affect currency values. A central bank can influence the value of its currency by moral suasion or by directly buying or selling the currency in the market.

Currency transactions involves two sets of payments, one for each of the two currencies involved in the trade. Banks in one nation settle their foreign currency transactions through correspondent banks in the foreign country. Foreign exchange transactions involving a bank's domestic currency will settle though that nation's domestic payments system. Spot market transactions settle one or two business days after the trade date, while the settlement of forward market transactions can occur from one week to 10 years after the trade date. This delayed settlement usually leads to forward prices that are different from spot prices.

The forward premium or forward discount between two currencies is the annualized difference between the spot and forward exchange rates. Interest-rate parity means that the currency of a country with a low interest rate should trade at a forward premium relative to the currency of a country with a higher interest rate. Interest-rate parity effectively eliminates the interest-rate differential between countries after foreign exchange risk has been eliminated with a forward contract. Covered interest arbitrage forces the forward discount or forward premium on a currency to approximately equal the interest-rate differential between the two currencies.

REFERENCE

Alexander, C and Sheedy, E (2008b). *The Professional Risk Managers' Guide to Financial Instruments* (New York: McGraw-Hill).

NOTES

1. Bank for International Settlements "Triennial Central Banks Survey: Foreign exchange and derivatives market activity in 2004", March 2005, available at www.bis.org
2. Oxford Dictionary of Finance

3. A correspondent bank is a member of a national payments clearing system that clears and settles transactions on behalf of a foreign customer. Each bank involved in the interbank market has at least one correspondent bank in each country in which it conducts forex transactions. All of a bank's foreign exchange balances are held by its correspondent banks on its behalf.

4. The actual delivery date is the number of months after the spot delivery date. For example, a one-month CAD/USD forward settles in one month and one day.

5. See Chapter 3 for the correct day-count conventions for interest rates. Here we use 360/30 for the CAD/USD quotes.

CHAPTER 5

The Stock Market

Andrew Street

INTRODUCTION

Stocks (also known as *shares* or *equities*) represent an interest in the ownership of companies or corporations. These securities may exist as paper certificates "bearer form" or notional entries in the computers of the share register ("book entry form"). These stocks are bought and sold (traded) among different market participants, including investors, hedge funds, and investment banks. Stock are issued and sold by companies or corporations on their formation as a way of raising working capital and spreading the risk of ownership among shareholders according to their individual risk appetite. Companies and corporations are often founded as small private ventures with a limited number of shareholders who know each other and are often directly involved in the business. As the business grows and the need for capital expands, the existing shareholders frequently "float" the company on the stock market by issuing new shares to new investors. This typically dilutes their shareholding and they often sell some of their own stake at the same time. This process is often known as "listing" or doing an initial public offering (IPO). Alternatively, as corporations grow, they may need more capital. One way of raising extra funds for a company that is already listed it to make a "secondary" or "rights offering." Here existing shareholders are offered the right to subscribe to new shares in a corporation, usually at a substantial discount to the current market price.

Access to the stock market is regulated in most developed economies so that a company applying for a listing has to achieve and maintain minimum standards of capitalization, disclosure, and financial standing. The other market participants, such as professional traders, investment banks, and investors, are also required to operate within the rules of the market, which may include refraining from activities such as "insider trading."

A stock market is therefore, in general, a regulated marketplace for the buying and selling of the ownership of corporations for the purpose of spreading risk and raising capital. The corporations benefit by having a large liquid market in which to raise capital, and investors benefit by having the ability to spread and control their investment risk via the liquidity that a large and deep market offers. Intermediaries such as investment banks benefit by generating commissions and fees on stock trades and participation in the movement in price of the individual stocks.

The details of stock that are listed on the various stock markets are generally available via daily official lists from the market controller (e.g. the London Stock Exchange or New York Stock Exchange) which are often reproduced in whole or part in newspapers such as the *Financial Times* or *Wall Street Journal*. This information is also invariably available electronically via data vendors such as Reuters and Bloomberg and includes statutory disclosures (part of the listing requirement) by the listed company of information affecting shareholders, such as dealings in shares by a director of that company.

The market may itself have divisions into "senior" or "junior" listings with higher or lower listing requirements, and therefore potentially more or less investment risk. For example, the UK has the Alternative Investment Market, which has less onerous listing and capitalization requirements than a full stock exchange listing. Other stock markets, such as Luxembourg or Johannesburg, may have higher or lower listing standards and requirements than, say, London or New York. Some very large companies may be listed on more than one stock exchange: for example, HSBC is listed in Hong Kong and London. The total value of stocks traded on the world's stock markets is approximately US$30 trillion dollars (US$3 $\times$ 10^{13}) with the USA having the largest single market (approximately 50% of the total), followed by the Eurozone, UK, and Japan.

In the following sections we will look in more detail at the characteristics of the stock market and its participants, the properties of common equities, the primary and secondary markets, and the mechanics of trading, including costs, strategies (such as going short), and the use of leverage via margin trading or exchange-traded derivatives.

THE CHARACTERISTICS OF COMMON STOCK

As we have seen above, common stocks represent the ownership of a company or corporation. More specifically, the equity holder has a *claim on the residual assets* of a company after all other claims have been paid in the event of a liquidation of the company. If we consider a simplified company balance sheet, we can illustrate this point more easily (Table 5.1).

The balance sheet equates assets to liabilities; the balancing item is the shareholders' funds. The shareholders' funds represent the value that the equity shareholders would be entitled to if the company were liquidated. Clearly, the greater the assets of the company and the smaller the creditors, the greater the value of the company and therefore the greater the value of the shares to the shareholder. However, practically speaking, this value is directly accessible only by breaking up or liquidating the company. When this happens, there is a strict hierarchy of pay-out (see Table 5.2) to the creditors of the firm based on seniority.

This means that senior creditors such as the Inland Revenue or the bond holders will be paid in full prior to any remaining assets being distributed to the equity holders. In this sense the equity holders have a *residual claim* on the company based on seniority. They are the most *junior* and therefore the *bearers of the most risk* on liquidation. Generally, this liquidation or break-up of the company would occur only when the company became insolvent and could no longer operate. In those circumstances it is unlikely that the residual value available to shareholders would be significant and is likely to be close to zero. This explains why, when a company announces a serious operating problem or potential insolvency that

T A B L E   5.1

Simplified balance sheet of a company

Assets	Liabilities
Fixed assets	Creditors/bond holders
Debtors	Shareholders' funds

TABLE 5.2

Pay-out hierarchy on liquidation

First in the queue	Inland Revenue/tax authorities
	Secured creditors (mortgagor)
	Trade creditors
	Senior bond holders
	Junior bond holders
Last in the queue	Equity holders

is not widely known, the equity share price rapidly falls towards zero. Similarly, when the company has a sudden windfall success (e.g. an oil field find or successful drug trials) the equity price often jumps substantially.

Share Premium and Capital Accounts and Limited Liability

Shares usually have a nominal value, typically in the UK 25p. These shares are known as "ordinary shares of 25p nominal value." At primary issue the shares are often sold at a premium, say £1, in which case 25p of the sale price goes into the *share capital account* of the shareholders' funds and 75p goes into the *share premium account*. Both of these accounts, along with the profit-and-loss account, constitute the shareholders' funds in the company balance sheet. Under certain accounting/regulatory circumstances, the "surplus" in the share premium account can be used by the company to offset some costs such as "goodwill" on the purchase of other companies. After the initial issue of shares, they then trade in the secondary market at the "market" price. This price then simply reflects the amount agreed by both counterparts to buy a share and this amount is paid to the seller in exchange for the equity share.

Once the shares are sold in a primary issue, the equity holder's liability to the debts of the company is limited to the amount already paid for the shares, i.e. the value of the share premium and share capital accounts. Occasionally, shares are issued "part-paid," which means that only a fraction of the issue price is paid upfront, with further payments due in the future, or, in the event of company default, due immediately. In this sense the owner of the company, the equity shareholder, has *limited liability* to the debts of the company, the amount of this liability being the fully paid-up share capital. This is the fundamental idea of a "limited-liability corporation."

Equity Shareholder's Rights and Dividends

The ordinary shareholder usually has voting rights associated with his holding in the corporation's stock at special company meetings such as the annual general meeting (AGM). Therefore, a shareholder with 30% of the issued equity would carry a 30% weight in any vote or resolution. This means that decisions regarding the company's management and overall direction are controlled by ballot weighted by ownership. There are exceptions where voting rights are not evenly distributed throughout the equity shareholders, although these are increasingly rare.

The shareholders are responsible for electing the company's board of directors, who in turn control the day-to-day activities of the company. The AGM provides a regular forum for shareholders to air their views and ultimately control their company by the support (or otherwise) of the managing director and the rest of the company board of directors. The directors run the company on behalf of, and with the permission of, the shareholders, who, with sufficient voting numbers, can remove them at any time.

In addition to voting rights, the equity shareholders will also receive dividend payments on their stock if the board of directors decide that a dividend can be paid. This decision is based on the financial standing of the company. Dividends are declared annually and may be varied or stopped completely if the directors decide that it is in the company's interest to do so. Typically, in the UK, dividends are paid twice a year (usually an *interim* and then a *final dividend*, the former usually being smaller); in the USA dividends on large companies are paid four times a year in equal instalments. Dividends are usually announced and a record and payment date set, such that all holders of the equity on the record day qualify for the dividend payment. After that date the share trades "ex-dividend" and the payment of the dividend is made at some later date to the holder on the record date, who by then may have sold his or her shares on as "ex-dividend" stock.

For instance, suppose Glaxo Ordinary 25p shares are trading at £12.50 mid (£12.45 bid, £12.55 offered) and a final dividend of 25p is announced. The record date is September 15 and pay day is October 5. If an interim dividend of 15p has already been paid six months earlier, the total dividend payment for the year is 40p. Then the simple annual dividend yield is $(40/1,250) \times 100\% = 3.20\%$.

Therefore, the holders of common stock have voting rights to control their company and they receive dividends if they are considered appropriate for the company by the board of directors. The board is ultimately controlled via the shareholders' votes. The return on an investment in equity is a combination of dividends received and any capital appreciation (increase in price) realised when the stocks are eventually sold. Equity shares can therefore provide a combination of income (which is uncertain) and capital gain (which is also uncertain). This makes equity valuation relatively difficult!

Other Types of Equity Shares—Preference Shares

In addition to ordinary shares, a company may issue other classes of equity such as *preference shares*. These shares are usually senior to the ordinary equity, but junior to bonds, and usually carry a *fixed dividend* such as 5% per annum based on their face value or a fixed amount such as US$5. This dividend can be *cumulative* or *noncumulative*. In the case of cumulative shares, if a declared dividend is not paid in one year, then when the next dividends are paid the missed dividend is also paid, i.e. the dividends are rolled up for cumulative preference shares. Missed dividends are not made up in the case of noncumulative preference shares. It is important to note that, if the dividends are not paid on the preference shares, no dividends can be paid on the ordinary (or common) stock since preference shares are senior to common stock. In the case of cumulative preference shares, all outstanding dividends have to be paid prior to any dividend payment to the common stock holders. Generally preference shares carry either limited voting rights or no voting rights at all. Usually the total amount of preference shares issued is much smaller than the common stock: for example, IBM-A preference shares represent less than 2% of the IBM-issued common stock. The smaller amounts naturally lead to lower trading volumes and less liquidity (i.e. wider bid–offer spreads in quoted prices and smaller trade lot amounts).

TABLE 5.3

Equity data *Pharmaceuticals & Biotech*

Share	Price	Change	1 year High	1 year Low	Yield	P/E Ratio	Volume
Glaxo 25p Ord.	1267 xd	−11	1,530	1,265	3.6%	14.7	18,941,000

Dividend payments by the company are not generally considered a business expense in the way that interest on bonds is tax-deductible/offsettable as they are a distribution of benefits of company ownership. However, some holders (typically companies) of preference shares may benefit from a lower rate of tax on preference dividends compared with the common stock dividend.

Equity Price Data

Details of trading activity of stocks in the market are distributed widely via electronic and print media. This may be "real-time" (almost as it happens), or delayed, or summary statistics. Daily summary statistics are produced by journals such as the *Wall Street Journal* and the *Financial Times* and contain information typically like that given in Table 5.3.

The volume is the total number of shares bought and sold on the day, and in this case the total volume traded was close to 19 million shares. With a price of £12.67 per share, the value of this daily turnover was approximately (£12.67 × 18,941,000) £240m. This information is usually grouped by market sector, and in this case Glaxo is a member of the Pharmaceutical and Biotech group.

Market Capitalization (or "Market Cap")

The market capitalization value of a listed company is the total amount of issued share capital multiplied by the current share price. This represents the total value or worth of the company. For example, a company with a share price of £10 and total number of shares issued of 100,000,000 would have a market capitalization of £1 billion. The sum of all the market caps of all the listed shares gives the total stock market value. The market cap is often used as the weighting factor in the calculation of stock market indices such as the Standard and Poor's (S&P) 500 and the Financial Times Stock Exchange (FTSE) 100.

Stock Market Indices

Stock market indices such as the S&P 500 and the FTSE 100 are used to measure broad equity market performance and to benchmark investment portfolios. Most indices are weighted by market cap, although simple price-weighted indices do exist (e.g. Nikkei 225, Dow Jones). Price-weighted indices are generally avoided due to the ease with which they can be manipulated by unscrupulous traders. With a simple price-weighted index a price movement in the smallest and most illiquid stock has the same effect on the index as the same move in price of the most liquid and largest company. When derivatives contracts such as futures and options are settled from this type of index, the index value may be pushed up or down relatively easily (and cheaply) by trading in the illiquid stocks. Vastly more profit is made from the derivatives' settlement value than the cost of manipulating the index. This type of market manipulation is illegal in many jurisdictions. A cap-weighted index is based on the sum of all the cap-weighted prices of the constituent companies. In this case movements in price are scaled by the economic size of the company and so it is much harder (and more expensive) to manipulate its value. In the case of the FTSE 100, the index contains the largest 100 companies listed on the London Stock Exchange, the "largest" being defined by market cap.

For instance, suppose ABC plc has a market cap of £100m and that the total market value of the top ten stocks is £2,000m. Then the weighting of ABC in the 'top ten index' will be 5% (i.e. 100/2,000). If the mid-price of ABC is £5.00 at close of business, the index calculation is:

$$I = k \times \left(£5 \times 5\% + \sum_{i=2}^{10} p_i w_i \right) \tag{5.1}$$

where k is a 'starting factor' that sets the index to 1,000 on the starting reference day, p_i are the stock prices and w_i the market-cap weights of the other nine stocks in the index.

The FTSE 100 index started in the early 1980s and had a starting reference value of 1,000. The index has risen to almost 7,000, fallen back to around 3,000 and risen again to close to 7,000 in the intervening 25 years. The index today does not contain the same 100 stocks as at the start due to changes in market cap (old businesses merging/failing or new companies growing).

Summary statistics can be produced for the index in the same way that they can for a single stock, thus we talk about the market yield or the market P/E ratio, which is usually based on an index such as the FTSE 100 or FTSE All-Share Index. These indices often form the reference underlying price for derivatives contracts such as futures and options. On the FTSE 100 and the S&P 500 there are both exchange-traded and over-the-counter (OTC) derivative transactions.

Some indices such as the DAX 30 are based on "total return," so that they are adjusted to include dividend payments over time. An index including both price movements and dividends is sometimes referred to as an *accumulation index*.

Equity Valuation

Clearly, one way to establish the value of a company is to analyze the balance sheet and calculate the net book value of its shares. This value is frequently much less than the market price of the stock as it does not take into account future earnings and the value of the company as a going concern. An alternative approach is to value the equity as the present value (PV) of all future dividend payments—this is the so-called "dividend discount model":

$$PV = \sum_{i=1}^{\infty} \frac{D(1+g)^{i-1}}{(1+r)^i} \tag{5.2}$$

where D is the expected next annual dividend, g is the growth rate of dividend payment, and r is the discount rate. The discount rate should represent the rate required by investors to compensate them for both (a) the time value of money and (b) risk of loss. It could be determined using the capital asset pricing model (see Alexander and Sheedy (2008a), Chapter 4), for example.

This dividend discount model can be simplified to the "Gordon growth" model:

$$PV = \frac{D}{r - g}$$

(5.3)

So, for example, with an expected Glaxo dividend of 40p, a dividend growth rate of 2.5% p.a. and a long-term discount rate of 5%, the Gordon growth model would imply a price for Glaxo of £16.00 compared with a market price of approximately £12.00. Clearly this valuation method is critically sensitive to long-term discount rates and the future growth rates of dividends.

Valuation of equity shares is very difficult due to the many sources of uncertainty and the long-term nature of the business enterprize. Ultimately, the market mechanism determines the price of equity by matching supply and demand at the "market price." This is underpinned theoretically by techniques such as net book value, P/E ratios, and the dividend discount model, as well as more complex corporate and market analysis.

STOCK MARKETS AND THEIR PARTICIPANTS

The stock market exists to bring together buyers and sellers of equity risk. This facilitates the efficient raising of capital and diversification of risk necessary for capitalism to thrive. When a company needs to raise new capital it may do so by selling shares; when an investor wishes to deploy excess capital to earn a return he or she may do so by buying shares. As simple as this sounds, it requires substantial resources, such as capital and technology, along with regulation to ensure an efficient and fair marketplace in which the participants have confidence. Confidence is an essential component of the market, since, if it considered corrupt or unfair, it will rapidly lose favour with the disadvantaged party and fall into disuse.

The Main Participants—Firms, Investment Banks, and Investors

Companies (or "corporations" or "firms" issue equity to raise capital and diversify their risk among a wider ownership group. This capital raising can occur at the commencement of the business or at some time later when extra funds are required for expansion or to shore up existing activities. The initial issuance of new equity capital by a company is called a *primary issue* and companies access the stock market via a *listing* (or *float*) of their equity securities on the stock market. This listing requires compliance with specific stock market rules and regulations and is usually undertaken by a specialist financial company (an *intermediary*) such as an *investment bank* or *stockbroker*.

The intermediary will use accountants and lawyers as necessary for compliance with both company law and stock exchange listing requirements (sometimes referred to in the UK as the *yellow book*). In the USA, compliance is with the Securities Exchange Commission (SEC) and the New York Stock Exchange (NYSE). Once a listing can be achieved, details of the new issue will be circulated to *investors* by the financial intermediary, who will be asked to subscribe to (i.e. to *buy*) the issue. Frequently, the deal is "bought" in its entirety by the financial intermediary, who then takes the risk of selling it on, so guaranteeing the amount of capital raised to the issuing company. Alternatively, the financial intermediary may *underwrite* the issue, so that, if not all the "paper" can be placed with the investors, the intermediary buys up the surplus "rump," usually at a slight discount to the issue price. A fee is charged by the intermediary for the work involved in listing and for the risks taken in undertaking a bought deal or underwriting. This fee is usually realized by buying the equity securities at a discount to the expected market price. Fees are negotiable and there is intense competition for "big-name" issues.

Once stocks have entered the market via a primary issue they trade in the secondary market via financial intermediaries such as investment banks and brokers. Commissions are charged by the intermediaries for arranging and settling secondary market trades. The secondary market activity may be organized in two basic ways:

- *Matched market.* Orders for sale or purchase with amounts are entered into a system or "order book" with a *limit price* at which the investor is happy to sell or buy. The system matches trades at the best price that is acceptable to both counterparts and "crosses" the trade at the matched price. This system can lead to wild swings in prices and periods of illiquidity.
- *Market maker.* Financial intermediaries make two-way prices (bid and offer prices in market lot sizes) which can be *hit* (i.e. to hit the bid is to sell) or *taken* (to take the offer is to buy) by investors, leaving the market maker with a risk position that he or she must manage. The market maker therefore uses their own

capital to create a more liquid market and to damp wild price swings.

Often, secondary market trading is a mixture of these two methods, with larger stocks trading via a market-maker approach and smaller, less liquid stocks trading on a matched-market basis.

Market Mechanics

The market requires secure communication between qualified participants. In earlier times the right people met in a designated secure room or place at an agreed time and traded directly with each other. Today the market is largely electronic or telephonic so that details of stock prices and trade amounts are communicated between financial intermediaries and transactions agreed either electronically or by phone. Investors deal through a broker of their choice, who may also "hold" the equity securities on their behalf in *custody* systems. These allow rapid movement of stocks electronically to settle trades. In the most advanced systems, settlement of trades can be achieved almost in real time. Once a trade is agreed, secure electronic messages can be generated and sent, which debit the buyer's cash account and credit his securities account with the purchased stock, while simultaneously doing the reverse to the seller's accounts. In less developed markets, the settlement process involves the movement of physical paper securities, with attendant delays and risk of a failed trade.

When referring to trading and settlement, brokers typically refer to T+1 or T+3 settlement. In this terminology a trade originated on "trade day" (T) will be settled (i.e. stock transferred and payment made) on a settlement day sometime later. So T+3 settlement denotes a three-day delay between trade day and settlement day. This is sometimes called "rolling settlement" as opposed to the old system of an account period where all trades made within an account were settled at the same time. Historically, the UK stock market had a three-week account period, which has now been changed to a rolling settlement of T+3. Ultimately the goal is to reduce this to T+1 or even same-day settlement. Shorter settlement periods are very useful in reducing the risk of default by a counterparty prior to settlement and in helping to minimize the effects of "out-trades" or dealing mistakes, as these are spotted earlier and rectified before the stock price has moved too far.

THE PRIMARY MARKET–IPOs AND PRIVATE PLACEMENTS

Initial public offerings (*IPOs*) is the name given to a formerly privately owned company selling equity securities to third-party investors for the first time, sometimes known as *floating on the market* or *listing*. *Seasoned new issues* (*SNIs*) is the name given to companies issuing securities after they have floated. Both IPOs and SNIs may be made via a *public offering*, which makes the securities available to the general investor population, or via a *private placement*, in which the issue is placed directly with a few specially chosen investors and is not widely traded after issue. IPOs and SNIs are examples of the *primary securities market* or *new issues market.*

Basic Primary Market Process

We will use US market practice as our example, but the approach is broadly similar to the approach taken in other major markets such as the UK or Eurozone.

The firm wishing to float contacts a number of investment banks to negotiate terms with regard to an IPO. Terms include fees and costs in addition to marketing strategy and experience. The firm chooses a bank to be the lead player in the IPO; sometimes this will involve underwriting the new issue if they fail to place all the paper at launch. Often an underwriting syndicate, headed by the lead manager, will be formed to share the risk and broaden the distribution of the securities. The lead manager advizes on terms and pricing of the IPO. A preliminary notice is filed with the SEC (one of the listing authorities in the USA), giving basic terms and details of the issuing company. This is a preliminary prospectus, which has to be finalized and approved by the SEC prior to its becoming the IPO prospectus. This is then used to market the securities to the investors and the issue price is fixed. This process may take several weeks or longer.

If the issue is *fully underwritten*, the entire issue is bought at launch by the underwriting syndicate at a discount to issue price and then distributed to investors; this is also known as a "firm commitment." Compensation for bearing this risk is the size of the discount to issue price and the tightness of the pricing. This method is more common for bond issues of high-quality borrowers than for equities.

If the issue goes ahead on a *"best efforts"* basis, the price risk remains with the floating company and not with the bank. The bank collects a fee for arranging the IPO and a sales commission for stock sold (at the height of the dotcom boom, it was not unusual for banks to be paid in stock rather than cash). This method is the more common approach for an IPO of common stock.

Initial Public Offerings

The lead manager is responsible for marketing the new issue once the SEC has accepted the issues registration document and preliminary prospectus. This marketing may take the form of a "road show" to investors, having two main aims:

- informing investors of the floating company and its activities, emphasizing its attraction as an investment; and
- sounding out the investors as to likely price levels at which they will purchase the securities at launch.

Talking to investors and getting them to commit to purchase securities at launch is called *book building*, and this process allows fine tuning of the offer price. Strong early commitment by investors is usually rewarded with a large allocation of shares and possibly even a discount. This can lead to substantial underpricing and a large jump in price at issue. At the height of the dotcom bubble, one share closed up nearly 700% on issue day!

Typically, a lead manager will charge around 7% in fees for an IPO, but this does not include any discount to the market price on issue, which as we have seen can be very substantial. In general, IPOs tend to be "cheap" on issue, but not in every case are all the securities sold at issue price. On occasion stock is left with the underwriters. Longer-term studies have shown that many IPOs, particularly those coming from the dotcom era, have proved to be relatively poor long-term investments. Money was made by those participating in the float and then selling into the market demand that followed very shortly afterwards.

There have been initiatives to move away from the investment-bank-led IPO due to the large fee involved and the potentially substantial underpricing. These have included internet book-building exercizes and do-it-yourself IPOs. So far they have had limited success and have focused on the smaller end of the market. At present, Wall Street still dominates the IPO business and enjoys relatively generous fees in the process.

Private Placements

Private placements of common stock are much cheaper than IPOs since the entire issue of securities is sold to a small group of investors under rule SEC 144A (in the USA), which permits a simpler (and therefore cheaper) registration and listing process. The need for extensive road shows is obviated. However, it is difficult to place large issues this way due to the limited risk appetite of a small investor group. Furthermore, these issues tend not to trade in the secondary market, making it difficult for the investor to liquidate his position at short notice. This in turn means that investors in private placements demand a discount price for bearing this additional risk.

THE SECONDARY MARKET–THE EXCHANGE VERSUS OTC MARKET

The secondary market consists of the buying and selling of already issued securities and represents by far the largest volume of activity by value on a day-to-day basis. This activity is effectively investor-to-investor trading via a financial intermediary (in the case of on-exchange and OTC activity) and directly with each other on a peer-to-peer basis.

The Exchange

Usually each developed country has at least one national stock exchange. In the USA there are two major ones—the American Stock Exchange (AMEX) and the NYSE—and several regional exchanges dealing in smaller local companies. Only members of the exchange are allowed to trade on it, and the membership is called a *seat*. Seats are owned by brokers and banks who in turn deal with their own clients (the investors). Members of the exchange charge a commission for executing trades on the exchange on behalf of their clients. The NYSE has approximately 3,000 members and trades in about 3,300 common and preference stocks, which represent the vast majority of large and medium-sized corporations in the USA. In order to be listed on the NYSE, in addition to SEC registration, the company needs to meet the minimum requirements as to size and profitability; the market cap requirement is more than $60m.

The basic trading mechanism on an exchange is illustrated for the NYSE as an example (other exchanges may vary somewhat):

- an investor places an order with a broker (who owns a seat on the exchange);
- the order is passed to the firm's commission broker on the floor of the exchange;
- he approaches the *specialist*, who is responsible for market making (making two-way prices and managing the order flow) in that particular stock (on the NYSE there is only one specialist per stock);
- the order is placed and dealt; and
- confirmation of the "fill" flows back to the investor via the broker chain.

This process may be partly physical (i.e. real people in a real room) or electronic via trading monitors (e.g. the Stock Exchange Trading System (SETS) in London, or the SuperDOT system in New York). In some markets the role of broker and market maker can be carried out by one firm and there may be multiple market makers in one stock.

There are essentially two types of order for buying or selling stock on exchange:

- *Market order*—deal the stock at the current market price and size. If the order size is larger than the quoted size (e.g. 55.20 bid/55.25 offer in 1,000 shares) then the order is executed at multiple successive prices until it is filled.
- *Limit order*—deal the whole order at a pre-fixed price. Variations on this include "fill or kill," which means that the entire order must be filled immediately at this price in one go or not at all.

The market maker "specialist" in the USA) in each stock has a responsibility for maintaining the market in that stock (monitored by the exchange authority). Many transactions, however, will actually be "crosses" from one broker (buying) to another broker (selling) at a price within the market makers' bid–offer spread. Frequently, very large orders called "blocks" are traded. Some brokers specialize in taking the other side of such transactions at discounted prices to provide liquidity and to profit from (hopefully) unwinding the large position over time.

The Over-the-Counter Market

Transactions on exchanges all go via the central market maker(s) or specialists. In the OTC market, deals are done directly between broker/dealers who make two-way prices to each other in the stocks that they trade. Without a central market maker this means that the broker/dealer initiating the transaction has to search for the best price for the deal from a large number of potential counterparts. The North American Securities Dealers Automated Quotation (NASDAQ) in the USA is an OTC market and brokers/dealers display their quotes via the electronic system, but must actually contact the dealer directly to obtain a firm quote and deal. A trading system called the Small Order Execution Service (SOES) exists alongside the NASDAQ and fills small trades at the stated ("screen") price. NASDAQ is working to upgrade this system with its SuperMontage development. In the UK, the Stock Exchange Automated Quotation System (SEAQ) and SETS perform similar, but not identical, roles.

By their nature OTC markets are diffuse and noncentralized and are therefore ideal for electronic information and trading platforms. This noncentralization, however, sometimes means that deals are not done at the best market price (sometimes called *trading through*) since not all deals go through a central market maker or specialist. Some may slip through unnoticed by a better buyer or seller (i.e. someone prepared to buy at a higher price or sell at a lower price than that actually dealt). It also makes OTC markets potentially more difficult to monitor and regulate and they may not provide true *price discovery* (i.e. making sure that *all* potential participants have the opportunity to quote), which is a feature of a centralized market such as the exchange.

TRADING COSTS

The costs of buying and selling common stock are a combination of explicit costs, such as commissions and brokerage fees, and more hidden costs, such as the width of the bid–offer spread. There are also market impact costs, when the size of the transaction is sufficiently large that executing it moves the price away from the indicated quote. Total trading costs will therefore vary by market and indeed by stock, and may increase or decrease over time depending on market conditions. Trading costs are significant, not only from the point of view of reducing total return, but also in determining the viability of arbitrage trades such as stock-index/future arbitrage.

Commissions

The commission paid to brokers is normally negotiable and will depend on the size and volume of trades to be placed via the broker and the level of service expected. This can vary from an execution-only service for large volumes of large-value trades to a bespoke, "full-service" fund-management process for a small investor, with information, detailed reports, and analysis. The latter is clearly more expensive to provide. Some exchanges/markets insist on minimum commission rates to safeguard the smaller broker, but some larger firms may find a way to rebate some of this to their customers, lowering the real cost. Typically, the execution-only broker charges a fixed fee. For orders placed via the Internet (the cheapest method) this can be as low as US$10–20 or alternatively a smaller flat fee plus a small cost per share (e.g. 2 cents per share). Full-service brokers may charge as much as US$300 for the same trade placed by telephone to one of their trading assistants.

Bid–Offer Spread

A major cost difference between on-exchange and OTC deal execution is that on the former many trades will be crossed between brokers inside the indicated market maker bid–offer spread. This is called *price improvement* because the actual deal price is below the initial quoted offer or above the quoted bid when struck—i.e. it is dealt "inside" the spread and is therefore an improvement on the quoted price—whereas, on the OTC market, the client will pay or receive the dealer's quoted price and thus always be subject to the full bid–offer spread on any "round trip" (buying and then later selling) in the stock. The client of course just "sees" the price dealt at and may never explicitly recognize this cost. Typical bid–offer spreads in large liquid common stocks are of the order of 0.5–1.0%, and so Glaxo with a mid price of £12.00 may have a quoted bid–offer of £11.97–12.03 in, say, 200,000 shares.

Less liquid stocks and less busy market makers and exchanges tend to increase the market bid–offer price in a stock and hence the costs of trading. In OTC markets there is always the risk that deals are being routed to dealers who do not offer the best prices, and it is difficult to ensure "best execution." Estimating the real cost of the bid–offer spread is clearly not simple.

Market Impact

When a trade is executed it represents new information in the market and the market price reacts. Buying stock should drive up the market price, all else being equal. If the deal is large and the stock is illiquid, the actual trade execution price will be higher than the indicated bid–offer price due to its "market impact." Market impact is a function of the "depth" (number of potential buyers and sellers outside of the bid–offer) of the market at the time of execution and will vary over time and by stock. Estimating market impact is usually the result of studies of market price reactions with trade size over a suitably large number of market conditions, usually indicated by share turnover or futures volume. Estimating market impact, as with real bid–offer costs, is potentially complex and requires data and modelling.

BUYING ON MARGIN

Essentially, buying stock on margin consists of taking a loan from the broker (a *broker call loan*) to buy more stock than his own funds would allow. The investor *leverages* his position in a stock through a combination of his own and borrowed funds. Once purchased, the stock remains with the broker as collateral for the loan. The investor has to pay interest on the loan and a fee or commission to the broker for the arrangement.

Leverage

Leverage is the use of borrowed funds to allow an investor to take a larger risk position than he would ordinarily be able to do with his own funds. An investor with $10,000 who buys a position in securities worth $20,000 is leveraged two times and has borrowed $10,000 in order to achieve this. In this case the investor has $10,000 of his own equity and $10,000 of broker call loan in his margin account. Synthetic leverage can be obtained by using derivative products such as futures and options. For example, the payment of option premium will give the investor the right to buy or sell a much greater value of stock than would be possible with a direct transaction.

Some regulatory authorities set limits on the amount of leverage that can be offered by margin trading. In the USA, the Federal Reserve set a limit of 2× so that only up to 50% of the money invested can be borrowed.

This limit is varied from time to time, dependent on the perceived risks of too much or too little gearing in the system. In other markets the degree of leverage offered is at the discretion of the broker/dealer but subject to regulatory oversight/control via the firm's capital adequacy. If the regulator considers that a firm is offering too high a leverage to its clients, thereby increasing its risk of default, the regulatory supervisor may insist on an increase of qualifying capital set aside to cover this risk.

Percentage Margin and Maintenance Margin

Once the loan has been agreed, subject to the maximum leverage not being exceeded, the money is invested in the stock. The value of this stock may rise or fall and this will affect the amount of the investor's "equity" or "own funds" in the position.

For instance, suppose an investor uses £5,000 of his own money and a loan of £5,000 to buy £10,000 of stock. Then his leverage is two times and his percentage initial margin (equity/stock value) is 50%; if the value of the stock falls to £8,000, the investor has £3,000 of equity or own funds remaining (he has lost £2,000 on a mark-to-market basis) and a percentage margin of £3,000/£8,000 = 37.5%. Clearly the collateral is still sufficient to cover the loan of £5,000.

If the value of the stock falls sufficiently far that the investor's equity is close to zero, the broker makes a *maintenance margin call*. That is, she requires that the investor *top up* his account so that his percentage margin is above a minimum value (say, 10%). This is known variously as the *trigger* or *margin call rate*. If the client did not respond immediately (in cash or by pledging securities) and pay his margin call, the broker could liquidate or close out the position in the stock to protect her collateral on the loan. Clearly the more volatile the stock price, the more urgent the margin call can become and sensibly the higher the trigger rate should be set. Typically, investors would have, at most, a few days to meet a margin call and in times of extreme volatility the broker/dealer generally has the right to close out the client without notice.

Why Trade on Margin?

By borrowing and buying a larger stock position than the investor would ordinarily be able to, he can create a leveraged risk position. Clearly, a necessary requirement for the investor is that the expected rate of return

T A B L E   5.4

Margin trade—risk and return

Stock Price	Investor A	Investor B
+15%	+15%	+20%
0%	0%	−10%
−15%	−15%	−40%

on the investment be greater than the cost of the loan. We consider a stock that rises 15%, 0% and minus 15% over one year and two investors A (who is unleveraged) and B (who is two times leveraged and borrows at 10%). We compare their risk–return ratio in Table 5.4.

Clearly, the leverage position increases both upside and downside, but the relatively high interest costs (10%) drag down the returns for investor B. Margin trading works best for investors who are able to use it for very short-term positions (e.g. a week) where a rapid movement in the stock price may yield an annualized return very much higher than the interest costs.

SHORT SALES AND STOCK BORROWING COSTS

Short-selling is the process of selling a security that the investor does not own with the intention of buying it back more cheaply later to make a profit. The *short sale* is the method by which an investor can speculate on the fall in share prices rather than their rise. In order to sell short it is necessary to *borrow stock* for delivery in the initial sale trade. Then, when the position is to be closed out, the shorted shares are bought in the market and returned to the counterparty who lent the stock. This is called *covering the short*. Clearly, the lender of the stock demands a fee for this service, and this is known as the *stock-borrowing cost* or *repo* cost. The word "repo" is an abbreviation of "sale and repurchase agreement," which is a more common form of managing short positions in the fixed-income market. In that market a repo involves an agreement to sell and buy back rather than borrow and return securities.

Short Sale

In some markets, notably the USA, there are restrictions on when a short sale can occur. The so-called *up-tick* rule prevents a short sale unless the last price move in the stock was positive. This rule is designed to limit the volatility of market swings. Further rules prevent brokers/dealers from investing the proceeds of the short sale in other positions, thus limiting the amount of leverage that can be generated this way. In other markets (e.g. the UK) the up-tick rule does not apply and overall leverage of the firm is controlled via capital adequacy. Under the Capital Adequacy Directive rules, firms calculate their potential loss exposure to investors using either a simple rules-based approach or a more complex risk model (which simulates movements in the value of collateral) and then allocate capital against this requirement. As a firm's capital is finite, this places an upper limit on the total risk the firm can take and in turn the degree of leverage it can offer to clients. In some markets short selling is restricted or may not be allowed at all from time to time in an attempt protect the market. This occurred in markets in the Far East such as Malaysia and Thailand during the turmoil of the late 1990s.

An investor selling short via a broker/dealer is required to post margin as in the margin-trading example above. This is due to the fact that a rise in the stock price will leave the investor exposed to a mark-to-market loss, which the broker/dealer will need to cover. Hence the usual leverage, initial margin and maintenance margin considerations apply in short selling as well as margin trading.

Stock Borrowing

Typically, stocks are lent by brokers/dealers from securities that are pledged or held in custody on behalf of their clients. Large investors who hold their own stocks (e.g. insurance companies) may lend directly in the market. The loan may be at *call*, which means that it may be terminated at any time by the lender (which is the market standard), or a *term* loan for a predefined period (e.g. one month). Note that the loan is for a specific number of shares, not for a specific value, since any change in share price will change the value of the loan. Stock borrowing is normally a secured loan activity so that, when shares are lent, cash or more likely securities are pledged in return as collateral. Typical stock borrow/loan fees in large European stocks are 30 basis points (0.3%) per annum. If a particular stock is in short supply to lend—e.g. when the market is very bearish on the company and many investors are "short"—this rate may rise to 20% or 30% p.a. When stocks are borrowed over a dividend payment date the stock has to be returned to the lender along with a payment for the dividend paid while on loan.

Usually the arrangements for stock borrowing, collateral, and fees are handled directly by the broker/dealer for the investor. All the investor sees are the net interest costs on his account and the margin calls. In certain markets (notably the Far East) stock borrowing is restricted or not allowed. This has a profound effect on trading activity. For, example, arbitrage strategies that involve short-selling stock against a long position in convertible bonds may not be possible.

EXCHANGE-TRADED DERIVATIVES ON STOCKS

The pricing of options and futures, along with their risk characteristics, is discussed in Alexander and Sheedy (2008a), Chapters 7 and 8. We will focus here on describing some of the stock derivatives available and how their markets operate.

Single Stock and Index Options

Tens of derivatives exchanges exist across the world, but we will focus on two of the major stock option exchanges. These are the Chicago Board Options Exchange (CBOE) in the USA and London International Financial Futures Exchange (Euronext.LIFFE) in the UK. These markets offer a range of derivative products that have common stocks as their underlying asset, either single stocks or stock indices, which in effect behave like baskets of stocks.

On the CBOE, single-stock options exist on approximately 500 individual companies, most of which are in the S&P 500 index. These stock options allow the holder the right but not the obligation to buy (call option) or sell (put option) 100 shares (which is a normal lot size) of the underlying stock. On exercise (these options are American style, so may be exercised at any time up to expiry) the contract is settled by physical delivery of shares rather than in cash. In addition to single-stock options, there are options on stock indices such as the S&P 500—these options are cash-settled—and also options on the S&P 500 futures contract. On LIFFE, single-stock options exist on approximately 90 individual companies, most of which are in the FTSE 100, and there are options on the FTSE 100 stock index itself, which are cash-settled.

Expiration Dates

CBOE stock options expire at 10.59 p.m. (Central Time) on the Saturday following the third Friday of the expiration month. There are January, February, and March cycles. The January cycle is January, April, July, and October, and the other cycles lag by one and two months respectively. This means that generally the maximum maturity of the option is nine months. Longer-dated options—long-term equity anticipation securities (LEAPs—on stocks do exist, with expiries in January out to three years. There is a similar three-month cycle for the Euronext.LIFFE stock options.

Strike Prices

The strike prices are chosen when a new expiry series is introduced, normally with $2.50, $5.00, and $10.00 spacing on either side of the current spot price to give five option strikes in both puts and calls. If the stock price moves outside of the range of existing strikes, a new series is introduced at the new spot strike price.

Flex Options

These options are agreed individually between brokers with an OTC-like flexibility in expiry and strike price, along with a choice of American or European exercise. They are an attempt to win on-exchange business (with the attendant safety from on-exchange margin arrangements) from the OTC options market. There is an exchange-specified minimum size.

Dividends and Corporate Actions

CBOE exchange options are not adjusted for cash dividends, so any payments that reduce the stock price are not adjusted in the strike price of the options. If there are corporate actions, such as a stock split (e.g. two new shares for one old one), these are adjusted for in the strike price of the exchange options and the number of shares involved. In this case (i.e. a two-for-one stock split) each strike price would be halved and the number of shares deliverable doubled.

Position Limits

There are maximum numbers of contracts that can be held by individual investors or groups of investors working in concert. This is to prevent the market being cornered and manipulated to the detriment of other market participants. On the CBOE the largest limit is 75,000 contracts for the largest single stocks.

Trading

Both the CBOE and LIFFE use market makers to facilitate trading who are committed to maximum bid–offer spreads to aid market liquidity. The markets these days are largely electronic, having evolved from pit trading in the 1980s and 1990s. The trading process is via a broker/dealer through a market maker. Settlement and margin management is via the exchange clearing house. On the CBOE this is the Options Clearing Corporation, whose members are the clearing brokers on the exchange. For further details and contract specification, contact the CBOE or Euronext.LIFFE via their websites (see References and Bibliography).

CONCLUSIONS

In this chapter we have looked at the structure and organization of the stock market and the common stocks that trade on it. We have considered the characteristics of common stock and the role of the participants in the market. We have studied in detail how new issues come to the primary market (or float) via IPOs or private placements, and how they then trade among investors via brokers/dealers in the secondary market. We have looked in detail at the costs of trading, including short selling and trading on margin. We have also seen how exchange-traded derivatives are organized to trade stock risk via futures and options. For further information and details see the References and Bibliography.

REFERENCES AND BIBLIOGRAPHY

Alexander, C and Sheedy, E (2008a) *The Professional Risk Managers' Guide to Finance Theory* (New York: McGraw-Hill).
Bodie, Z, Kane, A, and Marcus, AJ (2002) *Investments* (Boston: McGraw-Hill/Irwin).
Chicago Board Options Exchange—Stock Option Details, http://www .cboe.com/OptProd /EquityOptions.asp.
Hull, JC (2003) *Options, Futures and Other Derivatives* (New York: Prentice Hall).
London International Financial Future Exchange—Stock Option Details, http://www.liffe .com/products/equities/index.htm.
London Stock Exchange—Listing Requirements, http://www.londonstockexchange.com/.
New York Stock Exchange—Listing Requirements, http://www.nyse. com/.
Reverre, S (2001) *The Complete Arbitrage Desk Book* (New York: McGraw-Hill).

CHAPTER 6

The Futures Markets

Canadian Securities Institute

INTRODUCTION

This chapter provides an introduction to futures markets where exchange-traded, forward-based derivatives are traded. Forward-based derivatives represent contracts made between two parties that require some specific action at a later date. Most often, this action takes the form of delivery of some underlying asset and payment for the asset. All forward-based contracts have a buyer and a seller, a maturity or expiration date, and a formula for exchanging payments set up when the contract is initiated that takes effect at some later date. Apart from a performance bond, no up-front payment is required. All forwards are in effect zero-sum games. The buyer's gain will be the seller's loss and vice versa. The gain and loss will always have a linear relationship with the price of the underlying interest. It should be noted that all forwards facilitate the use of leverage.

A forward-based derivative can trade on an exchange or over the counter (OTC). When it is traded on an exchange, it is referred to as a *futures contract*. There are two general types of futures contracts. Contracts that have a financial asset as their underlying interest are referred to as *financial futures*. These would include interest-rate, currency, and equity futures. Contracts that are based on a physical or "hard" asset are generally referred to as *commodity futures* contracts. Examples of commodity futures are gold, soybeans and crude oil. A detailed description of spot and future commodity markets is given in Chapter 7, while energy contracts are described in Chapter 8.

HISTORY OF FORWARD-BASED DERIVATIVES AND FUTURES MARKETS

Forward-based derivatives have been around for centuries. Initially, they were largely based on agricultural products. Volatile financial markets in the 1970s led to the concept of forwards being applied to financial products such as stocks, bonds, and currencies. In 1968, approximately 15 million futures contracts were traded worldwide, predominantly based on agricultural commodities on US exchanges. In 2006, about 5,280 million futures contracts and 6,580 million options on futures contracts were traded.[1] The vast majority of these contracts were based on nonagricultural assets. Turnover on non-US exchanges now significantly exceeds trading on US exchanges, and is growing at a much faster pace.

The agricultural industry was largely responsible for launching forward trading as producers (farmers) and consumers (millers) sought to minimize price uncertainty. Although agricultural prices fluctuate with supply and demand like most other prices, seasonality and weather conditions tend to make these fluctuations more severe and unpredictable. For example, an unusually large harvest can overwhelm markets with excess supply, causing prices to fall. Similarly, as supplies are drawn down after harvest, shortages and escalating prices can result. The concept of forward buying and selling was developed to help producers and consumers protect themselves against seasonal price fluctuations.

The Japanese were the first to introduce forward trading in the 1600s with rice forwards. In North America, the grain industry was the first to embrace forward-based contracts. Initially, contracts were developed in which a buyer and seller agreed privately, in advance, to the terms of a sale that would be consummated when the goods *arrived*. These agreements, known as *to-arrive* contracts, had their origin in the Liverpool cotton trade in the late 1700s. In the beginning, buyers and sellers met in the street to conduct business, but as volumes grew, a more permanent marketplace was sought.

Although the to-arrive contracts helped smooth out seasonal boom and bust cycles, they were not a perfect solution. Disputes often arose at delivery over the terms of the contracts, and the threat of default was always present. The private nature of the contracts meant pricing information was limited. The buyer and seller in a particular deal were generally unaware of prices from other contracts and therefore would have difficulty determining the current market price. Another problem concerned contract resale. Early contracts were not transferable. Even when they became

TABLE   6.1

Top 15 futures exchanges

2006 Rank	2005 Rank	Exchange	Volume of Contracts Traded in 2006* (millions)
1	1	Chicago Mercantile Exchange	1,102
2	2	Eurex	961
3	3	Chicago Board of Trade	678
4	4	Euronext.liffe	430
5	8	Mexican Derivatives Exchange	275
6	5	BM&F (Brazil)	258
7	6	New York Mercantile Exchange	216
8	7	National Stock Exchange of India	171
9	9	Dalian Commodity Exchange (China)	118
10	14	ICE Futures (U.K.)	93
11	15	JSE Securities Exchange South Africa	87
12	10	London Metal Exchange	79
13	12	Sydney Futures Exchange	74
14	11	Tokyo Commodity Exchange	64
15	13	Korea Exchange	60

Source: *Futures Industry*, March–April 2007
*Volume figures exclude options on futures.

transferable, it was difficult for a buyer or seller to find a third party willing to accept the risk.

Many of these problems, with what were essentially OTC forwards, were resolved with the introduction of exchange-traded forwards which became known as futures contracts. The Chicago Board of Trade (CBOT) became North America's first organized futures market in 1848 when buyers and sellers moved off the street and into the exchange. However, it was not until the 1860s that the innovative concept of standardized contract terms was introduced.

Listed futures contracts were standardized in terms of size, quality, grade, and time and place of delivery. Standardization, together with the requirement that all trading take place in a single location via the *open outcry system,* facilitated accurate and immediate price dissemination. Soon, a margining system was developed to guarantee the financial integrity of each contract.

The development of futures trading attracted not only the merchants involved in the grain trade, but also individuals who were only interested in the market for its profit possibilities. The influx of *speculators* greatly improved liquidity, which helped enhance market efficiency. Liquid futures markets helped eliminate the risk of being unable to resell and also helped to minimize wide price fluctuations.

The success of exchange-traded grain contracts led to tremendous growth in new futures contracts and new exchanges. Cotton, lumber, livestock, coffee, and orange juice futures were eventually followed by industrial and precious metals. In the early 1970s, the first foreign currency contracts were developed, followed by contracts on debt instruments starting with the Government National Mortgage Association futures (GNMA or "Ginnie Mae"). In the early 1980s, the next generation of futures complexes, stock index futures, was initiated with the introduction of the Value Line and S&P 500 index contracts. Energy-based futures began trading in the mid-1980s.

It is evident that futures contracts developed to solve some of the problems associated with OTC forward agreements. Their growth was so rapid that, not too long after their inception, futures markets became the predominant market for transacting forward-based contracts in many markets. This predominance became even more pronounced with the inception of precious metal and then financial futures contracts. From non-existence in the early 1970s, financial futures (interest-rate, currency and equity contracts) now account for approximately 90% of all futures trading. They have been primarily responsible for the almost exponential growth in overall futures volumes. Table 6.2 highlights the relative importance of financial futures in world markets as of 2006.

FUTURES CONTRACTS AND MARKETS

A futures contract is an agreement between two parties to buy or sell an asset at some future point in time at a predetermined price. This section describes the characteristics and mechanisms that are common to all futures contracts, and the highly organized and structured markets in which these contracts are traded.

T A B L E   6.2

Global futures and options volume by sector

	2006 Volume in Millions	% Change on 2005
Equity indices	4,454	9.16
Interest rate	3,193	25.89
Individual equities	2,876	22.05
Currency	240	43.59
Agriculturals	486	28.37
Energies	386	37.78
Metals	219	27.84
Other	4	66.69
Total volume	11,859	18.90

Source: *Futures Industry*, March–April 2007

General Characteristics of Futures Contracts and Markets

Since futures contracts trade on an exchange, all futures contracts are *standardized* in terms of their size, grade, and time and place of delivery. Other features of futures contracts that are standardized include their trading hours, minimum price fluctuations, and, for contracts that have them, maximum daily price limits. All contract terms, except price, are defined by the exchange on which they trade. This standardization can have an impact on hedging, as delivery dates and terms are not flexible. Table 6.3 provides an example of the standard specifications of a typical futures contract—canola futures that trade on the Winnipeg Commodity Exchange.

The *contract size* describes the number of units that underlie the futures contract. This is the amount per contract that must be delivered or accepted for delivery if the contract is held to the delivery month. For instance, in the example in Table 6.3, if the current canola price was $400 per tonne, the value of the contract would be $8,000 ($400 × 20 tonnes). At delivery, the seller would deliver $8,000 worth of canola that the buyer would have to pay cash for.

The minimum *tick size* represents the smallest price increment the futures contract can move up or down. In the case of canola, it is 10 cents

T A B L E   6.3

Contract specifications of Canadian canola futures

Contract size:	20 metric tonnes
Minimum tick size:	C$0.10 per metric tonne (C$2 per contract)
Daily price limit:	C$30 per metric tonne above or below previous settlement
Dynamic price limit:	80 ticks or C$8.00 per contract
Delivery months:	January, March, May, July, and November
Trading hours:	9:30 a.m. to 1:15 p.m. (Central Time)
Delivery point:	Areas in Saskatchewan at par; a premium applies to other delivery areas of C$2.00-6.00/tonne
Deliverable grades:	Contract deliverable grades shall be based on primary elevator grade standards as established by the Canadian Grain Commission (CGC). Non-commercially clean Canadian canola with maximum dockage of 8%; all other specifications to meet No. 1 Canada canola. Premium/discount prices apply to other grades of canola.

per tonne. If the current price of an October canola futures contract is $400 per tonne, the next trade could take place at a price of either $400, $400.10 or greater, or $399.90 or less. The 10 cent per tonne increment translates to $2.00 per contract (20 tonnes × 10 cents).

Exchanges set *limits* on the amount by which most futures can move, either up or down, during one day's trading session. If the price moves down by an amount equal to the daily limit, the contract is said to be limit down. If it reaches the upper limit then it is said to be limit up. The limits are designed to calm market panic, and to give market participants time to absorb new information that may have been disseminated.

In addition the exchange imposes a dynamic price limit which relates to intra-day trading. This prevents large price moves between orders. In the case of the canola contract, a dynamic price limit applies of 80 ticks (or C$8.00/contract) between orders.

Example 6.1: Daily Trading Limits

A severe drought on the Canadian prairies resulted in volatile trading in the canola futures contract that trades on the Winnipeg Commodity

Exchange. After a settlement price of C$450 per metric tonne on the previous trading day, July canola futures moved up by the daily limit of C$30 to C$480. The C$30 limit prohibits any trading from taking place over C$30 above or under C$30 below the previous day's settlement price of C$450. In this particular case, no trades may take place above C$480 or below C$420.

When a futures price moves by its daily limit, there still may be some trading at the limit price. Most often, however, trading comes to a complete halt as *bids* (the highest price at which someone is willing to buy) or *offers* (the lowest price at which someone is willing to sell) are nonexistent when the market moves limit down or up, respectively. This kind of situation can be very dangerous for traders holding losing long or short positions because they are unable to liquidate. If the limit situation lasts for several days, huge losses can result.

Partially in recognition of this risk, most exchanges have adopted procedures to deal with limit moves. One procedure expands price limits after a few days of limit moves. *Expanded limits,* for example, may widen out to 150% of regular limits so as to give traders holding losing long or short positions a greater chance to liquidate. Another procedure removes limits entirely for futures contracts trading in their delivery month. Finally, some exchanges have abolished limits on some contracts altogether.

Futures contracts are *settled daily.* Profits are credited daily to accounts that have winning positions, and losses debited daily to accounts that have losing positions. The size of the daily amount depends on the relationship between the current futures price and the initial entry price. If the futures price is higher, the holder of the long position receives a payment from the short for an amount equal to the difference. If the futures price is lower, the holder of the short position receives a payment from the long for an amount equal to the difference.

A futures contract only gains or loses value as the futures price changes. The payoff from a position in a futures contract is *linear* and, because of margining and daily mark-to-market, there may be significant cash flows associated with futures contracts. Cash flows can be positive or negative and, if not properly anticipated, can affect a party's ability to effectively use futures as a hedging tool.

The *delivery months* are also set by the exchange. In addition, the exchanges set specific deadline days for when trading in a contract ceases and for when the delivery period begins and ends. In the case of canola, the last trading day for a particular delivery month is always the trading day preceding the fifteenth calendar day of the delivery month.

The exchange also sets the deliverable grade (the quality of an asset that will be accepted for delivery in terms of grade, weight, or other characteristics), and other alternative grades that are acceptable for delivery. The deliverable grade for canola is Number 1 Canada canola. However, some other grades will be accepted with an appropriate price discount/premium to the final settlement price.

A *clearing association* stands between the parties to a futures contract. As a result, counterparties' identities are irrelevant. Companies A and B, which may have equal and opposite positions in futures contracts, can easily terminate their respective futures contracts at anytime following onset up to contract expiration by what is referred to as an *offsetting transaction* (see the next section). Company A could independently sell and company B independently buy the contract in the secondary market, which would have the effect of liquidating their respective positions and have no dependence upon each other because of the clearing association: if A or B defaulted on their obligations, the exchange would assume the obligations of the defaulted party. The following section gives more details about the activities of clearing associations.

The financial integrity of the futures markets is protected by requiring that each party to a contract post a performance bond, which is called the *margin*. Through a daily *marking-to-market* process with corresponding transfers of margin, each party to a contract is assured of the other party's performance. The initial value of a futures contract to both buyer and seller is zero, but initial margins, which are discussed in the section on Market Participants are not.

Finally, futures markets are *regulated* by governmental agencies and self-regulatory organizations. Regulations are very specific and detailed. Before any futures contract can be listed for trading it must be approved by regulatory authorities. For example, in the USA all new contracts must be approved by the Commodity Futures Trading Commission; in Singapore all new contracts must be approved by the Monetary Authority of Singapore.

Settlement of Futures Contracts

This section takes the reader through the trading and settlement of futures through a sequence of examples. Not all futures contracts involve delivery of a physical asset in exchange for payment. Some futures contracts dictate that delivery be conducted with an exchange of cash. This type of contract is typically referred to as a *cash-settled futures contract*. An example of a futures contract that is cash-settled is a stock index futures contract. Those who are long on a stock index futures contract do not have to accept delivery of the stocks that make-up the index, nor do the shorts have to make delivery. Instead, if the position is held to expiration, the long and short must either pay or receive the difference between the initial entry price and the expiration price. If the futures price increases, then the holder of the long position receives a payment from the short for an amount equal to the difference. If the futures price decreases, the holder of the short position receives a payment from the long for an amount equal to the difference.

Example 6.2: Buying a Futures Contract

Suppose trader A places an order with a futures representative to buy one November canola futures contract on the Winnipeg Commodity Exchange. The order is relayed to the floor of the exchange, where it is filled at a price of C$420 per tonne. The speculator is now long, and if the contract is held to expiration in November, he/she is obligated to accept delivery of 20 tonnes of canola from the short based on the terms of the contract at an effective price of C$420 per tonne.[2] The terms of the contract are standardized as to the quantity (20 tonnes) and quality of the canola that will be delivered and the location(s) to which it will be delivered.

Although a futures contract represents an obligation to deliver or accept delivery of cash or an underlying asset, in 98% of futures trades that obligation is terminated prior to the delivery period through what is known as an *offsetting* trade. Settlement by offset is accomplished by the holder of a long position independently selling the contract, or the holder of a short position independently buying back the contract. The payoff from settling the contract prior to delivery is calculated as the difference between the offsetting and original entry prices.

Example 6.3: Settlement by an Offsetting Transaction

Prior to the start of the delivery month, trader A (who is long one November canola futures contract) places an order with the same futures representative to sell one contract of November canola futures. The order is relayed to the floor of the exchange where it is filled at a price of C$430 per tonne. By selling November canola, the trader has in effect cancelled out or offset the earlier long position. As the offsetting price is higher than the original delivery price, the speculator has earned a profit of C$10 per tonne, which is based on the difference between the buying and selling prices. As a contract represents 20 tonnes, A's profit is C$200.

Many individuals unfamiliar with the workings of the futures market visualize receiving physical delivery of the underlying asset. Needless to say, the thought of having 20 tonnes of canola, for example, dumped on one's doorstep is enough to steer anyone well clear of the futures markets. But, in fact, nothing could be further from the truth. The delivery period only begins with the first delivery day, which is typically near the end of the month prior to the delivery month. As long as a contract is offset prior to this important date (and, as mentioned above, 98% of all contracts are offset) there will be no need for any involvement with delivery. Even if an individual decides to take delivery, what is received/delivered in the case of most physical commodities is a *warehouse receipt* that the seller endorses over to the buyer. The receipt is issued by a storage point, authorized by the exchange, which confirms the presence and ownership of the underlying asset.

Contracts that have not been offset prior to the delivery period are subject to physical delivery (with the exception of cash-settled futures which will be discussed later in this chapter). There are several considerations to keep in mind with regard to physical delivery.

First, it is the short party that controls the delivery process. Within what is allowed by the terms of the futures contract, the short party determines the time and location of delivery as well as the quality or grade of the underlying asset to be delivered. Most contracts allow for multiple delivery points and for the delivery of grades that may be slightly better or worse than what par delivery specifications demand. The allowance of premium or discount grades is designed to increase the amount of a commodity available, and to help prevent one group from controlling or "cornering" the market.

A second consideration is that the delivery process begins with what is known as *first notice day*. The exact day depends on the particular futures contract, but typically it occurs near the end of the month preceding the delivery month. If a long futures holder such as trader A does not offset a position prior to this day, there is a risk of receiving a delivery notice. The risk grows the further into the delivery month the contract is held. If the contract is held to the end of last trading day, delivery is guaranteed.

At any time on or after first notice day, shorts will notify the exchange's clearing house of their intention to deliver, the location of delivery, and the deliverable grade. Upon this notification, the clearing house will then allocate delivery notices among clearing members who have long positions on or after first notice day. One method of allocation that clearing houses use is the "first in, first out" method, whereby the oldest long positions are given notices first.

Once the party with the long position receives a notice, actual delivery typically will take place a few days later. On the delivery day, the party with the long position in the contract issues payment by certified cheque to the short position and in exchange takes delivery. Rather than receiving the actual physical commodity at that time, the long will receive a warehouse receipt that represents the amount and the grade of the commodity that is stored at one of the acceptable delivery points. If the underlying asset to be delivered is a financial product such as a currency or bond, in exchange for the certified cheque, the party with the long position will receive documentation that verifies ownership of the asset at an exchange-approved bank.

Example 6.4: Settlement by Delivery

Instead of offsetting the long position in November canola futures, trader A decides to carry the position past first notice day. In early November, A receives a delivery notice. The notice, which has been delivered to the clearing corporation the previous day by the short, calls for A to accept delivery of a warehouse receipt that represents 20 tonnes of delivery grade canola at an exchange-approved warehouse at a price of C$440 in two days' time. On the delivery day, A accepts delivery of the warehouse receipt in exchange for a certified cheque in the amount of C$8800.

Notice that the delivery process is initiated by the short party, who delivers a notice of intention to deliver to the clearing corporation in early November. In actual fact, the notice will be delivered by the short party's broker on instructions from the short party. The notice includes details as to the timing of delivery, the grade of canola to be delivered (in this case par value), and the location where the canola is stored. The notice does not specify to whom delivery is to be made. The clearing corporation allocates delivery notices to the various member firms showing long positions. The member firms will then in turn allocate them to their clients who are long.

Readers should note that the delivery price in this example, rather than being trader A's entry price of C$420, is actually C$440, which represents the settlement price on the day the short issued the delivery notice. Based on a price of C$440, A issues a cheque for C$8,800 to the short (C$440 × 20 tonnes). While a cheque is issued for C$8,800, the net cost of the canola to A is only C$8,400. A profit of C$400 is earned on the long futures position which is automatically closed out the day the delivery notice is issued. The profit is the difference between the settlement price on this day (C$440) and the entry price (C$420). The effective net price A pays is C$420 per tonne (C$8,400/20 tonnes), being the initial entry price.

As has been mentioned, most market participants have no desire to accept or make delivery of an underlying asset. The best way to avoid making delivery is to offset the position before first notice day. If the market participant still wishes to maintain the same exposure to a particular futures contract, "rolling over" into a more distant contract can be done by offsetting the old contract, while simultaneously entering into a new contract. In the canola example above, if trader A does not wish to take delivery, but wants to maintain a long exposure, the November contract will be sold prior to first notice day while at the same time a deferred canola contract such as March will be bought.

Member firms have procedures for notifying their clients that first notice day is approaching. Typically, the client will be notified several days prior and advized to either liquidate the position or roll over to a more distant month. In order to encourage their clients to offset or roll over their positions, margin requirements are typically raised significantly on and after first notice day. Occasionally, however, a long client, who has no intention of taking delivery, accidentally holds on to the position through first notice day and receives a delivery notice. Most exchanges do have a mechanism that allows those clients to offset their obligation by selling an equivalent number of futures contracts, and then "passing along" the delivery notice to the clearing corporation, which in turn allocates it to another long position. This procedure, however, can be costly to the client, entailing extra commission costs as well as the possibility of the carrying costs of the physical commodity if the delivery notice cannot be passed on right away.

Types of Orders

When placing an order in the futures markets, there is some common terminology that is essential to understand in order to be sure that orders are executed properly. Below is a list of some of the most common order types. This terminology applies whether buying or selling a contract.

- *Market order.* This order is used to buy or sell immediately at the "market price." There is no guarantee what that price will be, so you rely on the broker and trader for timely and effective execution.
- *Best efforts or worked order.* This order is placed when you wish to give the broker or trader some discretion in executing the transaction. It is often used for large orders where a "market" order might disrupt trading. Again, you rely on the broker and trader for timely and effective execution and there is no guarantee as to the price at which the trade is executed, or even if the trade is executed at all.
- *Good 'til cancelled (GTC).* This is an order to execute a trade that stays "live" until the customer cancels the trade. Many firms will cancel all GTC trades at the "close of business," but others will not. It is important to understand the difference in how your brokerage treats GTC trades.
- *Market on open (MOO).* This is a "market" order that will be executed when the market opens, at a price within the opening range of prices. Opening price ranges can be quite wide, so this type of trade is to be used with discretion.
- *Market on close (MOC).* This is a "market" order that will be executed when the market closes. The price of the trade will be within the closing range of the day, which may be quite large and vary substantially from the settlement price. As with an MOO order, MOC orders are to be used with discretion.

- *Limit order.* This order is placed when you are looking to buy or sell at a specific price "or better." This tells your broker or trader in the pit that you are looking to purchase the futures contract at a price no higher than your limit or to sell at a price no lower than your limit. When using this type of order, you should be aware that the market may trade at your limit price for substantial periods of time and you may still not be filled at your order. You are only guaranteed to have your order executed if the market trades through the limit price, either above your sell limit or below your buy limit.

- *Stop order.* This is an order to buy or sell when the market reaches a certain price. Once that price has been reached, the order becomes a "market order." A buy stop is placed above the market and a sell stop is placed below the market. Stop orders are commonly used to protect profits or to attempt to limit losses. One should note that markets have a tendency to "find stops," meaning that when a market price is reached that triggers "stop orders," the market will often reverse price trends.

- *Market if touched (MIT).* Much like a stop order, an MIT order becomes a "market order" if the price reaches a specified level. Unlike the "stop order", an MIT order to sell is placed above the current market price, and an MIT order to buy is placed below the current market price. Not all firms or exchanges will accept MIT orders.

- *Fill or kill (FOK).* This order is a limit order that is sent to the pit to be executed immediately and if the order is unable to be filled right away, it is cancelled.

- *Spread order.* A simple spread order involves two positions, one bought and one sold. The trades generally involve the same market with different months (calendar spread) or closely related markets, such as interest rates of different maturities. An order is entered at a "spread" between the prices of the two contracts. The final execution prices of each contract may not be the same as current "market" prices of each individual contract, but each contract's price will be within the day's trading range for that contract.

- *Fast markets.* Of note to anyone who is executing trades on futures markets is a condition known as "fast markets." Such a condition means that there is excessive price volatility, usually in combination with a lack of normal liquidity. During "fast markets," the normal rules that cover whether a trade will be executed according to specific orders are suspended. There are no guarantees of prices or execution. In general, one should be very cautious about entering any type of order during "fast markets."

Margin Requirements and Marking to Market

Futures transactions are typically margin transactions. But unlike margins on securities (which are a counterpart to the maximum loan value that a dealer may extend to its customer to purchase a security), a futures margin is the amount of money that a customer must deposit with a broker to provide a level of assurance that the financial obligations of the futures contract will be met. In effect, futures margins represent a good faith deposit or a performance bond.

The minimum margin rate for a client who wishes to establish a position in a futures market is set by the exchange or clearing house, but a member firm may impose higher margin rates on its clients. The member firm, however, may not charge the client *less* than the exchange's minimum requirements.

Two levels of margin are used in futures trading—*original* and *maintenance margins*. Original or *initial* margin represents the required deposit when a futures contract is entered into. Maintenance margin is the minimum balance for margin required during the life of the contract.

Readers will recall that one of the characteristics of a futures contract is its daily settlement or what is referred to as *marking-to-market*. As mentioned earlier, at the end of each trading day, the long makes a payment to the short or vice versa, depending on the relationship between the current futures price and the initial entry price. In fact, this is a slight simplification. First, the payment is not made directly between the long and short, but takes place between the counterparties' respective investment dealers (member firms) through the clearing house. Second, while the long and short's respective accounts are debited or credited each day by the amount of loss or gain, the party who is in the losing position will only have to deposit additional margin when his or her account balance falls below the maintenance margin level. The margining process is explained in further detail in the section on Marking-to-Market and Margin.

Leverage

Since futures prices only reflect the prices of their underlying interests, the question to ask is why futures trading is considered riskier than trading the underlying interests themselves. The main reason is leverage. Leverage describes the amount of capital that must be put up in order to buy or sell an asset. In mathematical terms, it is simply the ratio of the investment relative to the amount of capital needed to purchase it. If a $100,000 house is purchased with a $25,000 down payment and a $75,000 loan, the purchaser has a 4:1 leverage ratio. Since futures trading requires smaller margins than equity trading, more leverage is available.

Investors can buy or sell equities with margin deposits ranging from 30% to 80%. For example, a $10,000 long position in a security eligible for reduced margin can be arranged with only a $3,000 deposit. That same $3,000 deposit, however, could secure a futures position with a value of $100,000 (futures margin requirements are typically from 3% to 10% of a contract's value). If the equity investor sees the value of the stock rise by 10%, the sale of the stock would yield a 33% return on margin. If the futures price increases by the same 10%, the return on margin would be 333%. Of course, leverage would magnify losses if prices moved in the wrong direction.

While leverage is often associated with futures trading, readers should understand that it is not inherent in a futures contract. A futures trader could decide to deposit a contract's full value as margin rather than the minimum margin required. For example, a trader who goes long a gold futures contract could deposit the contract's value of US$40,000 (100 ounces at an assumed price of $400 per ounce) as margin. If this decision is made, the trader would not be leveraged at all.

In practice, most traders will take advantage of the leverage that is offered. It is one of the attractions of trading futures. Leverage, however, should be thought of as separate to a futures contract. It is a feature that most participants will exploit, but some may choose not to use. For example, pension funds in Canada are regulated in a way that prevents them from taking leveraged positions in futures contracts.

Reading a Futures Quotation Page

End-of-day futures quotations are available in most daily financial publications and their websites. Real-time or delayed intraday quotations are available on most exchanges' websites. Table 6.4 duplicates an intraday

TABLE 6.4

Live cattle futures (prices in US cents)

Month	Current Session							Previous Session		
	Open	High	Low	Last	Settle*	Change	Volume†	Settle	Volume	Open††
FEB03	81.350	81.675	81.050	81.675	—	+475	2,936	81.200	3,325	3,328
APR03	77.150	77.375	76.550	77.350	—	+250	10,701	77.100	8,182	53,791
JUN03	70.500	70.900	70.200	70.900	—	+450	3,557	70.450	4,404	22,709
AUG03	67.450	67.800	67.175	67.800	—	+525	880	67.275	779	9,498
OCT03	69.550	69.975	69.525	69.975	—	+350	216	69.625	387	6,337
DEC03	70.850	71.100	70.750	71.100	—	+400	95	70.700	144	3,146
FEB04	72.250	72.300	72.250	72.250	—	+75	2	72.175	156	1,049

*The current session's settlement price is not known until the day's trading has concluded. The settlement price should not be confused with the price of the last trade of the day. The exchange's Pit Committee determines the settlement price, which is most often an average of the prices for trades made towards the end of the session.

†The estimated number of contracts that have traded during the current trading session.

††The open interest at the close of the previous trading session. Open interest represents the number of outstanding contracts (i.e. contracts that have not been liquidated by an offsetting transaction or by delivery). Due to the nature of the calculation, open interest is available only after the trading session concludes.

quotation on live cattle futures from the website of the Chicago Mercantile Exchange (CME); see www.cme.com.

Calculating the value of the underlying interest represented by one futures contract is a relatively simple task. It is just a matter of multiplying the contract size by the latest price. Most of the financial press includes contract sizes within their end-of-day quotations. The exchanges tend to post this information separately from their quotations. In the case of live cattle futures, the standard size of one contract is 40,000 pounds. With the April 2003 contract trading at a price of 77.35 US cents per pound, the value of the underlying interest per contract is $30,940 ($0.7735 × 40,000). Open interest and volume figures are analyzed quite carefully in conjunction with price movements to give traders an indication of the technical strength or weakness of a particular market.

Liquidity and Trading Costs

Liquidity, low trading costs, and price transparency are some of the main attractions of futures trading. Some of the most actively traded contracts have trading volumes in excess of 300 million contracts per annum[3] (e.g. Euro-Bund Futures on Eurex and three-month Eurodollar Futures on CME). In such circumstances it is possible to trade large parcels without adversely affecting the price, and bid–offer spreads are minimal. The spread in the liquid contracts is usually the minimum price fluctuation, called a tick. In contrast, some futures contracts are not at all liquid; days may pass when not a single contract is traded. Exchanges often introduce new contracts, of which the majority fail to attract sufficient liquidity. Those that do not attract liquidity are eventually cancelled. Trading costs also can include commissions paid to brokers and exchange/clearing fees.

OPTIONS ON FUTURES

Options on futures contracts were introduced in October 1982 when the CBOT began trading options on Treasury bond futures. These have added a new dimension to futures trading. While both futures and futures options can provide protection against adverse price movements, the purchase of futures options (as with other types of options) provides the ability to both guarantee a purchase or sale price and, at the same time, allow a hedger to participate fully in favorable movements in the price of the underlying asset. Of course, this feature of options comes at a cost—the premium.

T A B L E   6.5

Specifications of FTSE 100 index contracts

	FTSE 100 Index Futures	FTSE 100 Index Options (European Style)
Unit of trading	Contract valued at £10 per index point	Same
Delivery months	March, June, September, December (nearest four available for trading)	Same
Quotation	Index points (e.g. 6,500.0)	Same
Minimum price movement (tick size and value)	0.5 (£5.00)	Same
Last trading day	Third Friday in delivery month	Third Friday of the expiry month
Delivery day	First business day after the last trading day	NA
Trading hours	08:00–17:30	08:00–16:30
Trading platform	LIFFE CONNECT	Same
Exchange delivery settlement price (EDSP)	The value of the FTSE 100 Index is calculated by FTSE International with reference to the outcome of the EDSP intra-day auction at the London Stock Exchange carried out on the Last Trading Day	Same
Daily settlement price	NA	The daily settlement price is based on the 16:30 price of the FTSE 100 index
Settlement day	NA	Settlement day is the first business day after the Last Trading Day.
Exercise day	NA	Exercise by 18:00 on the Last Trading Day only
Contract standard	Cash settlement based on the EDSP	Same
Exercise price intervals	NA	The interval between exercise prices is determined by the time to maturity of a particular expiry month and is either 50 or 100 index points.

Continued

T A B L E   6.5

Continued

	FTSE 100 Index Futures	FTSE 100 Index Options (European Style)
		The Exchange reserves the right to introduce tighter strike intervals (e.g. 25 points) where necessary.
Introduction of new exercise prices	NA	Additional exercise prices will be introduced on the business day after the underlying index level has exceeded the second highest, or fallen below the second lowest, available exercise price
Option premium	NA	Payable by the buyer in full on the business day following a transaction

Source: www.euronext.com

Options on futures are just like any other option except that the underlying interest is a futures contract rather than a stock, bond, currency, or stock index. A *call option* gives the holder the right to purchase a particular futures contract at a specific price (the exercise price) at any time during the life of the option. A *put option* gives the holder the right to sell a particular futures contract at a specified price at any time during the life of the option. Most options on futures are American style, although some exchanges offer European options on futures (see Alexander and Sheedy (2008a), Chapter 8).

At most futures exchanges the option premium is paid by the buyer at the time of purchase. No margin is required as the losses are limited to the extent of the option premium. The seller of the option must, however, post a margin. Margining arrangements for options will be discussed in the section on Marking-to-Market and Margin. There are some exchanges (e.g. the Sydney Futures Exchange) where option purchases, in addition to sales, occur on a margined basis.

Table 6.5 provides an example of contract specifications for FTSE 100 index contracts. Note that the specifications of the options contracts are closely aligned with the underlying futures contract. The exchange (in this case Euronext-LIFFE) has to establish rules for the selection of exercise prices.

Euronext-LIFFE (like many exchanges these days), allows for even greater choice of contract terms through the availability of *flex options*. A flex option is designed to offer the flexibility of the OTC market, but with the advantages that exchange trading brings such as price transparency and reduction in counterparty risk. Participants may request a price quotation on an option with much longer maturity than standard contracts and with the exercise price of their choice.

Table 6.6 provides an example of pricing for FTSE 100 index options as at the close of trading on July 16, 2004. In this table put prices are shown on the left hand side and call prices on the right. On this day the underlying asset (FTSE 100 index futures expiring on September 17, 2004) closed with a bid–offer spread of 4,339–4,340. This tight bid–offer spread reflects excellent liquidity, total volume traded for the day being 55,086 contracts. Liquidity is less impressive in the corresponding option contracts, partly because there are so many. Options on futures expiring in August were the most actively traded, with a total of 38,379 contracts. These are split, however, between puts (20,171) and calls (18,208) and 25 strikes. Note that trading is typically the most active for strikes close to the current underlying. Strike prices that are out-of-the-money are more popular than those that are in-the-money (presumably because they are less expensive). The series with the greatest trading activity on July 16 was the call option with a strike of 4,525, having total daily volume of 5,479. While the bid–offer spread at the close for this series was only 0.5 point, spreads of 3 points or more are common.

When a futures option is exercised, the buyer and writer of the option will receive a futures position in their respective accounts the following day at the exercise price of the option. If a call is exercised, the buyer will receive a long futures position and the writer will receive a short futures position. The entry price for both the long and short position will be the exercise price.

Example 6.5: Exercise of a Futures Option

An investor who feels that canola prices are about to rise decides to buy on November 5, 400 canola call options at a price of C$2.00. The investor chooses the futures options rather than the outright futures because of the limited risk feature of the former. As with all futures options, the terms of the contract are characterized by the underlying futures.

TABLE 6.6

FTSE 100 index option pricing (European-style), August expiry, prices as at July 16, 2004. Underlying asset FTSE 100 index futures expiring September 17, 2004, last trade price 4,340

Put Options										Strike	Call Options									
Settle[a]	OI[b]	Total Daily Vol[c]	Vol[d]	Last Trade at	Last Trade	Bid	Offer	AQ[e] Bid	AQ Offer	AQ Strike Offer	AQ Bid	AQ Offer	Bid	Offer	Last Trade at	Last Trade	Vol[d]	Total Daily	OI[b]	Settle[a]
609.5	—	0	—	—	—	—	—	598.5	610.5	3,725	0	4.5	—	—	15:59:06	1.5	6	106	2,054	2
560.5	—	0	—	—	—	—	—	549	561	3,775	0	5	—	4	08:35:34	3	15	15	1,532	2.5
511.5	—	0	—	—	—	—	—	500	512	3,825	0	5.5	2.5	—	—	—	—	2,000	3,069	3.5
463	5	0	—	—	—	—	—	450.5	462.5	3,875	1	7	—	9.5	16:27:56	4.5	100	230	4,628	5
415	—	0	—	—	—	—	—	402.5	414.5	3,925	2	8	5	7.5	15:59:06	6.5	6	3,193	22,381	6.5
367	—	0	—	—	—	—	—	354.5	366.5	3,975	4	10	5.5	8.5	15:50:28	8	40	273	6,467	8.5
320	22	0	—	—	—	310.5	315	307	319	4,025	6	12	8	11	16:07:46	10	38	2,986	11,164	11
273.5	32	0	—	—	—	264.5	268	260	272	4,075	9.5	15.5	12	13.5	16:29:22	12.5	10	3,145	12,242	14.5
228	30	0	—	—	—	219	223	213.5	225.5	4,125	12.5	20	16.5	17	15:37:13	17	4	1,912	6,103	18.5
185	30	0	—	—	—	175.5	179.5	171	183	4,175	18.5	26	22.5	24.5	16:15:03	23.5	2	364	4,469	25
144.5	479	838	398	13:20:40	142	134.5	138.5	130.5	142.5	4,225	27.5	35	31.5	34	16:09:16	33.5	25	1,562	10,527	34.5
107.5	150	7	2	15:20:10	101	98	101	95	104	4,275	40	49	44.5	46.5	16:29:22	45	10	368	2,461	47.5
74.5	3,206	525	40	16:22:14	69.5	66.5	69.5	64	73	4,325	58.5	67.5	62.5	64.5	16:22:14	62	40	2,666	11,637	64.5
49	1,289	297	148	15:40:49	38.5	41.5	44	37.5	46.5	4,375	82.5	91.5	86.5	89.5	14:30:25	78	5	144	1,639	88

28.5	5,821	1,492	5	15:39:16	22	23	26	20	27.5	4,425	112	124	118	121.5	15:35:38	119	10	754	4,074	117.5
15	3,717	4,450	5	16:28:51	12	11.5	13.5	8	15.5	4,475	149.5	161.5	156.5	158.5	15:35:26	158	10	368	1,850	154
8	11,226	5,479	5	16:29:00	6	5.5	6	3	9	4,525	193.5	205.5	199	202	10:33:53	204	2	30	4,075	197
4	1,844	2,477	2	15:38:19	2.5	2	4	0	5.5	4,575	240	252	–	–	10:58:15	252	5	55	270	242
2	6,712	218	148	15:40:49	2	–	2	0	4	4,625	288.5	300.5	–	–	–	–	–	0	234	290
1	2,554	6	3	08:42:02	1	–	–	0	3.5	4,675	337.5	349.5	–	–	–	–	–	0	55	338.5
0.5	8,793	2,373	13	15:28:53	1.5	0.5	–	0	3.5	4,725	389.5	401.5	–	–	10:41:18	397	4	4	74	388
–	5,471	24	10	14:49:42	1	–	–	0	3	4,775	437	449	–	–	–	–	–	0	–	437.5
–	11,053	40	35	14:42:09	1	–	–	0	3	4,825	486.5	498.5	–	–	–	–	–	0	–	487.5
–	1,978	0	–	–	–	–	–	0	3	4,875	536	548	–	–	–	–	–	0	5	537
–	1,295	0	–	–	–	–	–	0	3	4,925	586	598	–	–	–	–	–	0	–	–

[a]Settle – the previous day's settlement price.

[b]OI (open interest) represents the outstanding long and short positions of the previous trading day updated in the morning each day.

[c]Total daily volume is the number of trades that have taken place within the respective strike in the trading day. This figure updates as the day progresses and more trades take place within the same strike.

[d]Vol (volume) is the number of contracts traded in the most recent trading session.

[e]AQ (Autoquote) is the Exchange's theoretical pricing model for options.

In the case of canola futures, the underlying interest is 20 tonnes of canola. Each dollar move in the price of canola represents C$20. The total dollar value of the option is therefore C$40 (C$2 × 20) per contract or C$200 for five contracts. The call option gives the investor the right to buy five contracts of canola futures at the exercise price of C$400 up to the expiry. If a decision is made to exercise, the call holder will receive five canola futures contracts the day after exercise with an initial entry price of C$400. If at the time of exercise, the November canola futures price is at C$410, for example, the call buyer has an immediate open profit of C$10 per tonne or C$1,000 on five contracts. The buyer can, at that time, decide to liquidate some or all of the contracts and take the profit or maintain some or all of the contracts. If the contracts are maintained, margin has to be deposited. Of course, as with all options, the buyer (or seller) can—and indeed most do—offset the position rather than exercise it. The writer of the call option upon assignment receives five short November canola futures contracts and has an immediate open loss of C$1,000.

Options on futures can be used to either speculate on or hedge an underlying futures contract or the asset underlying the futures contract. An investor who is holding a profitable long gold futures contract, for example, may want to buy a gold futures option put for profit protection (married put). By the same token, an investor who is bullish on gold may just want to buy a futures call option rather than buy the outright futures. As far as speculating or hedging cash price movements, the decision to use options on futures or outright futures depends on the investor's risk and return profile. If a limited risk strategy is desired, long futures options would be the choice. If the investor wants to lock in a price with no up-front costs, futures would be the choice.

Example 6.6: Using Bond Futures Call Options to Provide Insurance against Falling Interest Rates

A treasurer of an investment firm that anticipates having funds available at a later date to purchase $1 million of US Treasury bonds is worried that bond interest rates may decline (bond prices rise) before they can execute the purchase. The treasurer would like to have temporary insurance against a sudden price increase, but also wants to avoid paying too much if bond prices decline. To achieve these goals, the treasurer can buy call options on Treasury bond futures (each call option represents US$100,000 par value). Suppose that in May the price of a specific cash Treasury bond is 88–00. Ten September 90–00 futures calls are purchased by the treasurer for US$10,000. By September, interest rates on long-term Treasury bonds have declined and the price of the cash bond is 96–00, and the ten September 90–00 calls are priced at US$60,000. The treasurer decides to offset the position by selling the ten September 90–00 calls. The profit on purchase and sale of the calls is US$50,000 (US$60,000–US$10,000). This profit offsets most of the US$80,000 increase in the cost of buying the Treasury bonds (US$960,000–US$880,000).

The treasurer in this example, instead of using bond futures options, could have bought bond futures. The futures contract, due to its linear relationship with the underlying asset, would have locked in a price, with no up-front cost, regardless of whether the cash bond moved up or down. If bond futures were used, and bond prices did increase, the futures profit would have offset most if not all of the treasurer's increased cost. The negative side is that the treasurer would not have been able to benefit if bond prices decreased instead of increasing. The savings generated by buying the bond cheaper would have been offset by losses on the futures contract. Of course, the futures contract could have been offset prior to the end of the hedge period, but that would have required the treasurer to go unhedged from that point on.

Here options guaranteed a maximum buying price, but also gave the treasurer the ability to profit if prices declined. The downside of using options is that there is an up-front price to pay. In the example above, it was US$10,000. Also, an option does not have a linear relationship with its underlying asset the way futures contracts do. If, in Example 6.6, the price of the cash bond rose to 90 at expiration, the option would have no value. The treasurer would not only have paid more for the purchase of the cash bond, but also have incurred a US$10,000 option loss.

FUTURES EXCHANGES AND CLEARING HOUSES

This section describes the basic features and functions of organized futures exchanges and clearing houses. The trend to electronic trading is one of the most significant affecting the operation of exchanges at the present time. The world's second largest futures exchange, Eurex, has *only* electronic trading. With its lower trading costs, it has gained an important competitive advantage, even entering the Chicago market to compete with CBOT.

When an order is placed to buy or sell a futures contract, the order is relayed to the futures exchange where that contract is listed. If the futures exchange uses a trading floor, the order is relayed to the contract's trading pit. For the more active futures contracts, several hundred traders surround the octagonal-shaped pit. The action around the pit is frantic, with traders shouting, waving their arms and signaling with their fingers orders relayed to them by runners, who run or signal the orders received via phone lines or other communication facilities. Once a trade is consummated between two traders, details are filled out on a trading card and the confirmation is given to the runner who relays it back to the broker who then notifies the client.[4]

If the futures exchange uses an electronic trading system, orders are entered directly into the system where they are matched on a price–time priority, which simulates the auction system used on trading floors. When an order has been filled, the trading system automatically notifies the brokerage firms from where the orders originated. Each brokerage firm would then notify the broker who then notifies the client.

Exchanges

Futures exchanges provide a forum for market participants to buy and sell futures contracts. Traditionally, this forum consisted exclusively of a trading floor with pits in which traders bought and sold futures contracts through an open outcry auction process. Not so any longer. The late 1990s witnessed a big migration of futures volume from so-called physical trading floors to the electronic trading platforms developed or acquired by most futures exchanges. Some exchanges, like the Bourse de Montreal, went all out and completely shut down their trading floors. Others such as the CME and CBOT created "side-by-side" trading whereby some of the exchanges' contracts simultaneously trade in both open outcry and electronic trading venues. In these cases, customers are able to direct their orders to either the trading floor or the electronic trading system. A smaller number of exchanges, including the New York Mercantile Exchange (NYMEX), decided to offer electronic trading only in an overnight trading session when the trading floor is closed.

Regardless of the type of futures exchange, the price buyers and sellers agree upon is arrived at through an *auction process*. The term *open outcry auction process* is used to describe trading on a physical exchange. In this type of auction system, bids and offers are communicated between *floor traders* in a trading ring or pit through both verbal and hand communications. Once a trade is consummated, *market reporters*, who operate from strategic locations around the floor of the exchange, record and input the information into a communications system. Once inputted, the price information can be disseminated almost instantaneously around the world.

On an electronic exchange, a specific futures contract's best bid and offer prices are displayed on computer terminals located in member firms' offices. The terminals also allow member firms' traders to enter orders for any contract trading on the system. As orders are entered, the exchanges' trading systems will sort, display and, when the rules of auction trading say so, match them (i.e. create a trade). Only registered members of an exchange have privileges to trade on that exchange. On a physical exchange, there are two types of floor traders. Those who primarily trade on their own account are referred to as *locals*, while those who fill orders from customers are referred to as *floor brokers*. Locals either own an exchange membership, known as a *seat*, or lease one from an owner. The large number of locals that trade on the US exchanges have been among the most significant opponents of the trend away from physical floor trading.

Futures Exchange Functions

The primary function of a futures exchange is to provide the facilities for the buying and selling of futures contracts through the open outcry auction system. This means providing the physical space, in the case of physical futures exchanges, and the communications infrastructure, for both physical and electronic futures exchanges, to transmit information between the exchange and the rest of the world. In order to ensure the maintenance of fair and competitive markets, exchanges publish and enforce rules and regulations that meet both regulatory and internal requirements.

Another primary function of an exchange is the development of new contracts, and the revamping and sometimes elimination of existing contracts. It is typically the responsibility of the new products committee of an exchange to study the feasibility of new futures contracts in terms of their economic viability. The exchange then submits new contract proposals to the regulatory authority for approval. In addition to recommending new contracts, exchanges are also responsible for establishing the details of all futures contracts traded on its floor. Those details include contract size, delivery standards and location, tradable months, price increments, and margin requirements.

Clearing Houses

Although an exchange provides the setting for the purchase and sale of futures contracts, no money actually changes hands there. Instead, each futures exchange has an associated organization that takes care of financial settlement, and helps ensure that markets operate efficiently. This organization, which is called a *clearing house,* can be set up either as a separate corporation or as a department of the exchange. In Canada, the Canadian Derivatives Clearing Corporation is responsible for clearing Bourse de Montreal futures and option trades. The Winnipeg Commodity Clearing Corporation has sole responsibility for clearing Winnipeg Commodity Exchange trades.

A clearing house guarantees the financial obligations of every contract that it clears. It does this by acting as the buyer for every seller, and the seller for every buyer (*principle of substitution*). A participant who has bought or sold a futures contract has an obligation not to the party on the other side of the transaction, but to the clearing house, just as the clearing house has an obligation to the participant. The existence of the clearing house means that market participants need not be concerned about the honesty or reliability of other trading parties. The integrity of the clearing house is the only issue. As clearing houses have a good record in honoring their obligations, the counterparty risk in futures trading is considered to be negligible. This is one of the principal advantages of futures trading as opposed to OTC trading.

Clearing houses are able to guarantee the financial integrity of futures contracts through a layered system of financial protection. Margin deposits provide the first layer of protection. Parties to a futures trade must deposit an initial or original margin when the contract is first entered. Through the life of the contract, gains are credited and losses debited to the long and short holder accounts on a daily basis. If losses result in an account's net equity (defined as cash deposited plus/minus any open futures positions' profit/loss) falling under the maintenance margin level, the losing party must make a margin deposit to replenish net equity to at *least* the original margin level.

A primary activity of a clearing house is to *match trades* submitted by clearing member firms. Throughout each trading day, clearing members report the details of executed trades, whether they are on behalf of their clients or are on their own accounts, to the clearing house. Once the clearing house verifies the accuracy of all reported transactions, ensures that there is a buy for every sell, and receives original margin from clearing members, it takes over the financial obligations inherent in the futures contract.

The clearing house does not need to know the actual identities of the parties to the transactions. It only needs to know the net positions of the clearing members. The clients are financially responsible to the member firms, while the member firms are financially responsible to the clearing houses. Once a transaction is consummated and confirmed, the clearing house substitutes itself as the buyer for the seller and as the seller for the buyer. This substitution enables the individual trader to liquidate a position without having to wait until the other party to the original contract decides to liquidate. The trader has in effect bought the contract from or sold it to the clearing house.

It is also the job of the clearing house to ensure that all deliveries are carried out smoothly, as explained earlier. It is important to keep in mind that the principle of substitution does not apply to deliveries. The clearing house merely matches up the buyers and sellers who then can make arrangements for delivery either outside the clearing house or within the clearing house (in which case the clearing house merely acts as custodian). Once the long accepts the delivery notice, the clearing house's obligation is honored. The clearing house does not take on the obligations of delivery if one side does not satisfy the conditions of delivery. The clearing members must settle any disputes between themselves in accordance with regulatory by-laws. Neither member has any recourse to the clearing house.

Marking-to-Market and Margin

Suppose that client A has just entered a long December gold futures contract on NYMEX. The contract calls for delivery of 100 ounces of gold. The price that A and the counterparty to the trade (client B) arrived at through the open outcry auction system was US$385 per ounce. Therefore, A has contracted to buy and B to sell at the maturity of the contract in December 100 ounces of gold at an effective price of US$385 per ounce. To give each counterparty to the trade a higher level of assurance that the terms of the contract will be honored, each must deposit margin of, in this case, $2,000 into their respective trading accounts. In turn, the member firm(s) where the accounts are being held will submit the $2,000 to the clearing house.

The $2,000 is *initial* or *original* margin. Futures margins are set at only a small percentage of a contract's underlying value to give market participants, particularly hedgers, reasonable access to a market.

Assume in this example that the *maintenance* margin level is $1,500. The $2,000 that client A initially deposits in the account is equity. If the gold futures price moves higher, net equity will increase. If, for example, the gold futures price rises to $386 the day after the contract is initiated, A's equity will increase by $100 ($1 × 100 ounces) to $2,100. The $100 increase will be at the expense of the counterparty to the trade (client B), whose equity will have declined by $100 to $1,900 (assuming $2,000 was initially deposited). Client A's account will be automatically credited with $100 by the clearing house and B's debited by the same amount. Client A can withdraw this amount because the account's net equity would exceed the initial margin requirement of $2,000. Client B, however, would *not* have to deposit $100 into the account because the account's net equity of $1,900 would still be higher than the maintenance margin level of $1,500. Client B would only have to make a deposit if the account's net equity fell under the maintenance margin level. If, for example, gold futures rise to $391, B's net equity would fall by US$600 to US$1,400, which would take it under the maintenance margin level. Client B would then have to make a deposit of $600 so that net equity is replenished back to the original margin level. The deposit of $600 would then go from the member firm to the clearing house to A's member firm and finally to A. Member firms and clearing houses typically net out the amount of margin to be paid or received and make this net payment in a lump sum.

It should be noted that if the original and maintenance margin levels were exactly the same, every dollar lost would have to be physically transferred from the losing party to the winning party. This would be quite onerous and difficult to administer. One of the reasons for having a lower maintenance margin level is convenience. It means that clients do not have to run to their respective member firms to make a deposit every time there is a small fluctuation in their accounts.

Daily transference of margin from losers to winners gives the clearing house, in its capacity as third party guarantor and party to the transaction, a high level of confidence that performance will be honoured. Putting clearing houses in an even stronger position to act as guarantor are the *guarantee deposits* which must be maintained by each clearing member. In addition, the clearing house receives income to support its operations by charging fees for clearing trades and for other services performed.

The size of the initial margin will vary according to the contract and the trader's position. Initial margins are determined by the clearing house and may vary from time to time with reference to historical prices and volatilities or in anticipation of forthcoming price-sensitive events. In the case of option contracts, the choice of initial margin is complicated by the fact that option prices are exposed to multiple risks (Alexander and Sheedy (2008a), Chapter 8), the most significant being changes in the underlying futures price and changes in the volatility. Finally, the appropriate initial margin will depend on the exact position held by the investor. For example, a spread trade (see the discussion in the section on Spreaders, below) is less risky than a position in a single contract as the two positions partially hedge one another.

To take account of all these factors, many exchanges now use the Standard Portfolio Analysis of Risk (SPAN) framework which was originally developed by the Chicago Mercantile Exchange. The SPAN framework takes a portfolio of futures and options held by an investor and simulates how its value would react to a series of market scenarios. For example, the portfolio might be revalued for 16 different scenarios with various combinations of up/down movements in the price of the underlying and its volatility. The scenario with the worst outcome for that particular portfolio is used to set the initial margin. Various adjustments may also be made to take account of other factors such as basis risk in spread strategies and extra volatility which is common in the spot contract.

MARKET PARTICIPANTS—HEDGERS

The primary function of a futures market is to allow participants who wish to reduce or eliminate risk to do so by shifting the risk to those who want to assume it in return for the possibility of earning a profit. A market participant may need to either reduce the risk of holding a particular asset for future sale or reduce the risk involved in anticipating the purchase of a particular asset. This section covers only the most basic ideas of hedging with futures. More details on hedging with futures can be found in Alexander and Sheedy (2008b), Chapter 3.

A *short hedge* is executed by someone who owns or, in the case of a farmer or miner, anticipates owning an asset in the cash market that will be sold at some point in the future. In order to protect against a decline in price between the present and the time when the asset will be ready for sale, the hedger can take a short position in a futures contract on the same underlying asset which matures approximately at the time of the anticipated sale. By taking this action in the futures market, the hedger will be able to receive an amount equal to the price agreed in the contract, despite the fact that the spot price of the asset at the time of the sale might be considerably different.

Example 6.7 illustrates a short (or selling) hedge example. In this example, a grain elevator locks in its selling price in advance of selling the actual canola. By hedging, the elevator eliminates the risk of reduced profits due to falling prices by the time the physical canola will be sold. As the hedge is lifted at expiration of the futures contracts, the price of the physical canola and the canola futures is the same.

Example 6.7: Short Hedge

On October 1, a farmer sells 1,000 tonnes of canola to an elevator at a price of C$420 per tonne. The elevator now has an inventory of 1,000 tonnes of canola which it expects to sell in December at whatever price is prevailing at that time. In order to protect this inventory against a decline in prices over the next three months, the elevator sells 50 contracts (each contract represents 20 tonnes) of December canola futures at C$430 per tonne. By December, at the expiration of the futures contract, the price of canola has fallen to C$400 per tonne, and the elevator sells 1,000 tonnes at this price. At the same time as it sells the physical canola, the elevator offsets the short futures position at C$400 per tonne. The cash and futures market gain and loss for Example 6.7 are illustrated in Table 6.7.

Net result: The C$30 per tonne futures profit more than offsets the C$20 per tonne cash sale loss. The hedge earns a C$10 per tonne gross profit. On a net profit basis, the hedge breaks even as carrying costs (assuming the futures are priced at fair value) will be C$10.

By hedging, the elevator has actually locked in a C$10 per tonne *gross* profit (i.e. not including the cost of carry) regardless of what happens to prices between October 1, and December 1, as long as the canola is not sold or the futures contracts offset prior to December. For instance, if canola prices rise instead of falling, the net sale price is still C$430 per tonne. If canola rises to C$450 per tonne, for example, the elevator gains C$30 per tonne on the physical canola sale, but loses

TABLE   6.7

A short hedge

Time	Cash market	Futures
October 1	Buys 1,000 metric tonnes of canola at C$420 per tonne	Shorts 50 December canola futures contracts at C$430 per tonne
December 1	Sells 1,000 tonnes of canola at C$400 per tonne, losing C$20 per tonne	Offsets the 50 canola futures contracts at C$400 per tonne *Profit = C$30/tonne*

C$20 per tonne on the short futures position. The C$10 gross profit and net break-even result are locked in regardless of whether prices rise or fall. This is an example of a *perfect* short hedge.

Note that in this hedge the futures contract is offset (on the last trading day). The elevator does not deliver canola, but just uses the futures market to lock in a price by taking an opposite position to the canola inventory. In most hedges this is the case. Hedgers use futures contracts, in most cases, not as a delivery mechanism, but rather as a vehicle to offset adverse changes to the price of assets being carried in their normal course of business. As much as possible, hedgers try to fix future sales prices by short hedging, and fix future purchase prices by long hedging.

A long hedge is executed by someone who anticipates buying the underlying asset at some point in the future. In order to protect against rising prices between the present and the time when the asset is needed, the hedger can take a long position in a futures contract on the underlying asset which matures approximately at the time of the anticipated purchase of the asset. By taking this action in the futures market the hedger has fixed the purchase price, even though delivery does not need to be accepted until some point in the future.

The following example illustrates a long hedge where a dental supply company locks in its purchase price in advance of buying the physical silver. By hedging, the company has eliminated the risk of its net purchase price rising between January and April when the silver will be purchased. It can lock in a net purchase price regardless of what happens to prices between January and April, as long as the silver is not bought or the futures contract offset before April.

Example 6.8: Long Hedge

In January a dental supply company estimates that it will need 10,000 troy ounces of silver in April. The firm is concerned that prices will increase in the interim, and would like to lock in a price. The current spot silver price is $5.00 per ounce. One way of locking in a price that the company has considered is to buy the physical silver immediately and hold it until it is needed. To do so, however, would tie up considerable working capital. Another alternative for the company is to hope that silver prices will fall in the interim. The risk, however, that prices will increase is just too great. The company decides that it is not in the speculation business and chooses to hedge the price risk instead through the futures market. On January 25, the company buys two April silver futures (5,000 troy ounces per contract) that trade on the NYMEX at $5.20 per troy ounce. Three months later at expiration of the futures contract, the dental supply company buys the physical silver at $5.40 and offsets the long futures position at US$5.40 per ounce.[5]

The cash and futures gain and loss are illustrated in Table 6.8.

Net result: The company pays $0.40 more for the silver than expected. It makes a $0.20 profit on the rise in silver futures from $5.20 to $5.40. The effective purchase price is $5.40 − $0.20 = $5.20.

In this example, the $0.40 rise in the price of silver is at least partially offset by the $0.20 profit on the futures contracts. If instead of rising, silver prices fall, then the net purchase price is still $5.20. If silver falls to $4.80, for example, the company pays $0.20 less per ounce than the January price, but it experiences a $0.40 loss in the futures contract

T A B L E   6.8

Long hedge example

Time	Cash position	Futures position
January 25 at	Anticipates the need for 10,000 ounces of silver in April. Current spot price is $5.00 per ounce	Buys two April silver futures $5.20 per ounce
April 25	Silver prices rise to $5.40. The company buys 10,000 ounces at this price	Offsets futures contracts at $5.40 for profit of $0.20 per contract

which has been offset at $4.80. The net result is the same. By implementing this hedge, the company has locked in a net purchase price of $5.20.

The hedges demonstrated in Tables 6.7 and 6.8 are examples of *perfect* hedges. They are perfect because the futures price behaves in a way that is expected relative to the cash price. In other words, the basis did exactly as expected: it narrowed to the point where futures prices and cash prices are the same at expiration.

Prior to onset, a hedger will know with certainty that a hedge will be perfect if both of the following two conditions are met:

1. The hedger's holding period matches the expiration date of the futures contract (a *maturity match*).
2. The asset being hedged matches the asset underlying the futures contract (an *asset match*).

Under these conditions, the hedger will know with certainty how the futures contract price will behave relative to the price of the asset being hedged and thereby will have eliminated the risk associated with a future market commitment. On expiration, the spot and futures price will be the same. But if, at the outset of a hedge, at least one of the two conditions above is not met, the hedger is exposed to what is known as *basis risk,* that being the risk of *unexpected* movements in the basis. This does not necessarily mean that a hedge will not be perfect, only that the chances of an imperfect hedge are significant. In retrospect, a hedge may turn out to be perfect even if the two conditions above are not met, if one of the following occurs:

1. A hedge, where the asset being hedged matches the asset underlying the futures contract, is lifted early (the futures contract is either bought or sold), but the basis behaves in a way that was expected by the hedger at the onset of the hedge.
2. The asset being hedged does not match the asset underlying the futures contract, but the basis behaves in a way that was expected by the hedger at the onset of the hedge.

Consider Example 6.7. The three-month canola futures basis is C$10 per tonne, or C$3.30 (rounded) per tonne per month. If the hedge is lifted with one month left to expiration of the futures and the basis is at C$3.30 at that time (as expected), the hedge is still considered to be perfect because it behaves exactly as expected when first implemented. If the canola is sold at C$410 at that time and the futures contract is lifted at C$413.30, the elevator will still break even on a net profit basis. It will lose C$10 in the cash market, earn C$16.70 on the futures contract, and pay C$6.70 (rounded) by carrying the canola for two months.

MARKET PARTICIPANTS–SPECULATORS

Speculators are those market participants who, in the pursuit of profit, are willing to assume the risk that hedgers are seeking to shift. There are several different types of speculator who operate in the futures market. They are distinguished from each other by a number of factors, including the length of time they plan to hold a particular futures position, the amount of profit per position they anticipate, and the amount they are willing to risk.

Locals

Locals are also referred to as *scalpers*. This type of speculator operates right from the floor of the exchange and has the shortest time horizon of all. Taking advantage of the knowledge and "feel" gained from their proximity to the "action," the local attempts to profit from small price changes that take place in very short periods of time. The time horizon for a local can often be measured in minutes, rather than hours or days. Since the local is only looking to profit from very small price changes, the amount that is typically at risk on any given trade is small. Consequently, a local depends on relatively large volumes to make a successful living and is a unique feature of open outcry markets.

Day Traders

As the name suggests, day traders are speculators whose time horizon is a single day. Positions taken during a trading day are liquidated by the end of that day. Positions are not carried overnight. Day traders may trade on or off the floor. They are looking to profit from larger price moves than locals, and as a result they are willing to risk more. However, as is evidenced by their desire not to hold any positions overnight, they are not willing to tolerate a lot of risk. Overnight trading can entail considerable risk, particularly in futures contracts whose underlying assets trade 24 hours a day. Foreign currencies, for example, often see their greatest price moves in European or Asian trading. While a speculator sleeps, the value of a particular foreign exchange futures contract can change significantly. By the time North American trading is set to open, the speculator could be greeted with a significant open loss.

Another risk that day traders tend to avoid is that of holding positions going into major reports that could impact the price of a particular futures contract. Day traders involved with grain and oilseed futures, for example, typically go into major supply/demand reports (released on a regular basis by the United States Department of Agriculture) without any positions. These reports are typically released just before a market opening or just after a market close. Price movements in response to a report have the potential to be very significant, particularly if the data released are different from market expectations.

Position Traders

This type of trader has a time horizon that can be measured in terms of weeks or even months. Position traders attempt to profit from longer-term price trends. Timing is not as important for a position trader as it is for a local or day trader. The position trader is typically well financed and is therefore in a better position to avoid being *whipsawed* out of the market. This expression refers to a common occurrence in futures trading where a speculator is forced to close out a position due to an adverse price movement, only to see the price quickly rebound back in the favored direction. Position traders are willing and able to withstand adverse short-term price changes to a larger extent than locals or day traders, in order to maintain a position consistent with their long-term view of the market.

Spreaders

Spreading involves the purchase of one futures contract against the sale of another which is related in some fashion. Spread traders attempt to identify market situations where the price relationship between two related assets has deviated from its fair value. When such a situation is identified, the trader will take a spread position designed to profit from a move back towards a level or a range that is more in line with historical performance. The trader does this by simultaneously buying the "underpriced" asset and selling the "overpriced" asset. Spreads can be divided up into four broad categories, as follows:

Intramarket Spreads

Intramarket spreads are also known as *calendar spreads* or *time spreads*. This is a spread which involves the purchase and sale of futures contracts that have the same underlying asset, but different delivery months. They are very popular with agricultural futures where traders speculate on the relative changes in "old" and "new" crop prices.

Example 6.9: Intramarket Spread on Heating Oil

After reading the *Farmers' Almanac* prediction of a very cold northern hemisphere winter, a spread trader implements a spread strategy in November using heating oil futures. The trader feels that strong demand for heating oil during the winter months will force prices of contracts with delivery during this time frame to rise relative to the prices of contracts with spring or summer delivery. The trader buys the February contract at 59 cents per gallon and sells the May contract at 57 cents per gallon. The spread is lifted in January. The February contract is settled at 63 cents and the May contract settled at 58 cents. The trader earns a profit of 3 cents as the spread widens out from 2 cents premium February to 5 cents premium February. As each cent move represents US$420 (a heating oil contract is 42,000 gallons), the spread trader's profit is US$1,260.

Intercommodity Spreads

An intercommodity spread is between two different but related futures contracts. The two contracts may trade on the same exchange or on different exchanges. A trader would implement an intercommodity spread when he/she feels that the price of one asset has become under- or overvalued relative to the price of another asset which has a similar usage. For example, both corn and oats, which trade on the CBOT, are used for animal feed. Historically, corn trades at a premium of 50–200 cents to oats. If that spread rises, for example, to 250 cents, a trader may feel there is an opportunity to buy the "cheap" oats and sell the "expensive" corn, hoping the spread will move back down to its historical norm.

Perhaps the most popular financial futures intercommodity spread is what is known as the TED spread, which involves the purchase or sale of Treasury bill futures (T) against the opposite position in Eurodollar futures (ED). A trader buys the TED spread by going long on Treasury bills and short on Eurodollars, and he/she shorts the TED spread by going short on Treasury bills and long on Eurodollars. Generally, in times of economic and/or political turmoil, investors seek the safety of Treasury bills which are backed by the US government rather than Eurodollar deposits which are backed only by the bank that issues them. The collective action of investors during these periods forces Treasury bill rates down (prices up) relative to Eurodollars rates. The most extreme widening of the TED spread occurred during the Continental Illinois Bank crisis in 1984, the stock market "crash" of October 1987, and the Gulf crisis of 1990.

Intermarket Spreads

An intermarket spread involves the purchase and sale of futures contracts that trade on different exchanges, but which have the same underlying asset. Opportunities arise for various reasons. For example, in the case of wheat futures, which trade on the Chicago Board of Trade, Kansas City Board of Trade, and Minneapolis Grain Exchange, a spread opportunity may occur because of relative changes in supply and demand conditions of different deliverable grades trading in each respective market.

Commodity Product Spread

This kind of spread involves the purchase or sale of a commodity against the opposite position in the products of that commodity. The most common example of a commodity product spread is the *crush* spread, which involves taking a long position in, for example, soybeans against a short position in its products, soybean meal and soybean oil. The objective of the spread is to take advantage of any unusual price differences between soybeans, which are not often used in their natural state, and the products they are crushed into—soybean meal, which is primarily used for animal feed, and soybean oil, which is used as a vegetable oil.

MARKET PARTICIPANTS–MANAGED FUTURES INVESTORS

Individuals and institutions invest in managed futures products primarily to gain exposure to an asset class that is distinct from the traditional stocks, bonds, and cash. Research into managed futures has found that futures are a distinct asset class due to their low correlation with other asset classes. As a result, the addition of futures to a portfolio of other asset classes can provide diversification benefits. Investors looking to diversify their equity and/or bond portfolios are increasingly turning to managed futures products. Barclay Trading Group, which maintains one of the most widely respected managed futures databases, estimates that the amount of assets invested globally in managed products grew from just under $300 million in 1980 to $50.7 billion by the end of 2002.

Essentially there are two types of managed futures: *managed accounts* and *managed funds*. Managed futures accounts are used primarily by high net-worth investors and occasionally by institutions. For instance, an investor who wants some exposure to the futures market, but lacks the trading expertise or the time to trade, may give trading authority over to a trading adviser.

Managed futures funds are investment funds that employ strategies using specified derivatives, physical commodities and leverage. Managed futures funds generally focus on a wide variety of market sectors utilizing trading styles that may be based on fundamental analysis, technical analysis, or a combination of both. Fund managers may base their trading decisions on fully automated computer programs and/or some degree of personal judgement. Fund managers may also trade on the basis of trends, anticipated trend reversals or arbitrage. Unlike equity funds, for example, whose performance may be highly dependent on the direction of the overall stock market, the performance of managed futures is much more dependent on the skills of the manager.

In many ways hedge funds are similar to mutual funds (or unit trusts). Both hedge funds and mutual funds are professionally managed pools of money that may charge investors front- or back-end sales commissions. Both mutual funds and hedge funds charge management fees and can be bought and sold through an investment dealer at a price equal to the funds' net asset value per share. But in contrast to mutual funds, which are generally limited to buying securities or holding cash, hedge funds are structured as limited partnerships that allow the managers to use a wide variety of alternative strategies and investments. These include derivatives, short selling, leverage, arbitrage, currency trading, and more. Commodity pools are essentially managed futures funds that are structured and sold as mutual funds.

CONCLUSIONS

Futures contracts are instruments that allow users to lock in prices on assets that are to be delivered (or cash settled) at some point in the future.

When each contract is initiated, there is an entry price which is known as the futures price. Futures contracts are standardized with respect to the delivery date, and the quantity and quality of the underlying asset to be delivered, are traded on an organized exchange, and the transaction is guaranteed by the clearing house of that exchange. A small security deposit is required from the parties to a futures contract known as margin. This margin is held by the clearing house that guarantees the performance of the contract.

Futures contracts are settled mostly by offset and very few involve delivery of the underlying asset. In addition, a unique characteristic of a futures contract is its daily settlement, known as marking-to-market. At the end of each trading day, the long and short position holders' profit or loss is calculated, and the margin account is adjusted accordingly.

Futures contracts cover a wide range of underlying assets such as commodities, stock indexes, interest-rate products, and foreign currencies. They are used mainly for hedging purposes. However, since margin requirements are usually small relative to the value of the transaction specified in the contract, they have also become ideal vehicles for speculation.

Futures markets represent some of the most important forums for financial risk management. Institutional arrangements have been established to minimize counterparty risk and trading costs and to maximize liquidity and price transparency. All these features create an ideal environment for risk management and have contributed to the growing popularity of futures.

The markets for futures and options on futures continue to grow at a rapid pace—volumes have grown in excess of 13% per annum in 2004–6.[6] Growth in volumes has been assisted by a number of factors. Countries such as Korea, Brazil, Mexico, China, and India have rapidly growing futures markets, and they are now important markets in global terms. Electronic trading, with its low trading costs, has also been a factor supporting the overall market growth. Intense competition between exchanges (e.g. Eurex and CME) has created an environment in which futures markets continue to evolve to respond to market needs and trading costs are kept low. New contracts are regularly launched, and new initiatives introduced to increase market share. An excellent example is the introduction of flex options which allow for greater customization and therefore reduce the need for OTC trades.

It is likely, therefore, that futures will continue to be an essential tool for the management of financial risk.

REFERENCES

Alexander, C and Sheedy, E (2008a) *The Professional Risk Managers' Guide to Finance Theory* (New York: McGraw-Hill).

Alexander, C and Sheedy, E (2008b) *The Professional Risk Managers' Guide to Financial Instruments* (New York: McGraw-Hill).

NOTES

1. *Futures Industry*, March–April 2007.
2. The actual delivery price for a futures contract is the settlement price at delivery. The effective price, however, is the initial entry price as the contract profit or loss is netted from the settlement price
3. *Futures Industry*, March–April 2007.
4. Modern technology is quickly eliminating, in some cases, the need for runners. Orders are increasingly being entered into trading pits directly.
5. In reality, a delivery notice probably would have been issued to the dental supply company earlier in the month with respect to the long futures positions. For illustrative purposes, we show the long futures position being carried right to expiration day.
6. *Futures Industry*, March–April 2007.

CHAPTER 7

The Structure of Commodities Markets

Colin Lawrence and Alistair Milne

INTRODUCTION

Commodities are traded in both spot and forward markets. They are physical as opposed to financial assets, creating the need for storage and shipping. Because commodities are generally not perishable and can be stored, they are also an asset and can be used as a store of value. Gold and silver have been units of account and numeraires of the entire financial system, as well as a medium of exchange, and a store of value. Forward markets for commodities have existed for centuries because, with high volatility, risk-averse producers and consumers have attempted to hedge their inventories in forward and futures markets.

Risk managers in any market have a special interest in the pricing of forward contracts. One key observation regarding commodities is that the term structure of the forward curve has often been downward sloped, despite the fact that there are non-trivial storage and other transactions costs. This chapter will examine the reasons for this observed *backwardation* of commodity markets. Backwardation is something of a puzzle, since storage costs would normally be expected to raise future prices above spot prices. Explaining backwardation provides an excellent introduction to the special characteristics and risks of commodity markets.

We begin by describing the universe of commodities, the various delivery and settlement mechanisms, and the liquidity of their markets.

167

We further examine why gold is special due to its importance as a reserve asset. Next we introduce the reader to the famous arbitrage condition linking forward prices to spot prices and introduce the concepts of convenience yield, backwardation, and normal backwardation. The following section analyses the risks associated with short squeezes and provides some famous illustrations such as the Hunts Silver corner in 1979. We then provides an analysis of downside risk in a typical commodity trading book. Here we show how to estimate the value-at-risk of a commodity portfolio when taking account of the large volatility of borrowing and lending costs. Finally, we provide some further observations on the behavior of commodity returns before the Conclusions.

THE COMMODITY UNIVERSE AND ANATOMY OF MARKETS

Commodity Types and Characteristics[1]

Commodities are divided into four types: the *metals*, the *softs*, the *grains and oilseeds*, and *livestock*. These generally trade in the spot markets and most have evolved forwards, futures and option-based contracts. The metals can be decomposed into *base metals*, such as nonferrous metals (e.g. zinc, aluminum, lead, and nickel); *strategic metals*, such as bismuth and vanadium, and *minor metals*, such as cobalt and chromium; and *precious metals*, such as gold, silver, and palladium. The London Metals Exchange (LME) is one of the key spot-trading centres for both base and precious metals, while strategic and minor metals, having less homogeneity, tend to be traded over the counter (OTC) between producer and consumer. The buyers tend to be automotive, aerospace, pharmaceutical, and electrical corporations.

The softs include cocoa, sugar, and coffee, and minor softs include rubber, tea, and pepper. Most trading of soft commodities involves processors, roasters, refiners, distributors, and traders who are "inventory flow traders" or speculators. The grains and oilseeds category spans most edible agricultural products. It can be further decomposed into the *grains*, such as wheat, barley, rice, and oats; *oilseeds*, such as soybeans, rapeseed, palm kernel, and flaxseed; *fibers*, such as wool, cloth, and silk; and finally, *livestock and other*, including live animals and meat products such as pork bellies. Also included in the latter category are dairy products, such as milk and cheese, and citrus and tropical fruits, such as orange juice.

The Markets for Trading²

There are two types of markets: the spot commodity market and the market for commodity forwards, futures, and other derivatives such as options. Spot transactions take place *on the spot*. They are OTC transactions and could take place in auctions or sales rooms. Once the characteristics are agreed, the commodity is sold and payment takes place at settlement. Usually spot trades involve the exchange of cash for the specified commodity. One must distinguish between the cash for commodity exchange in contrast to settlement of difference. Even a spot transaction takes time to settle, usually in 2 to 45 days. The key problems in the spot or OTC market (which indeed are the key drivers for margin-based structures and exchanges) are: lack of contract transparency, transaction costs, search and time, and creditworthiness. These reasons are the drivers for more standardized contracts and clearinghouse management of credit risk in commodities exchanges.

We also need to distinguish between the markets for forwards and for futures. One important difference between the two is that forwards generally trade in OTC markets. They can be tailor-made contracts, with quantity, quality, and maturity all designed to the customer's requirements. Like spot, forward settles cash for the physical. In fact, since a spot trade can settle anywhere between 2 days and 45 days, the spot market is in essence a short-dated forward. Most forwards are not traded on exchanges, but there are anomalies. For example, on the LME, forwards are traded. Futures often (but not always) trade on the basis of *settlement of difference*. This is when the difference, for instance between the forward and actual cash settlement prices at maturity, is settled by a net cash payment. Futures are standardized exchange-traded contracts. They have historically been traded in pits under the *open outcry* system. Whilst it looks pretty chaotic, it is a well-regulated and institutionalized form of trading. With the impetus of technology, open outcry trading is giving way to newer forms of electronic trading (see Chapter 1).

Participants in commodity exchanges are brokers and traders acting on behalf of clients, and locals who act on their own behalf. The key distinction between a broker and a trader is that a broker executes on behalf of the client, whereas the trader trades on his own behalf. Often enough, trading and broking are performed by the same firm or individual. There have thus emerged a stringent set of exchange rules which attempt to prevent traders front-running positions or more generally not acting in the best interests of the customer (see, for example, Telser and Higinbotham,

1977). Members of the exchange must execute the orders of customers before they execute their own trades.

The incentive for trading on an exchange is high for all parties. Firstly, trading continually takes place under guaranteed conditions, the price is determined in a transparent manner and, due to posting of margins, counterparty exposure is minimized. The reduction of counterparty exposure through the posting of collateral is the chief function of a clearing house. The key disadvantage is that transactions are standardized and maturity dates are fixed. The standardization and lower counterparty exposure are critical ingredients in ensuring "liquidity" of trading, which is the ability to buy or sell a contract with relative low transaction costs.

Delivery and Settlement Methods[3]

Irrespective of whether the commodity is traded spot, forward or futures, the delivery and settlement methods are critical in determining the actual spot, forward, or futures price. There are at least six characteristics of delivery mechanisms:

1. *In store* is the simplest form of physical delivery. It is used for example, in softs such as coffee and cocoa. *The seller is responsible for delivery to an agreed warehouse.* As in all physical deals, quality, quantity and *location* are all negotiated or embedded in the terms of a standardized (futures) contract. A "warrant" is delivered in the form of a bearer document and is a warehouse claim on a physical commodity. When the trade is concluded the seller transfers ownership of the warrant to the buyer. The product is then shipped to the required location and the buyer exchanges the warrant for the physical or alternatively can transfer it to a third party. Once the contract changes title, the "warrant is cancelled."

2. *Ex store* is identical to in store except that the seller prepays the storekeeper for loading onto the buyers' transportation. Thus the price will be more expensive in ex store. This process is used in the UK for cocoa and grain. In all physical deliveries, the seller must deliver many documents including a grading certificate, the warrant and weight notes. When these are delivered to the buyer, then the latter pays cash.

3. *Free on board (FOB)*. Once the goods have passed over the ship's rail, the seller has fulfiled his obligation. The onus of risk

is shifted onto the buyer once goods are loaded, and hence an FOB price will be cheaper by the insurance premium for damage whilst on board as well as the transportation costs. FOB is used mainly when loading and shipping bulk such as gas oils, sugars and soybeans. Once on board a bill of lading is issued by the seller.

4. *Free alongside ship (FAS)* is similar to FOB. It is a form of delivery where goods are delivered alongside the shipping vessel instead of being loaded. The FAS price will be lower than the FOB price by the cost of loading. In both FOB and FAS it must be specified who pays the tax, import duty, docking fees, value added tax (VAT) etc.

5. *Cost, insurance and freight (CIF)*. This involves FOB delivery plus the costs of insurance and transportation. The following simple arbitrage equation relates the FOB to the CIF price:

$$CIF = FOB + F + I,$$

where F is the freight cost and I is the insurance premium. The most expensive element will be the freight cost. Markets have developed in shipping bulk and air cargo. The Baltic exchange is one of the important shipping exchanges. Due to the riskiness of transportation, a futures contract, the BIFEX which trades on LIFFE, has developed, enabling providers of transportation to hedge. The BIFEX is based on the Baltic Freight Index, which is a composite index of the 11 major dry cargo routes. The contract is settled by difference.

6. *Exchange for futures or physicals (EFP)*. It is possible to swap a physical position for a futures position, and this will be subject to off-exchange negotiation.

Commodity Market Liquidity

Liquidity, or lack thereof, is of critical importance in the trading of commodities.[4] We define liquidity as the ability to buy or sell at fair market value without changing transaction costs. A market is liquid when there are lots of sellers and buyers, and where large volumes can be executed with small transaction costs. We would expect bid–offer spreads to be smaller, the greater the liquidity of the market.[5] In trading forward or futures markets, how liquid is each market?

Table 7.1 shows a live trading screen of cocoa futures contracts on the New York Board of Trade (NYBOT). This gives the contract traded, the time the last trade was executed, the highest and lowest prices, the price at which the last trade took place, and the price change. The prices are quoted in dollars per metric tonne and each contract is for delivery of 10 metric tonnes. The price change ("Chg") is computed by subtracting the last trade price today from the previous day's last trading price. The current day's last trading price is the closing 12.22 p.m. price on July 19, 2007, i.e. $US2,114. This is shown under the column labelled "Sett" meaning settlement price. For example the December contract last traded today at 2,141 and this is 17 ticks higher than the previous days closing price. Additionally, the table displays the daily volume ("Vol") and the "Op Int" or open interest (the total amount of contracts outstanding) to explore the notion of liquidity.

T A B L E   7.1

NYBOT Cocoa Thursday July 19, 2007 at 12.22 p.m. Live screen display

Month Click for chart	Session								Pr. Day	
	Open	High	Low	Last	Time	Sett	Chg	Vol	Sett	Op Int
7-Sep	2,096	2,117	2,088	2,114	Jul 19, 12:22	2,114	17	4,536	2,097	88,002
7-Dec	2,120	2,141	2,120	2,141	Jul 19, 12:22	2,141	17	1,384	2,124	41,159
8-Mar	2,169	2,169	2,169	2,169	Jul 19, 12:22	2,169	17	230	2,152	19,160
8-May	2,184	2,184	2,184	2,184	Jul 19, 12:22	2,184	17	25	2,167	3,688
8-Jul	2,200	2,200	2,200	2,200	Jul 19, 12:22	2,200	17	18	2,183	2,950
8-Sep	2,216	2,216	2,216	2,216	Jul 19, 12:22	2,216	17	197	2,199	3,712
8-Dec	2,239	2,239	2,239	2,239	Jul 19, 12:22	2,239	17	9	2,222	9,272
9-Mar	2,256	2,256	2,256	2,256	Jul 19, 12:22	2,256	17	–	2,239	–
9-May	2,273	2,273	2,273	2,273	Jul 19, 12:22	2,273	17	–	2,256	–

As shown in Table 7.1 the front September contract is the most active with an open interest of close to 88,000 contracts and a current daily volume close to 4,500 contracts. Actually only the front three contracts out to March are relatively liquid, with an open interest of over 19,000 contracts. The most active trading is the front contract with 4,530 contracts traded on the July 19. There is very little liquidity beyond the first two contracts and open interest declines precipitously.

For this reason, hedgers who need to reduce exposure (long or short) for 2008 might well trade the September and December 2007 contracts if they need liquidity. This involves a trade-off between the benefits of the liquidity where there are active market makers and basis or contango risk. Thus if a long cocoa producer needs to hedge a sizeable physical position in March 2008, he might in the first instance hedge by shorting the September 2007 contract. With this hedge in place he is initially protected from any price collapse until the September expiry. But he has not eliminated his risk, as the basis can shift between September 2007 and March 2008, i.e. the delivery date. Currently the basis is $US55. Any deviation between September 2007 and March 2008 will lead to an imperfect hedge thus realizing losses or gains. One strategy would be to attempt to roll over his initial position into the long-dated contracts. He would execute this by buying the September 2007 to December 2007 spread. This is tantamount to closing out (or reducing) his September 2007 position and shorting the December 2007s. He could therefore buy the December 2007–March 2008 spread, which would leave him with a perfect hedge. But transactions costs are extremely high. Because the bid–offer spreads are generally wide due to lack of liquidity the further out the contract, this rollover strategy could be costly. So he is more likely to put in a sequence of spread buy orders and execute this quite slowly, hoping there is a ready seller of the spread. The speed at which he rolls over his trade will depend on the trade-off between transaction costs and volatility of the basis. The more volatile the basis, relative to the bid–offer spreads, the faster will be the rollover the position.

In Table 7.2 we depict the open interest and volumes in gold and silver futures contracts traded on the COMEX, on July 20, 2007. Just like cocoa, there are large volume trades in the gold front contracts especially in the current contract of August 2007 and December 2007, whilst silver's major liquidity is in the September and December contracts. As we move along the term structure of these metals we note that the volumes and open interest decline markedly.[6]

T A B L E   7.2

Liquidity in COMEX gold and silver futures contracts
(July 20, 2007)

Gold				Silver		
Contract	Volume	Open Int		Contract	Volume	Open Int
Aug-7	75,283	136,631		Aug-7	7	73
Sep-7	27	68		Sep-7	14,509	69,305
Oct-7	3,643	22,395		Dec-7	985	24,095
Dec-7	12,740	108,715		Jan-8	–	11
Feb-8	1,710	13,647		Mar-8	14	4,698
Apr-8	381	23,094		May-8	77	4,262
Jun-8	463	15,964		Jul-8	759	3,344
Aug-8	180	2,945		Sep-8	31	650
Oct-8	–	1,470		Dec-8	7	4,809
Dec-8	340	15,641		Jan-9	–	1
Feb-9	300	9,045		Mar-9	–	212
Apr-9	–	1,700		May-9	–	–
Jun-9	14	10,355		Jul-9	–	2,537
Dec-9	–	2,711		Dec-9	1	2,841
Jun-10	50	4,889		Jul-10	–	264
Dec-10	50	5,470		Dec-10	–	762
Jun-11	–	1,524		Jul-11	–	29
Dec-11	–	404		Dec-11	–	123
Total	95,181	376,668		Total	16,390	118,016

It is imperative that risk managers incorporate the bid–offer spreads and illiquidity of longer-dated contracts into measures of value-at-risk and stress testing.[7] And as we shall see, there is a further very serious liquidity risk which is hidden from these charts, and that is the squeeze or cornering risk in which the shorts have to deliver physicals as the front contract expires. Thus there is an implicit demand for warrants of the physical by the shorts who have to cover their positions. What happens when these inventories become scarce? This has happened throughout history as in the case of silver in 1979–80, when the silver price skyrocketed to US$50 per ounce due to a squeeze. This type of backwardation happened throughout the nineteenth and twentieth centuries, and the section on Short Squeezes, Corners, and Regulation examines these volatile price jumps and the ensuing limits imposed by regulators and exchanges.

The Special Case of Gold as a Reserve Asset[8]

Gold has special characteristics relative to other commodities because it is still a reserve asset of central banks and has a history of being pivotal to the international monetary system. As a consequence of the world's central banks' holdings of gold reserves, changes in central banking portfolio behavior can have profound effects on the gold price.

The international gold standard existed for a short time period from 1870 until the beginning of World War I.[9] This period was a relatively stable period, coupled with strong economic growth. Money was fully backed by gold, and investors were protected from inflation. It also meant that international investment was safer than under floating exchange rates. Capital flows were excessively large during the imposition of this standard. A key reason for this was the credibility of the regime. The problem with the standard, however, was that much depended on getting supplies out the ground, and indeed the demand for money could well have outstripped supply at times. The lack of credibility was widespread after World War I. Despite an initial fixing of US$20.67 per troy ounce, this was suspended in 1933. This culminated in one of the greatest hyperinflations, especially in the Austro-Hungarian Empire. As long as governments used money to finance budget deficits, inflation was a direct outcome. In 1934 gold was fixed at $35 per troy ounce.

In 1944 the Bretton Woods System of fixed exchange rates was created, with the US dollar as the fulcrum of the system. The dollar was pegged at $35 dollars per ounce, member nations of the International Monetary Fund had to deposit a share of gross domestic product in gold, and the major central banks all used gold as the core reserve asset. But the system came to a halt following the Vietnam War when the US government under Nixon abandoned the gold standard completely, and since 1971 the price of gold has floated freely. Figure 7.1 depicts the inventories of gold reserves held by central banks and supranational institutions. The USA has dramatically reduced its reserves from over 20,000 tonnes in 1950 to around 9,000 tonnes in 1971, while Europe built up its reserves. At the end of 2002, the USA held about 8,000 tonnes and Europe about 13,000 tonnes.

The total inventory of central banks' holdings is around 32,000 tonnes, about 22% of the above-ground reserves. This is huge relative to annual production, which is estimated at around 2,600 tonnes. As a consequence of this, speculators and hedgers of gold scrutinize the behavior

FIGURE 7.1

Official gold reserves, 1948 to 2005 (tonnes)

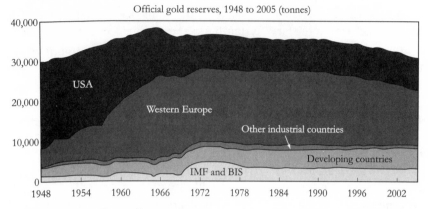

Official gold reserves, 1948 to 2005 (tonnes)

Source: World Gold Council, www.gold.org

of the central banks. On September 26, 1999 the Washington Agreement on Gold was announced, whereby it was agreed that uncoordinated selling of gold by central banks would destabilize its price. The Accord reached a pledge not to sell more than 2,000 tonnes as a "collective" over the next five years. The accord halted the decline in the price of gold at around $250 per ounce and certainly contributed to its subsequent rise to $400 per ounce.

Despite the fact that gold standard is a historical event, movements in inventories of central banks are critical not only in changing supply in the market but also in determining lease rates (the rates at which banks lend out their gold) and hence the gold basis. Central bankers lend gold to gold dealers with mismatched books in order to earn a return on their gold holdings. There is a ready demand for gold loans (from gold producers) as a cost-effective means of financing their gold production. The gold inter-est rate paid on gold deposits is called the gold lease rate or gold LIBOR. Thus while most commodities incur storage costs, gold deposits earn a positive return.

To summarize, gold is unique in the commodity universe for the simple reason that the above-ground reserves are so massive and they can earn a positive return. The large scale of these reserves makes it extremely unlikely that a short squeeze (caused by excessive short-term demand)

could ever occur. This has enormous implications for the spot–forward pricing relationship which is the subject of the next section.

SPOT–FORWARD PRICING RELATIONSHIPS

We have described cash, forward, and futures markets for commodities. In this section we review the relationship between futures/forwards and spot prices, sometimes referred to as "basis." Unlike "normal markets" where forward prices are generally higher than spot, forward commodity prices are often found to be below the spot price. Not only does the basis for commodities differ from most other markets, but it is also highly variable over time because of the possibility of short squeezes. This feature of commodity markets is a concern for risk managers because it can make hedging strategies less effective and create unexpected changes in the value of a portfolio (possibly giving rise to significant margin calls). Thus nonnormal distributions, stress testing, and scenario analysis prove to be critical ingredients in the commodity risk manager's toolkit.[10] We will ignore the institutional differences and treat the forwards and futures markets as equivalent.[11]

Backwardation and Contango

The relationship between forward and spot prices has been developed in Alexander and Sheely (2008a), Chapter 7; and Alexander and Sheedy (2008b), Chapter 3. Based on the analysis of typical markets, one might expect the pricing relationship for commodities to be defined as

$$Forward\ price = spot\ price + carrying\ cost, \tag{7.1}$$

where the carrying costs involve storage costs, transaction costs and all other characteristics in the section on Delivery and Settlement Methods, above, especially freight and interest costs.

In studying patterns of spot versus forwards, or short-dated versus longer-dated forwards, we find by empirical observation that the spot price often lies *above* the forward price. See, for example, the sugar and wheat prices in Table 7.3. Indeed in many commodities we find that the forward can switch from being at a premium to a discount and vice versa. If the forward or future is traded at a price higher than the spot price, then we say that the forward or future is at a *premium* or (equivalently) that the market is in *contango*. If the forward is below the spot price, then we say that the market is in *backwardation*.

Table 7.3 shows closing prices of three commodity futures listed on CBOT: corn, wheat, and ethanol. Corn is in contango, while wheat is mixed and ethanol is in backwardation; wheat shifts from contango to backwardation in March 2008. The daily percentage change is also shown. A key observation is that the changes are almost invariably non-uniform across the term structure. For example, September 7 corn has risen by 1.09%, while December 8 has risen by only 0.71%. The reason for the non-parallel shift is the relationship described in equation (7.1), namely that shifts in forward prices are due to both the change in the spot price plus a shift in carrying costs. The nonparallel shift must be caused by changes in carrying costs.

The data in Table 7.3 show how the basis can vary from day to day. A key point driving the yield curve or basis is that commodity buffer supplies can run out. We cannot import spot commodities from the future. The risk manager will have to scrutinize demand and supply data carefully. In the case of gold, we noted above that above-ground stocks are very large relative to flows. Hence any incipient excess demand can be met through an elastic supply of inventory, thus mitigating the kind of backwardation we observe in cyclical commodities such as oil and aluminium.

Gold is an exceptional commodity for the reasons cited above. The gold market is almost always in contango, as discussed in the previous section. But with a lack of inventory to cope with unexpected changes in the flow demand or supply, other commodities can experience shortages—and hence backwardation. For example, in the last decade there has been a surge in food consumption in China and, with her low area of green land per capita, imports fill the deficit. In the 1990s analysts were watching the near monopolization of grain containers out of Chicago by the Chinese. Chinese demand pushed prices of food products up by over 13% in 1997. Any gyrations in demand for imports can tilt the yield curve of foodstuffs.

Finally, backwardation is caused by either combinations of rapid demand for immediacy creating scarcity or by manipulation of the market. To illustrate the latter point, in 2003 the LME was concerned when the aluminum basis backwardation flared from 2% to about 5% in 2003.[12] On investigation they found that the market had been in over-supply since 2000. There was a surplus of 1 million tonnes in 2002 and about 400,000 tonnes in 2003; inventories had risen to over 3.5 million tonnes in July 2003 and a large share of this was in LME warehouses. A strong possibility of market collusion was investigated by the LME. The FSA also began

TABLE 7.3

Closing futures prices on the Chicago Board of Trade (CBOT) July 19, 2007

	Corn					Wheat					Ethanol			
Con-tract	Sett	% ch	Vol	Op Int	Con-tract	Sett	% ch	Vol	Op Int	Con-tract	Sett	% chg	Vol	Op Int
Sep-7	321	1.09%	20,705	33,7920	Sep-7	651	0.35%	19,670	19,8984	7-Aug	1.96	-0.76%	5	153
Dec-7	336 1/2	1.04%	24,050	52,3636	Dec-7	669	0.00%	13,230	15,3363	7-Sep	1.87	0.27%	5	127
Mar-8	351 3/4	0.92%	1269	97,535	Mar-8	663	-0.04%	1727	16,475	7-Oct	1.84	-0.33%	10	94
May-8	362 1/4	0.90%	692	28,042	May-8	643	0.31%	120	3574	7-Nov	1.82	0.00%	34	45
Jul-8	370 3/4	0.81%	1024	63,312	Jul-8	583 1/2	-0.13%	1070	42,765	7-Dec	1.79	0.00%	34	131
Sep-8	379	1.06%	246	9828	Sep-8	584	0.09%	9	679	8-Jan	1.79	0.00%	0	123
Dec-8	386 1/2	0.71%	2491	12,8162	Dec-8	589	-0.17%	377	13,133	8-Feb	1.77	0.56%	0	97
Mar-9	393 1/2	0.76%	225	4056	Jul-9	563	0.53%	39	3938	8-Mar	1.73	-1.73%	0	91
Jul-9	400 1/2	0.44%	6	1045	Dec-9	575	0.35%	1	280	8-Apr	1.73	-1.73%	0	31
Dec-9	400	0.56%	110	22,639	Jul-10	566	0.00%	26	59	8-May	1.73	-1.73%	0	30
contango					mixed					contango				

their own investigation but no charges were ever made despite the suspicious nature of the backwardation. By January 2004 the market was back in contango and it was suspected that the traders that were involved in this "short squeeze" had backed off.[13] Since this episode the LME has reduced the maximum size of the aluminum contract. Even so there have been further episodes of backwardation.

In 2006 the total inventory of cash aluminum in the LME warehouse was about 650,000 tons. A major hedge fund took a long futures position equivalent to owning over 93% of the total inventory. Despite otherwise normal conditions and sufficient supplies the market moved into a sharp backwardation, with a premium for cash over the 3 months futures contract of USD100. Allegations were leveled against the fund and there was no proof that this was a short squeeze. Of course shorts, fearing a squeeze, liquidated their positions exacerbating the situation. Then in yet another incident in May 2007 long call option positions were placed on the exchange with a notional size valued at over $US3 billion. The shorts of these options clearly expected the normal contango situation to resume before the options expired. But the cash roared to a premium of $US30 per ton.

Regardless of whether there has ever been actual market abuse the aluminum market has been subject to large volatility in lease rates with discrete jumps in cash relative to futures. The FSA have noted these squeezes in their market abuse regulations and risk managers have to assess the potential for short squeezes to create an artificial short supply. See below for more information on short squeezes and regulation.

Reasons for Backwardation

Keynes (1930) explained backwardation by the presence of speculators transacting in commodities in the hope of making short-term trading profits. These speculators should be viewed as selling insurance to hedgers. According to Keynes, speculators would demand a premium for providing this insurance, and this would generally drive the spot price above the forward price. This hypothesis has undergone a barrage of scrutiny by economists. At first glance it is puzzling how spot prices lie above forwards unless carrying costs are somehow negative. Indeed, for over a century economists have debated why the forward price could lie below the spot price.

Modern portfolio theory and subsequent empirical testing have refuted the Keynesian view of normal backwardation. Efficient market hypotheses have also rejected the premise of Hicks (1946) that forwards are biased estimators of expected spot prices. In fact, the theory which most successfully explains backwardation is the *convenience yield theory* (Kaldor, 1939; Williams, 1986). This focuses on the physical demand and supply of commodities as an input and/or output in the production process. It suggests that spot prices are driven above forwards because users of commodities cannot afford to run out of inventory. They are prepared to pay more in spot markets than the expected future price, in order to ensure that they have immediate access to supply (this is the *demand for immediacy*).[14] From the perspective of suppliers, they are also prepared to hold more than required inventory in case the market switches from backwardation into contango. Despite the apparent negative return to suppliers, there is a chance that they can get exceptionally high returns from shortages, where producers will borrow commodities and thus drive spot prices very high.

Furthermore, a major cause of sudden switches from contango to backwardation has been the fact that the deliverable commodity to any futures contract at maturity can be subject to manipulation. The examples that stand out include the infamous silver corner in 1979–80, the copper scandal in 1996s and the aluminum backwardation in 2003. Whilst the exchanges and regulators have attempted to stop these "corners" with an array of limits on movements in prices per day as well as ensuring the maximum open interest held by one investor is limited, history has been scarred by the omnipotence of squeezes. In the next section we explore these squeezes in more detail. They can be an Achilles heel for the risk manager and often they are very difficult to detect, and yet they could wipe out economic capital in one stroke!

Convenience yield theory suggests that shortages of physical delivery arise through either an unexpected shock or an anticipated (or unanticipated) act of Nature such as the seasonal harvest. Producers are willing to hoard commodities since they could otherwise suffer an opportunity loss if they do not have the commodity, especially if it is a key input in a supply chain. A consequence is that there are always premium prices at which producers will be willing to hold excess inventory even if they incur all the carrying costs.[15] In such circumstances they could earn huge returns if there is a market shortage and this creates a backwardation.[16]

Empirically, commodity markets can switch from contango to backwardation and back to contango, creating much volatility. Thus it is crucial for the risk manager to understand exactly what factors cause such volatility in prices. In the next section we give some current and historical examples of short squeezes, showing them to be a major cause of backwardation. Indeed, in stress situations real and artificial physical shortages are a major cause of backwardation.

The No-Arbitrage Condition

In an efficient market with no arbitrage, forward term structures such as those shown in Tables 7.1 and 7.3 will be influenced by the interest rate, storage costs, and the convenience yield. To see this, first note that the key arbitrage equation for commodity pricing is:[17]

$$(E(S)-S)/S = r + C-q \qquad (7.2)$$

where S is the spot price, $E(S)$ is the expected spot price, r is the risk-free rate of return, C is the storage cost (quoted as a percentage of the spot price) and q is the convenience yield. This is similar to the arbitrage equation for equities where the storage cost is zero and the convenience yield is analogous to the dividend yield. The left-hand side of equation (7.2) is the expected capital gain, while the right-hand side is the *carrying cost*. The higher the convenience yield, the lower will be the expected capital gain. If $q > r + C$ then the carrying cost can be negative.

If the expected capital gain from holding inventory is greater than the carrying cost then investors or producers will hoard inventory. Then, even if the market price is expected to fall, investors may hold stocks if the convenience yield is high enough to compensate for the loss.

Note that if markets are efficient, $E(S)$ is equal to the future price F. Then (7.2) becomes

$$(F-S)/S = r + C-q \qquad (7.3)$$

Hence the future price will lie below the spot price—and the market will be in backwardation—if the convenience yield q outweighs the other two carrying costs. The left-hand side of equation (7.3) is the *basis* (the spread between the future and the spot price) as a percentage of the spot price. It increases with r and C and decreases with q. More importantly, q is much more volatile than either r or C and so the changes in the convenience yield dominate the changes in the basis. This is a very useful insight. Variations in the carrying cost of commodities can be estimated using variations in the basis in the forward market.

The lease rate of a commodity is depicted by the right-hand side of (7.3). It is quite difficult to find data on storage costs and difficult econometrically to estimate the convenience yield. However under the assumption that the no-arbitrage condition holds we can estimate the gold lease rate via the left-hand side of (7.3) since cash and futures are readily available. Since Nixon's decision to de-link the dollar and gold the market has only briefly been in backwardation. When gold roared in the 1980s so did the contango, reflecting inflationary expectations and a bubble. Lease rates rose to over 30%. But as inflation subsided after the Fed's tightening policy of 1979 lease rate collapsed and at the time of writing is around 1 to 1.5%. In Figure 7.2 we show spot price of gold above and the lease rate of gold for four different maturities below, over the period 1995 to 2006.[18] We note that as the price of gold trended upwards

F I G U R E   7.2

The price of gold. Gold lease rates, 1995–2006 (quoted as an annualized yield)

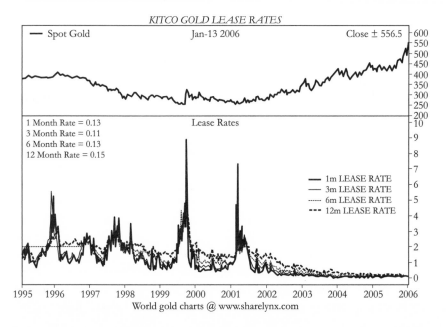

the lease rates for all terms declined to below 1%. During the bear market the lease rates were much more volatile, especially over short maturities.

SHORT SQUEEZES, CORNERS, AND REGULATION

Historical Experience

Commodity markets throughout history have been plagued by "short squeezes." The reason for a squeeze in the futures or forward markets is that the delivery of the physical to "longs" by the "shorts" is in an artificially short supply. We now examine some of these historical examples, focusing on the following questions:

a. Was there a fundamental exogenous shock such as a poor harvest or under-supply or increase in demand that drove prices up and created a backwardation situation?

b. Did any institution or individual or associated[19] party hold a long futures position and attempt to buy spot commodities prior to expiration?

c. How were these inventories financed?

d. What was the response of the exchange or/and the regulators?

e. What was the path of the price before and after expiration?

Clearly, the astute commodity risk manager should ask all five questions. Failing to do so can lead to substantial unanticipated risk exposure.

Example 7.1: Benjamin Hutchingson and the wheat squeeze, August 1866

It all began with poor harvest forecasts. Hutchingson built up long wheat positions in cash and futures markets. The average price was around 88 cents per bushel. In August the spot price started rising in Iowa and Chicago and by August 4 the price had hit 92 cents a bushel. But on expiration, Hutchingson's right to demand physical delivery raised the price to $1.87 per bushel. The Chicago Board of Trade (CBOT) deemed such transactions as fraudulent and declared that any member of the CBOT engaged in this activity would be expelled. This did very little to prevent transactions of these types (see Sikorzewski, 2001, pp. 2–3).

Example 7.2: The Great Chicago Fire and John Lyon, 1872

On October 6, 1872 six out of seventeen elevators burnt down in the Great Fire of Chicago. The storage capacity of Chicago fell from 8 million to 5.5 million bushels. An important merchant named John Lyon formed a coalition with two other brokers. In spring 1872 they began buying up physicals and futures. In July the August contract rose to $1.16 and by month's end to $1.35. The price stimulated a huge inflow of wheat into Chicago. Initially the train volume was around 14,000 bushels, and it rose steadily to 27,000 bushels in the first week of August. A further disaster struck when the Iowa elevator also burnt down, reducing storage by 300,000 bushels. Meanwhile further bad weather reports led to rumors that the new crop would mature too late for delivery into the August futures contract. The August futures price climbed to $1.51 on August 15.

As a consequence of the price hike, farmers started shipping wheat to Chicago at an accelerating rate. In the first week in August about 75,000 bushels per train reached Chicago, and by the 19th daily arrivals reached up to 200,000 bushels. The wheat coming in from Buffalo would usually have begun depressing the price. At this point, Lyons and his partners, who had been borrowing heavily from the banks to execute his cash trades and post margin, were turned down for more financing. Meanwhile, the building of new elevators raised the capacity to 10 million bushels, which was higher than the pre-fire capacity. When the banks turned him down on August 19, the price plunged to 25 cents per bushel. Lyons then announced that he was bankrupt and the price plunged a further 17 cents. This and similar squeezes—there were 15 such cases—ultimately led in 1922 to Congress passing legislation in the form of the Commodity Exchange Act outlawing squeezes.

Example 7.3: The Great Silver Squeeze by the Hunt Brothers, 1979–80[20]

In the summer of 1979 the Hunt brothers, together with their Saudi partners, began buying up silver. They bought about 43 million ounces of silver on the COMEX with delivery to be taken. Over the summer the silver price jumped from $8 to $16 as a result of their actions.

Other syndicates began to copy them. The COMEX and CBOT were in a panic. In 1979 the warehouses of the two exchanges only held 120 million ounces and that amount was traded in October alone. The Hunts moved a further 9 million ounces of silver to Europe through a silver swap. They were worried that US government would attempt to confiscate their inventory. Late in 1979 the CBOT changed its rules and stated that no investor could hold more than 3 million ounces of silver contracts and any investor with over 3 million would have to liquidate by February 1980. The margin requirement was also raised. The Hunts accused the exchange of vested interests. This was borne out by the fact that many CBOT members had "shorts." The Hunts, knowing that indeed the market was synthetically short, continued buying silver. At year's end the price had risen to $34.45 per ounce. The brothers at this time held 40 million ounces in Switzerland and 90 million ounces through their holding company, International Metals. On top of that they had longs for the March contract on another 90 million ounces. Lamar Hunt, the younger brother, had also accumulated an individual position $300 million position by the end of 1979.

Finally, on January 7, the COMEX changed their rules to only allow 10 million ounces of contracts per trader and to require all traders to reach this threshold before February 18. The Commodity Futures Trading Commission (CFTC) backed the ruling.[21] On January 17 silver had peaked at $50. Amazingly, the Hunts continued buying—their position was worth $4.5 billion and their profits were estimated at $3.5 billion. On January 21, the COMEX suspended trading in silver. They would only accept liquidation orders. Silver dropped to $39 per ounce and stayed there until the end of January. About 22 million ounces of scraps, including silver coins, silverware and jewellery, came to market. In early February the Hunts took delivery of another 26 million ounces from Chicago. The Hunts had substantial resources—their oil company, Placid Oil, was generating about $200 million in profits from North Sea oil. There were talks of taking over Texaco and rumours that their Middle Eastern partners were putting together a syndicate to buy silver. A new shock occurred. Paul Volker, the Fed chairman, had decided that inflation had gone too far and pushed up the Fed funds rate to over 21% as he tightened monetary growth. By March silver plummeted as the dollar roared, reaching $24 per ounce by March 14. Margin calls cost the Hunts about $10 million daily. They scrambled across Europe searching for buyers, but as the price dropped not only did their margin calls rise, but so did the cost of margins as a consequence of the higher interest rates.[22] It was all over on March 25, 1980 as they defaulted on a margin call to the tune of $135 million. By March 27 the price fell to $10.80 an ounce. They lost $1.35 billion and the Fed, worried about systemic risk, was willing to extend loans to the beleaguered brothers.[23]

The Exchange Limits[24]

The exchange rules, prodded by the CFTC, have changed dramatically. All commodity contracts have two sets of limits: the first are daily maximum movements in price of any contract; and the second are limits on each individual trader. Column 3 in Table 7.4 shows the daily limits on a sample of commodities traded on a number of exchanges: Coffee Sugar Cocoa Exchange (CSCE), CME, New York Coton Exchange (NYCE), COMEX, CBT, Kansas City Board of Trade (KCBT), Winnipeg Commodity Exchange (WCE). For pork bellies, for example, the contract size is 40,000 lbs. The minimum daily move is US$4.00 per contract and the exchange will suspend trading if the contract falls or rises by 200 ticks.

In addition to the limits shown in Table 7.4 there are a range of other restrictions. The most important control is the maximum exposure per trader. In pork bellies, for example, no trader is allowed 1,000 contracts net long or short in all contract months, and no trader can have (or control) over 800 contracts long or short in any one month. Furthermore, to avoid squeezes traders may not have more than 150 contracts long or short on the Friday in the first week of the expiration month.

RISK MANAGEMENT AT THE COMMODITY TRADING DESK

This section explains the first golden rule for commodities: that one must decompose risks into those associated with an outright spot position and those defined by the borrowing cost of commodities. Such decomposition can greatly ease the computational burden when calculating value-at-risk (VaR) for a portfolio of commodities. Furthermore, it enables the risk manager to assess where the concentration of risk is based. We show that for a typical market making commodity portfolio in cash and derivatives, most risk comes from volatility in the convenience yield. The portfolio includes all the hedges of the trading desk. and of course

Commodity Contracts and Daily Limits on Price Movements

Contract	Exchange	Limit	Tick move	Contract size	Units
Cocoa	CSCE	88	$10.00	10 tonnes	$/tonne
Hogs (lean index)	CME	150	$4.00	40,000 lbs	c/lb
Pork bellies, frozen	CME	200	$4.00	40,000 lbs	c/lb
Cotton #2	NYCE	300	$5.00	50,000 lbs	c/lb
Copper, hi-grade RTH*	COMEX	2,000	$2.50	25,000 lbs	c/lb
Corn RTH	CBT	120	$6.25	5,000 BU	c/BU
Coffee	CSCE	600	$3.75	37,500 lbs	c/lb
Oats RTH	CBT	100	$6.25	5,000 BU	c/BU
Orange juice	NYCE	500	$1.50	15,000 lbs	c/lb
Platinum	NYMEX	250	$5.00	50 troy oz	$/oz
Silver RTH	COMEX	1,500	$5.00	5,000 troy oz	c/oz
SoybeanS RTH	CBT	300	$6.25	5,000 BU	c/BU
Soybean meal RTH	CBT	100	$10.00	100 tons	$/ton
Soybean oil RTH	CBT	100	$6.00	60,000 lbs	c/lb
World sugar #11	CSCE	50	$11.20	112,000 lbs	c/lb
Wheat RTH	CBT	200	$6.25	5,000 BU	c/BU
Kansas City wheat	KCBT	250	$6.25	5,000 BU	c/BU
Lumber	CME	100	$8.00	80,000 BF	$/1000 BF
Gold	CBT	500	$10.00	100 ounces	$/oz
Stocker cattle	CME		$2.50	25,000 lbs	c/lb
Gold RTH	COMEX	750	$10.00	100 troy oz	$/oz
Feeder cattle	CME	150	$5.00	50,000 lbs	c/lb
Silver	CBT	1,000	$5.00	5000 troy oz	c/oz
Domestic sugar #14	CSCE	50	$11.20	112,000 lbs	c/lb
Oats	WCE	500	CAD 0.20	20 tonnes	CAD/ tonne
Rapeseed (canola)	WCE	100	CAD 2.00	20 tonnes	CAD/ tonne
Flaxseed	WCE	100	CAD 2.00	20 tonnes	CAD/ tonne
Feed wheat (domestic)	WCE	500	CAD 0.20	20 tonnes	CAD/ tonne

* RTH stands for Regular Trading Hours, meaning "trading hours on the exchange." Once the exchange closes, many contracts are traded CT (Trading Cycle) through electronic networks such as Globex or Access. See for example, http://www.cme.com/trd/calhrs/ tradehours3497.html, which defines RTH and CT hours.

if VaR limits or other limits are imposed then these will also affect the VaR of the observed portfolio. Generally, traders hedge out their spot exposure—the reason is that the market is relatively liquid but long-dated interest-rate risk is more expensive to hedge, and thus traders must balance transactions costs with the uncertainty of the unhedged exposures (see, for example, Lawrence and Robinson, 1995a, 1995b, 1996).

The no-arbitrage condition (equation (7.2)) in an efficient market, where the expected spot price is the future price, and when the storage costs are constant, gives

$$\sigma_F = \sigma_S + \Delta r - \Delta q, \tag{7.4}$$

where σ_F is the percentage change in the futures price, σ_S is the percentage change in the spot price and Δr and Δq denote the change in the interest rate and the convenience yield, respectively. The term $\Delta r - \Delta q$ is the borrowing cost (net of the immediacy premium) and we here refer to the percentage price changes as the volatility. An example of the decomposition of variance as measured by a standard deviation, for aluminum and gold futures at 3 months and 27 months, is given in Table 7.5.

Several features stand out. A position in a forward is analogous to a portfolio of two risk factors: spot plus borrowing costs. For shorter-dated base commodities, the spot affect dominates. In aluminum three-month forwards the outright volatility is 17.54%, indeed the borrowing costs reduce overall the risk. In contrast, aluminum long-dated 27-month contract risk is shared equally between net spot volatility of 8.48% and net borrowing cost of 8.19%. In gold the spot rate dominates the overall contribution of, risk with borrowing costs contributing little.

The immediacy premium is related to the volatility of net borrowing costs. The right-hand side of the table shows that the interest rate affect dominates the immediacy premium for gold. However, it is the convenience yield that determines the (much higher) immediacy premium for aluminum. Lawrence (2003) has analyzed the key reason why base metals tend to have more volatile convenience yields than gold. Gold essentially has extremely large above-ground stocks that can readily be converted into inputs to meet industrial demand. The law of diminishing marginal utility from liquid commodities such as gold leads to a small and less volatile convenience yield.

We have selected a real portfolio of aluminum, copper, lead, nickel, tin, and zinc to illustrate these ideas. Table 7.6 describes the spot and forward positions (in £000) of a real portfolio of a major trading bank.

T A B L E 7.5

Decomposition of risk in computing VaR

Commodity	Decomposition of Volatility			Decomposition of Net Borrowing Costs Volatility		
	Forward Volatility	Spot Volatility	Net Borrowing Cost	Net Borrowing Costs Volatility	Net Convenience Yield	Interest Rate
Aluminum 3M	17.54%	19.10%	−1.56%	2.48%	2.44%	0.05%
Aluminum 27M	16.67%	8.48%	8.19%	19.07%	19.40%	−0.33%
Gold 3M	4.86%	5.06%	−0.20%	1.05%	0.35%	0.69%
Gold 27M	4.82%	4.81%	0.00%	1.87%	0.62%	1.25%

T A B L E 7.6

A portfolio of commodities

Tenor	Aluminum	Aluminum Alloy	Copper A	Lead	Nickel	Tin	Zinc
Spot	98.9	9.1	4.8	9.8	8.6	2.6	151.3
1 wk	−15.1	−5	−10.3	−5.3	8.1	−1.8	−42.8
2 wk	−4	−1.6	−0.5	−0.3	−8.9	0.2	−65.1
1 m	−23.1	−2.1	−8.5	2.4	−4.8	0.1	−7.6
3 m	15.7	0.2	−4.2	−6	−2	−0.7	−6.9
6 m	−21	0.5	−4.7	−0.8	−0.7	−0.1	−19.3
12 m	−17.4	−0.9	14.9	−0.3	0	0	−8.5
15 m	1.5	0	6.5	0	0	0	−0.7
18 m	−3.2	0	0.6	0	0	0	−0.1
2 yr	−1.5	0	−4.8	0	0	0	0
27m	0.7	0	1.2	0	0	0	0
36 m	0	0	0.6	0	0	0	0

The portfolio is a diversified portfolio of long spot positions with hedges (short forwards) mainly concentrated in the short-dated maturities but extending out to three years. In order to compute the VaR of the portfolio one could use a covariance model, but this would be a cumbersome process: we would need over 2,500 parameters (correlations and variances) to estimate the VaR. The alternative approach is to decompose the forward risks into spot risk and the risk associated with carrying costs, as demonstrated above. To compute the overall spot position in each commodity, each forward must be discounted to an equivalent spot position (using equation (7.3). The overall spot positions are computed in Table 7.7.

In this table, the annual volatility in the centre column is translated into a daily VaR based on a normal distribution at the 98% confidence level. Of the individual VaRs for each commodity (termed "gross" VaR in the second last column) the largest is aluminum with a VaR of £181,450, and the second largest is copper with a VaR of £95,000.

The most interesting column, though, is the net contribution of each position to the overall risk. Diversification effects are captured using the correlation between spot returns. Aluminum risk declines to £163,000 and

TABLE   7.7

Overall spot exposures, volatility and VaR

	Physical Position (000s tonnes)	Value Physical (£ millions)	Volatility (annual %)	Individual ("Gross") VaR (£ 000)	Contribution to Total VaR (£ 000)
Aluminum	0.16	0.17	29%	181.45	163.59
Aluminum Alloy	0.28	0.26	15%	7.53	5.29
Copper Grade A	−4.35	−8.47	14.90%	95.76	−21.21
Lead	−0.57	−0.27	24.37%	7.19	−2.12
Nickel	0.1	0.54	23.41%	43.6	25.37
Tin	0.32	1.31	24.47%	43.34	26.33
Zinc	0.31	0.21	20.55%	64.23	37.3

the short copper position with an individual VaR of £95,000 reduces overall exposure by £21,000 since copper and aluminum have a positive correlation of 0.54.

By adding up the net risk contribution in the final column of Table 7.7 we compute the total VaR of the spot positions as approximately £230,000. The aggregate risk of £440,000 is the sum of the individual VaRs in the second last column of Table 7.7. This represents the risk if each position moved adversely against us. The risk reduction due to diversification is £440,000 − £230,000 = £210,000. This demonstrates that setting limits on each commodity can be too constraining and will exaggerate VaR. Indeed, diversification reduces risk by almost 50%.

This representation of spot risk assumes that the commodity yields do not change. To get a handle on the borrowing risk, Table 7.8 analyzes the borrowing cost sensitivities of each commodity at each tenor. The report first computes the sensitivity of each commodity at each tenor to a 100 basis point rise in commodity yields. These sensitivities are shown in the top part of the table. The sum of these sensitivities over all tenors gives the "bull–bear" sensitivity: this is positive for a bear sensitivity and negative for a bull sensitivity. For example, overall we have a "bull" position of £436,000 in aluminum.

A bull position in commodities is identical to selling spot and hedging with a forward position. With a bull position a rise of 100 basis points

T A B L E   7.8

Base metals borrowing/lending premium report

Change in Value for 1% in Borrowing/Lending Premium (£0000s)	Aluminum	Aluminum Alloy	Copper Grade A	Lead	Nickel	Tin	Zinc
Spot	−3	0	0	0	1	0	3
1 week	−3	−1	−4	0	8	−1	−5
2 week	−2	−1	0	0	−18	0	−17
1 month	−21	−2	−14	1	−22	0	−4
3 month	−44	1	−19	−7	−27	−7	−12
6 month	−119	3	−39	−2	−20	−1	−67
12 month	−202	−9	239	−1	−2	1	−60
15 month	22	0	128	0	0	0	−6
18 month	−55	0	15	0	0	0	−1
2 year	−34	0	−146	0	0	0	0
27 month	19	0	39	0	0	0	0
36 month	0	0	28	0	0	0	0
Bull–Bear Sensitivity	−436	−9	227	−10	−79	−8	−170
Adverse Risk	454	16	1215	37	88	18	184
Net Parallel Risk	301	4	443	25	102	8	143
Net Non-parallel Risk	59	5	−125	8	−66	5	9
Daily Value-at-Risk	360	9	319	32	36	12	152

Portfolio (£ millions)	
Adverse Risk	2.01
Less Diversification Effect	1.35
98% Daily Value-at-Risk	0.46
(Normality)	
Add Non-Normality Effect	0.18
98% Daily Value-at-Risk	0.64

across the whole yield curve would lead to a loss. This rise in the commodity yield could come about from either a rise in the interest rate, a fall in the convenience yield or a hike in storage costs.

Table 7.8 also provides data to traders on shifts in the term structure of interest rates. In the example shown most tenors have negative sensitivities. Now, using a simulation technique, we compute the borrowing risk VaR for each commodity. For example, at the bottom of the aluminum column, the VaR is £360,000 and this is composed of £300,000 in parallel shifts in the aluminum yield curve and £59,0000 in non-parallel shifts. The above numbers are estimates of the net contribution of risk to the borrowing cost portfolio, assuming that the spot price is held constant.

Table 7.9 shows the aggregate borrowing cost risk of the example portfolio. By adding up the gross VaR of each commodity we estimate the adverse situation where all yield curves shift adversely against us. This is estimated at £2 million. However, since the correlations between yield curves across commodities are generally low, the estimate of diversification at the 98% confidence interval is £1.44m. Thus the VaR of borrowing costs is estimated at £460,000.

In Table 7.10 we produce the overall VaR and decomposition of the portfolio by commodity into spot and carrying cost exposure as well as an estimate of the aggregate VaR. For the portfolio as a whole we noted that the borrowing rate VaR is about £460,000 and spot commodity VaR is £230,000. Most of the commodity risk is entirely due to the "convenience yield" risk.

For most commodities we note how the desk has much larger borrowing cost risk than spot risk. For example, in copper the spot VaR is £97,000 and carrying cost VaR is £280,000. This need not be the case, but it is something that typically occurs at trading desks due to hedging of spot exposure but inability to hedge term structure risk (particularly long-dated forwards) due to illiquidity and high transactions costs.

T A B L E   7.9

Aggregate borrowing cost risk

Gross Risk	£2,000,000
Diversification	−£1,440,000
VaR	£460,000

T A B L E   7.10

Decomposition of VaR

(£000s)	Aluminum	Aluminum Alloy	Copper Grade A	Lead	Nickel	Tin	Zinc
Spot Risk	181.5	7.5	96.8	7.2	43.6	43.3	64.2
Borrowing Rate Risk	367.4	9	280.3	31.1	33.2	12.1	143
Daily VaR (£000s)	409.8	11.8	296.6	31.9	54.8	45	157

Portfolio Risk (£ millions)		Decomposition of Risk (£ millions)	
Adverse Risk	1.98	Spot Commodity Risk	0.23
Less Diversification	1.46	Borrowing Rate Risk	0.46
98% Daily VaR (Normality)	0.51	Daily Value-at-Risk	0.51
Add Non-normality Effect	0.26		
98% Daily VaR	0.77		
Limit	2		

The demand for immediacy is a core risk factor contributing significantly to overall risk. In a simulation of the above portfolio, we found that if the convenience yield were held constant, the VaR of the portfolio would fall by 75%. A bank that is running a short metals position hedged by a longer-dated forward contract can be subject to a severe market squeeze if the market suddenly goes into backwardation. Stress testing and empirical scrutiny of borrowing rate (the forward–spot contango) behavior take on considerable importance for the risk assessment of a commodity portfolio.

If we added up all the individual VaRs this would total £1.98 million. But it appears that all these risks are empirically quite independent, so that diversification would reduce the exposure to £510,000. But this only applies if the portfolio returns are normally distributed. Re-estimating the entire portfolio under a nonparametric distribution, we do find significant nonnormality. The VaR now increases by 25% to £710,000. This suggests that nonnormality is absolutely vital in estimating VaR for commodity portfolios.[25]

THE DISTRIBUTION OF COMMODITY RETURNS

We have shown that commodity prices have been subject to sudden unexpected shocks such as harvest failures or production delays, leading to an increase in the convenience yield. We have further explored some illustrations of squeezes or potential squeezes on physical deliveries into forward or futures contracts. Consequently, we were not at all surprised to observe that normal distributions were inconsistent with empirical observation in the VaRs estimated in the previous section We further explore here the characteristics of the observed distributions.

Evidence of Non-normality

Table 7.11 presents summary statistics of quarterly data over the period 1982–2001 for financial instruments and some commodities. The series are returns on the three-month Treasury bill rate, the S&P index, bonds, gold, the CRB index, aluminum, copper, lead, zinc, oil, and silver. All data have

T A B L E   7.11

Sample moments of commodity return distributions

Asset	Mean	Volatility	Skewness	Kurtosis
R3M	4.38	5.16	0.39	0.21
RSP	6.78	32.21	−0.54	0.95
RBOND	5.5	21.32	0.12	1.18
RGOLD	−1.36	34.49	0.7	2.14
RCRB	−3.03	19.95	−0.14	0.09
RALUM	−1.63	45.59	0.11	2.1
RCOPPER	−2.71	46.07	0.67	2.22
RLEAD	−3.3	56.89	−0.09	1.23
RZINC	−3.21	44.71	0.03	0.19
RWTI	−0.98	59.76	−0.24	7.91
RSILVER	−2.8	53.91	0.56	2.95

been deflated by the wholesale price index so that we can examine real rates of return.

The commodities all have *negative* rates of return on average over this period. But, amazingly, the annual volatility of gold over the period is about the same as that of the S&P index and Dow Jones.

Commodity returns are also highly nonnormally distributed. The last two columns of Table 7.11 show the skewness and excess kurtosis estimates, again based on quarterly data. At this frequency the financial asset returns are near to normally distributed—the 1987 outlier being the main cause of nonnormality in the S&P index. However, aluminum, gold, silver, copper, and oil all have highly leptokurtic distributions (evidenced by the positive estimate of kurtosis). Hence their risk management requires the use of advanced VaR models (see Chapter 3)

What Drives Commodity Prices?

Lawrence (2003) has explored the key drivers of commodity prices. Using regressions of commodity returns on gross domestic product, inflation, monetary growth, short- and long-term yields as proxies of the business cycle, he examines how prices fluctuate with the business cycle for each commodity. Consequently, he categorizes commodities into two classes: those that are correlated with the cycle (through one or more variables) and those that are not. Most commodity prices are related to a business cycle, through varying channels. Only zinc and gold appear to have no systematic risk. Any commodity that does not have excessive above-ground stocks relative to production flows, such as aluminum or oil, will tend to be affected by cyclical movements. The astute risk manager should perform stress tests and scenario analysis and be aware that estimates of correlations vary dramatically over the cycle.

CONCLUSIONS

This chapter covers the markets for and the transaction characteristics of different types of commodities. As a risk manager it is important to recognize these characteristics, which focus on the delivery and settlement mechanisms for heterogeneous commodities. The key arbitrage equation which links spot prices with forward prices is the commodity equivalent of covered interest arbitrage in foreign exchange or interest parity in bonds.

Unlike other markets, the arbitrage equation for commodities contains a convenience yield which reflects the importance that is sometimes placed on immediate access to supply. This feature of commodity markets is no doubt related to the importance of commodities as factors of production and possible delays in supply/shipping. It is the presence of this convenience yield, and its variability, that make commodity risk management unique. Failure to properly appreciate these aspects of commodity markets can have disastrous consequences.

We have introduced the reader to the risk management of a commodity trading desk. We have shown how any forward commodity position can be decomposed into an outright spot position and carrying cost position. We have presented the reader with examples of the key value-at-risk and sensitivity reports that are produced by commodity trading desks. These reports highlight the importance of diversification for portfolios of commodities, a characteristic held in common with trading portfolios in other markets (such as stocks, bonds and currencies). Unlike these other markets, the main component of risk for a commodities portfolio is typically not spot risk, but changes in the cost of carry. The markets are also subject to extreme movements due to squeezes or corners. We showed two examples of the golden age manipulators in the nineteenth century. As a consequence, the CFTC and the exchanges responded by setting limits on maximum price fluctuations, maximum position size, and criminal legal action. These still did not terrify the Hunts, who allegedly created the greatest corner in 1979 and even had the central bankers lending them money.

Commodity risk managers should also consider the unique characteristics of the distribution of commodity returns. Compared with financial assets, commodities typically have high volatility and low returns. Many also exhibit nonnormality, with positive excess kurtosis. Examining the key risk factors that drive the prices of commodities, we conclude that the business cycle only affects commodities that have small aboveground stocks relative to production. In such cases an immediacy premium can arise due to sudden unexpected shortages in input supply. This can drive markets into backwardation. In contrast, when there is a ready supply of above-ground stocks that can be converted into production inputs, as in the case of gold, the business cycle has little effect on pricing and there is less chance of dramatic hikes in spot prices over and above forward prices.

REFERENCES

Alexander, C and Sheedy, E (2008a) *The Professional Risk Managers' Guide to Finance Theory* (New York: McGraw-Hill).

Alexander, C and Sheedy, E (2008b) *The Professional Risk Managers' Guide to Financial Instruments* (New York: McGraw-Hill).

Dusak, K (1973) Futures trading and investor returns: An investigation of commodity market risk premiums, *Journal of Political Economy*, **81**, pp. 1387–406. Reprinted in Telser (2000) pp. 597–617.

Geisst, CR (2002) *Wheels of Fortune. The History of Speculation from Scandal to Respectability* (Hoboken, NJ: Wiley).

Hicks, JR (1946) *Value and Capital*, 2nd edition (Oxford: Oxford University Press).

Kaldor, N (1939) Speculation and economic stability. *Review of Economic Studies*, **7**(1), pp. 1–27. Reprinted in Telser (2000) pp. 53–87.

Keynes, JM (1930) *A Treatise on Money*, Volume 2. (London: Macmillan).

Lawrence, C (2003) Why is gold different from all other assets? An empirical investigation. World Gold Council.

Lawrence, C and Robinson, G (1995a) Handbook of market risk management. Unpublished manuscript, Barclays Bank.

Lawrence, C and Robinson, G (1995b) Value at risk: addressing liquidity and volatility risks. *Capital Market Strategies*, no. 7 (November).

Lawrence, C and Robinson, G (1996) Incorporating liquidity into the risk-measurement framework, *Financial Derivatives and Risk Management*, no. 6 (June).

Reuters Limited (2000) *An Introduction to the Commodities, Energy and Transport Markets* (Chichester: Wiley).

Sharpe, W (1964) Capital asset prices: A treaty of market equilibrium under conditions of risk. *Journal of Finance*, **19**, pp. 425–42.

Sikorzewski, W (2001) Corners in the commodity futures markets in the XIXth century. Unpublished manuscript, University of Caen, France.

Telser, LG (1958) Futures trading and the storage of wheat and cotton, *Journal of Poltical Economy*, **66**, pp. 233–255. Reprinted in Telser (2000) pp. 119–48.

Telser, LG (2000) *Classic Futures—Lessons from the Past for the Electronic Age* (London: Risk Publications).

Telser, LG and Higinbotham, HN (1977) Organised futures markets: costs and benefits. *Journal of Political Economy*, **85**(5), pp. 969–1000. Reprinted in Telser (2000) pp. 321–53.

Williams J (1986) *Economics of Futures Markets* (Cambridge: Cambridge University Press).

NOTES

1. This section draws heavily on Reuters (2000) pp. 7–129.
2. See Reuters (2000) pp. 31–39.
3. See Reuters (2000) pp. 61–129.

4. For a useful methodology of both theory and practice in measuring liquidity, see Lawrence and Robinson (1995a, 1995b).

5. See, for example, Telser and Higinbotham (1977). They examined 23 commodities and found a negative correlation between commissions and volume.

6. Telser and Higinbotham (1977) find that as volumes and open interest increase, commissions decline. Furthermore, as volatility increases the ratio of volume to open interest also declines. The key driver for this is that uncertainty induces heavier turnover of positions.

7. See Lawrence and Robinson (1996) for a comprehensive methodology for working bid–offer spreads and illiquidity into value-at-risk measurements.

8. This section draws heavily on "Gold as a Reserve Asset", World Gold Council. See www.gold.org.

9. See www.gold.org for a chronology of events concerning gold as a reserve asset.

10. See the next section for a historical overview of short squeezes, in particular the famous silver squeeze of 1979–1980 manipulated by the Hunt brothers.

11. The reader is referred to Alexander and Sheedy (2008a), Chapter 7 for an analysis of the critical differences between the two types of markets. General historical and cross-sectional data can be readily obtained from the commodity futures exchanges.

12. The spot price of aluminum shot up to US$70!

13. See the next section.

14. Williams (1986) gives a persuasive and cogent analysis of the demand for immediacy and backwardation. Lawrence (2003) shows, however, that there is negligible backwardation in commodities such as gold where inventory supplies (above-ground stocks) are very large relative to production (flows), regardless of the convenience yield.

15. See Telser (1958) for a derivation of a commodity model with speculators and the behaviour of storage.

16. Normal backwardation, according to Keynes (1930), implies that the *forward price will lie below the expected spot price*. This hypothesis has been thoroughly scrutinized by economists. In the next section we will describe the key arbitrage equation linking spot and forwards/futures and how backwardation and normal backwardation come into play.

17. In this equation Kaldor and others have included a risk premium. We have omitted it since we believe that the evidence tends to refute it and thus is not that critical to incorporate it.

18. Note that one would proxy r by the interbank dollar rate such as LIBOR. The difference between the interbank rate and the LIBOR is measured by $q - C$. Since the volatility of C will generally be small, the difference is a good proxy for the convenience yield.

19. Associated in this context could be a family member, a subsidiary, an insider collusive customer, or any entity that is "party" to the squeeze.

20. For a delightful analysis of all the corners, scandals and squeezes in historical and modern times, see Geisst (2002). For an exposition of the Hunt silver scandal, see pp. 212–241.

21. The CFTC is the key regulator of commodities, exchanges and derivatives in the USA. Its key mission is to protect market users and the public from fraud, manipulation, and abusive practices related to the sale of commodity and financial futures and options,

and to foster open, competitive, and financially sound futures and option markets (see htpp://www.cftc.gov).

22. The risk manager will be aware that this is a "negative convexity" stress exposure. In this case both the cost and the quantity of margin demanded have risen at heightened rates.

23. Years later in 1998 the precedent set by Volker of lending the Hunts money to avoid systemic risk was emulated by Greenspan arranging support for LTCM. (See United States Treasury report on Hedge Funds, Leverage and Lessons from Long Term Capital Management, pp. 1–42. www.treas.gov/press/releases/reports/hedgfund.pdf and Shirreff on Lessons from the Collapse of Hedge Fund, Long-Term Capital Management. http://newrisk.ifci.ch/146480.htm)

24. For an insight into the setting of limits and the relationship between the exchanges and the CFTC, see Geisst (2002).

25. See Dusak (1973), who provides a methodology for testing whether or not commodity future prices are nonnormally distributed. For soy beans and other softs she rejects the normality assumption. For the risk manager this suggests that to estimate economic capital for a commodity desk using a normal distribution assumption could seriously understate risk.

CHAPTER 8

The Energy Markets

Peter C. Fusaro

INTRODUCTION

Energy trading began in 1978 with the first oil futures contract on the New York Mercantile Exchange (NYMEX). During the 1980s and 1990s, NYMEX and the International Petroleum Exchange (IPE), now called ICE Futures, successfully launched futures contracts for oil and gas futures trading. These successful energy futures exchanges have survived the trading debacles of recent years, of which Enron was the most notable. Oil companies and financial houses now provide the necessary trading liquidity through market-making on both the established government-regulated futures exchanges and over-the-counter (OTC) energy derivatives markets that can clear on the futures exchanges. They have considerable skill in the management of financial energy risks and the risks in the emerging global environmental markets.

This chapter introduces the energy markets from a risk management perspective. It first provides an initial overview of the market, its products and its risks. Next, it explains how risk management is conducted on energy exchanges, and then covers the OTC markets. In both cases a global perspective is given. Emerging energy markets are considered next, including brief coverage of coal trading, weather derivatives, green trading and freight swaps. Finally, it looks to the future of energy trading, before the Conclusions.

MARKET OVERVIEW

Crude oil and petroleum products have particularly active markets. Daily physical oil consumption is over 84.5 million barrels per day[1] and approaches $2 trillion in annual trade, which entices many active hedgers and speculators. Crude oil and petroleum products are now traded 24 hours per day every business day in both the physical and paper (financial) markets. Options and OTC oil price swaps are also well developed. The majority of financial oil trading still takes place in the United States and Europe. Although Asian energy trading markets in general are less developed, that is the region with the highest oil consumption growth rates. Natural gas has had a viable energy futures contract in North America since April 1990, and in Europe since 1999.

Electric power futures and OTC contracts have proliferated around the world since the 1990s but, frankly, these markets are much smaller than other markets, mainly due to the high price risk and the inability to store electricity. Moreover, there have been many failed electricity futures contracts in the USA and electricity futures exchanges in Europe. While paper market trading for oil and gas has grown considerably during the past decade, on both established futures exchanges and the OTC forward markets, electricity paper trading is still in its infancy. Electricity deregulation has driven the commoditization process whereby electricity becomes a fungible commodity, as it is in the Nord Pool market in Scandinavia (perhaps the best example of a working electricity market in the world). There is convergence of both gas and electric prices that has accelerated much more on the physical side of the market than the financial trading of power. In fact, the close relationship between natural gas and electric power markets cannot be understated. However, power is a more demanding market, as it is a next hour, next day, next week, and next month business. Power marketers and traders provide greater efficiency by buying and selling power and transmissions capacity. Electric power is a market that never closes, where prices change hourly, half-hourly, or quarter-hourly. It is the most volatile commodity ever created and therefore its financial markets are significantly smaller than the oil and gas markets. While there is much attraction in trading electricity, the fact is that it is a very hard risk to manage, with fuel inputs on one side of the equation and electricity outputs on the other side. Adding to this risk complexity is the fact that electric utilities are the main emitters of greenhouse gases and other air emissions. This will add costs and more trading complexity to trading electric power in the future as the environmental financial markets become better established throughout the world.

Today we are still only hedging about half of the global commodity price exposure of the physical energy markets. To put this statement into some perspective, the annualized notional value of all energy derivatives is over $3 trillion, compared to a physical energy market of $5 trillion annually. Commodities usually trade at least 6 and up to 20 times the physical market. Consequently, financial energy trading is still in its infancy. Ironically, most companies still do not hedge their energy price risk exposures. However, the new market drivers for energy hedging and active risk management are growing because of market liberalization, competitive markets, globalization, privatization of energy, and the internet, which is facilitating electronic energy trading. Increased price volatility due to the more active trading of hedge funds and investment banks makes this sector ripe for financial change.

The Products

The energy complex trades the following products on established futures exchanges, OTC markets and the internet:

- crude oil
- gasoline
- naphtha
- gasoil
- jet fuel
- home heating oil
- residual fuel oil
- bunker fuels
- freight-rate swaps
- natural gas
- electricity
- liquefied natural gas (LNG)
- petrochemicals
- coal
- emissions such as sulfur dioxide and nitrous oxides
- greenhouse gases, i.e. carbon credits

- renewable energy credits
- negawatts (value of energy efficiency)

Some of these products are quite illiquid (like greenhouse gases or negawatts) while others (like crude oil in the USA and Europe as well as North American natural gas) are very well established. The mature energy markets have more sophisticated financial instruments and recently have attracted the active participation of many hedge funds which are extending their trading platform from energy equities into energy commodities as they seek higher returns.

The Risks

Energy commodities are subject to numerous risks, including credit or counterparty risk, liquidity risk, event risk, cash-flow risk, basis risk, legal and regulatory risk, operational risks, tax risk, and most evidently geo-political and weather risks. There are also tremendous variations over time in many energy markets. The weather (seasonal) impacts supply and demand so that risks increase in the mid-summer and winter seasons as more energy is required for heating, cooling, and transportation.

Of all the different types of risks that affect the energy markets, market risk is still pre-eminent. Price volatility is caused by fundamental factors such as supply/demand, and weather and financial factors such as technical trading, speculators, and market imperfections. These factors are very well defined in energy markets and as a result they are the most volatile commodity markets ever created.

Figures 8.1 and 8.2 show the implied volatility of at-the-money options on light sweet crude oil and natural gas, both traded on NYMEX, for the period from January 1998 until July 2007. The prices of very short-term options are much affected by supply shortages, often during cold winter months. For instance, the one-month implied volatility for natural gas has exceeded 100% several times during the last decade, as shown in Figure 8.2. The volatility of crude oil is also related to economic conditions: the exceptionally high volatility experienced during 2002 and 2003 was related to the war on Iraq. Electric power volatility sometimes reaches 1,000% due to supply shortages and weather-related influences. Clearly, energy markets are the most volatile financial markets, and consequently risk management has become a core competency and fiduciary responsibility for many energy companies.

F I G U R E   8.1

At-the-money implied volatility, crude oil

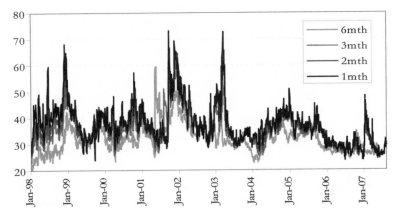

Source: Bloomberg

F I G U R E   8.2

At-the-money implied volatility, natural gas

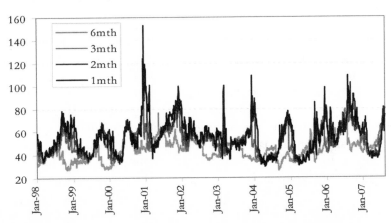

Source: Bloomberg

Developing a Cash Market

The most interesting and complex factor that differentiates energy trading from forex and other financial instruments is its need for a viable cash market to enable trading. Today, we have viable cash markets for the following energy commodities: crude oil, heating oil (also called gasoil in Europe), gasoline, propane, residual fuel oil, ship bunkers, natural gas, coal, and electricity. Energy market development always begins with opaque prices, little trading, poor liquidity, few participants, wide arbitrage opportunities, fat margins, and tremendous inefficiency. At this point in market development, deal flow is dominated by OTC brokers. As the cash market develops spot market price discovery there is more deal flow.[2] Eventually both OTC forward contracts and exchange-traded futures start to trade. There is no special time period for all markets to develop, but the evolutionary process is the same. Although energy price management is still in its early stages of development compared to the more developed and financially sophisticated markets of interest rates and foreign currencies, the future is indeed very bright.

ENERGY FUTURES MARKETS

A standardized energy futures contract always has the following characteristics. It has an underlying physical commodity or price index upon which the energy futures contract is based. There is a certain size for the amount of the underlying item covered by each futures contract. There is a predetermined and specified time given in months for which contracts can be traded. There is an expiration date. Finally, there is a specified grade or quality and delivery location for oil and coal futures contracts. Whereas oil varies by grade/quality, natural gas (methane), and electricity are more homogeneous commodities, obviating the need for the grade/quality to be specified in the contract. The settlement mechanism can be either physical delivery of the underlying item or cash payment. The trend in energy futures has been towards cash settlement, but in reality the only liquid futures contract that goes to cash settlement is the ICE Brent crude oil contract.

Partly because futures markets provide the opportunity for leveraged investments, they attract large pools of risk capital. As a result, futures markets are among the most liquid of all global financial markets, providing low transaction costs and ease of entry and exit. This fosters their use by a wide range of businesses and investors wishing to manage price risks.

Due to the continued geopolitical problems over oil supply, futures exchanges are currently experiencing unprecedented growth in their oil futures contracts. As explained in Alexander and Sheedy (2008b), Chapter 6, the institutional features of futures markets mean that counterparty risk is eliminated.

The Exchanges

Futures markets have been used by traders in commodities for hundreds of years, beginning with the trading of rice futures in Osaka, Japan, in the late 1600s. NYMEX, the world's largest regulated energy futures exchange, started life in 1872 as the Butter and Cheese Exchange of New York before being renamed 10 years later. Today, NYMEX is the largest energy futures exchange in the world, having introduced its first energy futures contract for home heating oil in 1978, and trades oil, gas, electric power, and coal contracts. Other oil and gas futures markets include the ICE Futures Market in London, which trades oil and gas contracts, and the Tokyo Commodity Exchange in Tokyo, which trades small oil futures contracts. The Singapore Exchange used to trade fuel oil futures contracts in the past and now has relationships with other energy futures exchanges for electronic trading. The Shanghai Futures Exchange (SHFE) launched a fuel oil futures contract in August 2004 and also has a number of linkages to NYMEX, the ICE Futures, and the Singapore Exchange.

There are a number of electricity exchanges which trade both physical spot electricity and electricity futures, including the APX Group (www.apxgroup.com) which provides markets in the UK and The Netherlands, NordPool in Scandinavia and the European Energy Exchange (EEX) in Germany. NordPool (www.nordpool.com) is the most liquid electricity trading market in the world. It trades OTC, bilateral, cleared OTC, and physical forward electricity contracts. EEX (www.eex.de) trades both physical spot electricity and electricity futures and is the consolidation of two German exchanges. Then there are several electronic energy platforms, the IntercontinentalExchange™ (ICE) of the USA being the largest. ICE bought IPE in June 2002 and is now the second largest energy exchange in the world; it has launched the Interchange, which trades during floor trading hours. The ICE trades many oil, gas, and power OTC contracts in North America and Europe, but its primary growth in recent years has been in Asia. There is another electronic exchange called the Natural Gas Exchange in Calgary, Canada, which has been profitable for many years and trades a western Canadian natural gas contract.

To round out the remaining energy futures exchanges, there is Powernext Paris (www.powernext.fr) in France which engages in day-ahead power trading, the Austrian Power Exchange (www.exaa.at) which has limited activity, the Warsaw Power Exchange (www.polpx.pl) which trades day-ahead physical electric power, and the Spanish Power Market (www.cne.es) in Madrid which trades physical power in Spain. None of these exchanges trade high volumes. The problem in the European Union is that all countries have developed electronic exchanges independently and have not figured out that the internet is borderless, and that all these exchanges are doomed to failure unless they link to or are subsumed by other exchanges.

The Contracts

The major oil futures contracts are NYMEX light sweet crude oil futures, NYMEX heating oil futures, NYMEX gasoline futures, ICE Brent crude oil futures, and ICE gasoil futures. Natural gas futures contracts are only traded on the NYMEX and ICE. The NYMEX Henry Hub natural gas futures contract is considered the global benchmark for gas trading, and recently has been used for LNG hedging purposes. It was launched in 1990. The ICE's natural gas futures contract is more regionalized for the UK's National Balancing Point (price reference) and was launched in 1997.

Example 8.1: Contract Specifications—Light, Sweet Crude Oil Futures (Physical)

Trading Unit: 1,000 US barrels (42,000 gallons).

Price Quotation: US dollars and cents per barrel.

Trading Hours (all times are New York time): Open outcry trading is conducted from 9:00 a.m. until 2:30 p.m. Electronic trading is conducted from 6:00 p.m. until 5:15 p.m. via the CME Globex(r) trading platform, Sunday through Friday. There is a 45-minute break each day between 5:15 p.m. (current trade date) and 6:00 p.m. (next trade date).

Trading Months: Thirty consecutive months plus long-dated futures initially listed 36, 48, 60, 72, and 84 months prior to delivery. Additionally, trading can be executed at an average differential to the previous day's settlement prices for periods of 2–30 consecutive months in a single transaction. These calendar strips are executed during open outcry trading hours.

Minimum Price Fluctuation: $0.01 (1¢) per barrel ($10.00 per contract).

Maximum Daily Price Fluctuation: $10.00 per barrel ($10,000 per contract) for all months. If any contract is traded, bid, or offered at the limit for five minutes, trading is halted for five minutes. When trading resumes, the limit is expanded by $10.00 per barrel in either direction. If another halt were triggered, the market would continue to be expanded by $10.00 per barrel in either direction after each successive five-minute trading halt. There will be no maximum price fluctuation limits during any one trading session.

Last Trading Day: Trading terminates at the close of business on the third business day prior to the 25th calendar day of the month preceding the delivery month. If the 25th calendar day of the month is a non-business day, trading shall cease on the third business day prior to the business day preceding the 25th calendar day.

Settlement Type: Physical.

Delivery: Free on board seller's facility, Cushing, Oklahoma, at any pipeline or storage facility with pipeline access to TEPPCO, Cushing storage, or Equilon Pipeline Co., by in-tank transfer, in-line transfer, book-out, or inter-facility transfer (pumpover).

Delivery Period: All deliveries are rateable over the course of the month and must be initiated on or after the first calendar day and completed by the last calendar day of the delivery month.

Alternative Delivery Procedure (ADP): An ADP is available to buyers and sellers who have been matched by the Exchange subsequent to the termination of trading in the spot month contract. If buyer and seller agree to consummate delivery under terms different from those prescribed in the contract specifications, they may proceed on that basis after submitting a notice of their intention to the Exchange.

Exchange of Futures for Physicals (EFP): The commercial buyer or seller may exchange a futures position for a physical position of equal quantity by submitting a notice to the Exchange. EFPs may be used to either initiate or liquidate a futures position.

Deliverable Grades: Specific domestic crudes with 0.42% sulfur by weight or less, not less than 37° API gravity or more than 42° API gravity. The following domestic crude streams are deliverable: West Texas Intermediate, Low Sweet Mix, New Mexican Sweet, North Texas Sweet, Oklahoma Sweet, and South Texas Sweet. Specific foreign crudes of not less than 34° API or more than 42° API. The following foreign streams are deliverable: UK Brent and Forties, and Norwegian Oseberg Blend, for which the seller shall receive a 55¢ per barrel discount below the final settlement price; Nigerian Bonny Light and Colombian Cusiana are delivered at 15¢ premiums; and Nigerian Qua Iboe is delivered at a 5¢ premium.

Inspection: Inspection shall be conducted in accordance with pipeline practices. A buyer or seller may appoint an inspector to inspect the quality of oil delivered. However, the buyer or seller who requests the inspection will bear its costs and will notify the other party to the transaction that the inspection will occur.

Position Accountability Levels and Limits: Any one month/all months: 20,000 net futures, but not to exceed 1,000 in the last three days of trading in the spot month.

Margin Requirements: Margins are required for open futures positions.

Trading Symbol: CL

Source: New York Mercantile Exchange

Electricity futures are traded on the NYMEX for the eastern United States in its PJM[3] and NYISO[4] electricity futures contracts (among others), APX for the UK power markets, NordPool for the Scandinavian power markets and EEX for the German power markets. There are many other minor electricity exchanges in Europe, including some in France, Austria, Poland, and The Netherlands. The ICE is preparing to launch its second attempt at a successful electricity futures contract.

It should be stated that most energy futures contracts fail. It takes several success factors to make an energy futures contract work. Most importantly, there must be active market participation. A successful energy futures contract needs 10,000 to 20,000 lots of open interest. If that is not attained, the contract will most likely fail or will need more time to gain industry acceptance. The other important feature about open interest is that exchange-traded options contracts can only be launched when we have enough liquidity in open interest in the futures market so that it can trade successfully.

Options on Energy Futures

As energy futures contracts become more liquid, exchanges usually launch options contracts. Exchange-traded options contracts are usually launched after 10,000 to 20,000 lots of open interest are developed in the futures contract. Options on energy futures are traded on the same exchanges that trade the underlying futures contracts and are standardized with respect to the quantity of the underlying futures contracts, expiration date, and strike price (the price at which the underlying futures contract can be bought or sold). As with futures, exchange-traded options positions can be closed out by offset, which is the execution of a trade of equal size on the other side of the market from the transaction that originated the position. Options trading models are very well developed for energy trading in oil and gas futures.

On NYMEX, for example, there is a wide range of option contracts. Aside from the traditional European and American style options, they offer:

- *Average price options* (also called Asian or average rate options). These are settled against the average of prices for an underlying commodity for a specified period. As explained in Alexander and Sheedy (2008b), Chapter 9, the averaging process reduces volatility and hence the option premium.
- *Calendar spread options.* This contract is on the price differential between two delivery dates for the same commodity. It helps market participants manage the risk of changes in the price spread.
- *Crack spread options.* The crack spread is the difference between the price of crude and refined products. This contract helps refiners and other market participants efficiently manage the risk of changes in this differential.
- *Inventory options.* NYMEX offers clearing services for over-the-counter options on the weekly crude oil storage number released by the Energy Information Administration (EIA) of the US Department of Energy. The options help market participants manage exposure to the impact of reported crude oil inventories released by the EIA each week.

Example 8.2: Contract Specifications–Light, Sweet Crude Oil Options

Trading Unit: One NYMEX Division light, sweet crude oil futures contract.

Price Quotation: US dollars and cents per barrel.

Trading Hours (all times are New York times): Open outcry trading is conducted from 9:00 a.m. until 2:30 p.m. Electronic trading is conducted from 6:00 p.m. until 5:15 p.m. via the CME Globex® trading platform, Sunday through Friday. There is a 45-minute break each day between 5:15 p.m. (current trade date) and 6:00 p.m. (next trade date).

Trading Months: Thirty consecutive months, plus long-dated options at 36, 48, 60, 72, and 84 months out on a June/December cycle.

Minimum Price Fluctuation: $0.01 (1¢) per barrel ($10.00 per contract).

Maximum Daily Price Fluctuation: No price limits.

Last Trading Day: Trading ends three business days before the underlying futures contract.

Exercise of Options: By a clearing member to the Exchange clearing house no later than 5:30 p.m. or 45 minutes after the underlying futures settlement price is posted, whichever is later, on any day up to and including the options expiration.

Strike Prices: Twenty strike prices in increments of 50¢ per barrel above and below the at-the-money strike price, and the next 10 strike prices in increments of $2.50 above the highest and below the lowest existing strike prices for a total of at least 61 strike prices. The at-the-money strike price is nearest to the previous day's close of the underlying futures contract. Strike price boundaries are adjusted according to the futures price movements.

Margin Requirements: Margins are required for open short options positions. The margin requirement for an options purchaser will never exceed the premium.

Trading Symbol: LO

Source: New York Mercantile Exchange

Hedging in Energy Futures Markets

Energy risk management does not eliminate risk. It only shifts it. Hedging is a strategy for price risk to be shifted by using financial instruments such as futures contracts, price swaps, or options to shift risk between buyers and sellers. The hedger takes a position in the financial market (futures or OTC) that is equal and opposite to the position that exposes price risk in the cash market, and locks in prices, costs, and profit margins. Physical delivery is not anticipated.

The hedger uses risk management tools such as futures and price swaps to protect a physical position or other financial exposure in the

(MWh), $23.50 and $24, respectively. Assuming a perfect hedge, the futures sales realise $169,280 for the April contracts (10 contracts × 736 MWh per contract × $23 per MWh = $169,280), $172,960 for May contracts (10 × 736 × $23.50), and $176,640 for June contracts (10 × 736 × $24), for a total of $518,880.

On March 29, the utility arranges to deliver 7,360 MWh of April pre-scheduled power in the cash market, the equivalent of 10 contracts, at the current price which has fallen to $22 per MWh, and receives $161,920. That is $7,360 less than budgeted when prices were anticipated at $23 per MWh.

Simultaneously, the producer buys back the April futures contracts to offset the obligations in the futures market. This also relieves it of the delivery obligation through the Exchange. The April contracts, originally sold for $23 ($169,280), are now valued at $22 per MWh, or $161,920. This yields a gain in the futures market of $7,360. Therefore:

the cash market sale of $161,920 (7,360 × $22/MWh)
plus a futures gain of $7,360
equals a net amount of $169,280, or $23 per MWh, the
                             budgeted sum for April.

As cash prices continue to be soft for the second quarter, the hedge looks like this:

	Cash Market	Futures Market
Feb. 1		Sells 10 Entergy electricity contracts in each of April, May, June for $23, $23.50, $24, respectively
Mar. 27	Sells 7,360 MWh at $22	Buys back 10 April contracts, at $22
Apr. 26	Sells 7,360 MWh at $23	Buys back 10 May contracts, at $23
May 26	Sells 7,360 MWh at $23.25	Buys back 10 June contracts at $23

Financial Result	April	May	June	Quarter
Expected revenue	$169,280	$172,960	$176,640	$518,880
Cash market sales revenue	$161,920	$169,280	$171,120	$502,320

market from adverse price movements that would reduce the val
position. The purpose of a hedge is to avoid the risk of advers
movements resulting in major losses in the physical market. Bec
physical cash markets and futures markets do not always have
price correlation relationship, there is no such thing as a perfect h
there is almost always some profit or loss. In futures markets,
involves taking a futures position opposite to that of a cash mar
tion. The seller of the commodity seeks protection against downsi
moves and a buyer seeks price protection against upside price mo
example, an oil producer would sell crude oil futures against its
tion. Thus, an energy producer or consumer might look at buying
ing energy futures against their price risk exposure in anticipati
market price increase/decrease.

The hedge position is established to buffer against day
market fluctuations. It is a form of insurance in that the hedger
upfront cost to ensure price certainty. The benefits of active ene
management using futures contracts are to stabilize cash flow
closely match balance sheet assets and liabilities, reduce transactic
decrease costs of storage, lock in "cost of carry" forward profit:
minimize the capital at risk needed to carry inventories.

Example 8.3: Electricity Producer Fears a F
Decline

In this example, an independent power production company
that falling prices will reduce profitability. It stabilizes cash
instituting a managed short hedging strategy on the electrici
market.

On February 1, the bulk power sales manager at a sou
utility projects that he will have excess generation for the secc
and notices attractive prices in the futures market for the A
and June contracts. The manager arranges to deliver this exc
at the prevailing market price in April, May, and June. H
wants to capture the market prices now, rather than be exp
risk of lower prices in the spot markets. The action the util
protect the company from this risk is to sell Entergy electri
contracts for those months.

In the futures market, the producer sells 10 futures c
each of three months, April, May, and June at $23 per me

Financial Result	April	May	June	Quarter
Futures market gain (loss)	$7,360	$3,680	$5,520	$16,560
Actual revenue	$169,280	$172,960	$176,640	$518,880 $23.50 per MWh

What happens to the power production company's hedge if prices rise instead of fall?

In that case, assume the cash market rises to $24, $24.50, and $25. The power producer realises $176,640 on the cash sale of 7,360 MWh for April, but sold futures at $23 in February, and now must buy them back at the higher price, $24, if it does not want to stand for delivery through the Exchange. The 10 contracts are valued at $176,640 which is what the company must pay to buy them back, incurring a $7,360 loss on the futures transaction. Therefore:

the cash market sale of:	$176,640 (7,360 × $24/MWh)
minus a futures loss of:	$7,360
equals a net amount of:	$169,280, or $23 per MWh, the budgeted sum for April.

As cash prices continue to be firm for the second quarter, the hedge looks like this:

	Cash Market	Futures Market
Feb. 1		Sells 10 Entergy electricity contracts in each of April, May, June for $23, $23.50, $24, respectively
Mar. 27	Sells 7,360 MWh at $24	Buys back 10 April contracts, at $24
Apr. 26	Sells 7,360 MWh at $24.50	Buys back 10 May contracts, at $24.50
May 26	Sells 7,360 MWh at $25	Buys back 10 June contracts at $25

Financial result	April	May	June	Quarter
Expected revenue	$169,280	$172,960	$176,640	$518,880
Cash market sales revenue	$176,640	$180,320	$184,000	$540,960
Futures market gain (loss)	($7,360)	($7,360)	($7,360)	($22,080)

Financial result	April	May	June	Quarter
Actual revenue	$169,280	$172,960	$176,640	$518,880
				$23.50 per MWh

The average price of $23.50 per MWh represents an opportunity cost of $1 per MWh because cash market prices averaged $24.50 during the period of the hedge. The producer is comfortable with this because it is within the tolerance for risk that the risk management committee set at the time the positions were opened. Managing a hedge strategy is an evolving process. While hedges serve to stabilize prices, risk management targets can be re-evaluated in future periods as market and financial circumstances change.

Source: New York Mercantile Exchange, *A Guide to Energy Hedging*

Example 8.4: Petroleum Marketer's Long Hedge, Rising and Falling Markets

On September 7, the New York Harbor price for heating oil is 55¢ and the cash market price at the fuel dealer's location is 54¢ a gallon, a 1¢ differential, or basis, between New York Harbor and the retailer's location. The dealer agrees to deliver 168,000 gallons to a commercial customer in December at 70¢ per gallon. On September 7, he buys four December heating oil contracts (42,000 gallons each) at 57¢, the price quoted that day on the Exchange's NYMEX Division, at a total cost of $42,000 \times 4 \times \$0.57 = \$95,760$.

Case 1. Rising Prices

On November 25, the fuel dealer buys 168,000 gallons in the cash market at the prevailing price of 59¢ a gallon, a 1¢ differential to the New York Harbor cash quotation of 60¢, at a cost of $99,120. He sells his four December futures contracts (initially purchased for 57¢) at 60¢ a gallon, the current price on the Exchange, realising $100,800 on the sale, for a futures market profit of $5040 (3¢ a gallon). His cash margin is 11¢ (the difference between his agreed-upon sales price of 70¢ and his cash market acquisition cost of 59¢ for a total of $18,480 ($0.11 per gallon × 168,000 gallons).

	Cash Market	Futures Market
Sept. 7		Buys four December futures contracts for 57¢ per gallon
Nov. 25	Buys 168,000 gallons at 59¢ per gallon	Sells four December heating oil futures at 59¢ per gallon for 60¢ per gallon

We have:

a cash margin of	$18,480 or 11¢/gallon
plus a futures profit of	$5,040 or 3¢/gallon
equals a total margin of	$23,520 or 14¢/gallon

Case 2. Falling Prices

On November 25, the dealer buys 168,000 gallons at his local truck loading rack for 49¢ a gallon, the prevailing price on that day, based on the New York Harbor cash quotation of 50¢ a gallon. He sells his four December futures contracts for 50¢ a gallon, the futures price that day, realising $84,000 on the sale, and experiencing a futures loss of $11,760 (7¢ a gallon).

	Cash Market	Futures Market
Sept. 7		Buys four December heating oil futures at 57¢ per gallon
Nov. 25	Buys 168,000 gallons at 59¢ per gallon	Sells four December heating oil futures at 49¢ per gallon for 50¢ per gallon

We now have:

a cash margin of	$35,280
minus a futures loss of	$11,760 (7¢/gallon)
equals a total margin of	$23,520 (14¢/gallon)

In summary, the fuel retailer guarantees himself a margin of 14¢ a gallon regardless of price moves upwards or down in the market. With the differential between cash and futures stable, as in cases 1 and 2, spot-price changes in either direction are the same for both New York and the marketer's location. As a result, a decline in the futures price, which causes a loss in the futures market, is offset cent-for-cent by the increase in the cash margin.

Source: New York Mercantile Exchange, *A Guide to Energy Hedging*

Speculators, on the other hand, are usually not active in the physical markets as either producers or consumers of the physical commodity. They take no physical commodity position. Their risk appetite is significantly higher than that of the hedger. What attracts the speculator is the potential for profit. In effect, the speculator assumes the hedger's risk and adds liquidity to the market. Markets would die without the active participation of speculators since their view on the market is important for market liquidity.

Physical Delivery

The energy futures markets have an active underlying physical market. Because of this factor, some futures contracts go to contract expiry for physical delivery. It should be remembered that futures contracts should not be used to gain physical supply but only to manage the price risk of that supply. Although generally no more than 2% of energy futures contracts ever go to physical delivery via the exchange, the NYMEX and ICE offer several methods for physical delivery of their expiring futures contracts. The NYMEX physical delivery point for its crude oil contract is Cushing, Oklahoma, for its heating oil and gasoline contracts is New York Harbor, and for natural gas contract is Erath, Louisiana. The ICE's gasoil contract was launched in 1981 and is delivered into the barge market for the Antwerp, Rotterdam, and Amsterdam (ARA) region (barge lots are typically 50,000 to 100,000 tonnes in the physical market). The ICE Brent crude oil contract is the only large energy futures contract that does not go to physical delivery on expiry, going instead to cash settlement.

Companies which do choose to deliver, however, have several options. They can choose standard delivery (as per the specification of the futures contracts laid down in the rule book of the futures exchange) or they can attempt to arrange an ADP. This would normally happen if someone wishes to deliver some energy which is not in keeping with the specifications of the futures contract (so it cannot be delivered via the exchange/clearing house procedure) or two parties are stuck with a position and they just wish to negotiate directly with one another on some cash settlement. In ADP transactions, market participants release both the exchange and their clearing broker member from all liabilities related to the delivery negotiated between parties. Traders and hedgers can also execute an EFP.

Companies using energy futures contracts for hedging purposes are often not interested in making or taking delivery at the specified locations. More often than not, a hedger using futures finds it more economical to make or take delivery of physical energy elsewhere, under terms that differ from those of the futures contract. An EFP provides the mechanism for such transactions and is usually the preferred method of delivery because it provides greater flexibility. EFPs allow companies to choose their trading partners, delivery site, the grade of product to be delivered, and the timing of delivery. The EFP mechanism allows buyers and sellers to execute their physical energy market transaction on the basis of negotiated price. After both parties to an EFP agree to such a transaction, the price at which the EFP is to be cleared is submitted to their futures broker who in turn submits it to the futures exchange which then registers the trade. The price of the futures position created by the EFP can be outside the daily trading range of that futures market. This is the nominal price of the EFP. The EFP parties can then effect the actual physical exchange at a price they negotiate between themselves.

Example 8.5: EFP to initiate a position

On August 7, an oil refiner who wishes to protect a portion of his products inventory wants to sell to protect against falling prices. At the same time, a diesel fuel distributor is concerned about rising prices and looks to buy to protect his forward purchases.

They agree to a price of diesel fuel, net the basis, and register the EFP with the Exchange. Once registered, both parties have instituted futures positions at a price which reflects the exact basis between NYMEX Division heating oil futures and the regional rack price for diesel fuel.

On September 16, the diesel refiner arranges with the distributor for the physical delivery of the fuel. At that time, the refiner and the distributor independently offset their futures positions on the Exchange.

In this example, the long and short hedgers have "swapped" futures obligations (thus terminating their contract obligations on the Exchange before their futures contracts mature) in consideration of their exchange of physical market positions. The transaction occurs at the price, location, and time negotiated by the parties.

In order to engage in an EFP, it is not necessary for both sides to be in the futures market when the EFP is initiated except during EFP-only sessions. A futures market long, for example, might effect an

EFP with a cash market long. The net result of the transaction would be delivery of a commodity to the futures hedger and the assumption by the physical market participant of the hedger's futures market contracts. *Source:* New York Mercantile Exchange, *A Guide to Energy Hedging*

Market Changes: Backwardation and Contango

The shape of the forward price curve has been explored generally in Alexander and Sheedy (2008a), Chapter 7; and Alexander and Sheedy (2008b), Chapter 3. Contango is a market condition where prices are progressively higher in future contract months; this is considered to be the "normal" condition of markets since cost of carry (funding, storage, and the like) is generally positive. Backwardation is a market condition where prices are progressively lower in future contract months. Thus, when the price for a contract month nearer to the present time is higher than the price for a contract further into the future, the market is said to be in backwardation. As explained in Chapter 7, this typically occurs when prices are high because supplies are tight. When markets are in backwardation the strike price for a calendar spread options contract will be positive. When the price curve is in contango, strike prices of calendar spread options contracts will be negative. A negative price is not unusual in spread relationships.

In contango markets, the producer, who is a seller of oil, would seek downside protection by buying puts; an oil buyer would purchase calls. A crude oil producer with excess storage capacity can make money when the price curve is in contango by purchasing the cheaper prompt month and selling the more expensive deferred contract month.

When the markets are in backwardation, however, spare storage capacity is an asset that generates no cash flow. Selling put options on calendar spreads generates cash flow, and having the asset as a backstop enables the oil company to sell the put. Additionally, in a steeply backwardated market, it can be costly to buy back a hedge after it has appreciated in value on its way to becoming the prompt month. Buying calls on the calendar spread can reduce such costs, and can complement the short hedge by allowing for participation in the rising market.

OTC ENERGY DERIVATIVE MARKETS

The previous section explained how energy risk can be managed using exchange-traded instruments, but much of the trading on energy derivatives is based on the OTC contracts.

Nearly all the key terms of an OTC derivatives deal are negotiable, which means that the pricing reference, the payment terms and the volume can all be adjusted to suit the counterparties to the deal. In effect, they are customized transactions. Fortunately, for risk management purposes, the core energy markets like the larger oil, gas and electricity (power) markets have some active and fairly standardized OTC contracts. They are standard both in their floating price reference and in the sort of minimum contract volume that would normally be traded. Brief explanations of some of the most common transaction types are given below, along with illustrations of their application in energy markets:

- *Forward Contracts.* A contract to buy/sell with future delivery. The contract sets the price (or price formula) in advance. For example, an oil refiner may purchase crude oil in the forward market to hedge against possible price rises. See Alexander and Sheedy (2008b), Chapter 3 for a general discussion of forward contracts.

- *Option Contracts.* A contract giving the buyer of the contract the right to buy or sell at a pre-specified price. For example, a gas supplier might buy a put option giving the right to sell gas at a pre-specified future price. In addition, option contracts can be based on the crack spread (the difference between the price of refined products and crude) or on the calendar spread (the difference between prices for different maturities). See Alexander and Sheedy (2008b), Chapter 5 for a general discussion of option contracts.

- *Swaps.* A swap contract provides for the parties to exchange a series of cash flows generated by underlying assets. See Alexander and Sheedy (2008b), Chapter 4 for a general discussion of swap contracts. There is no transfer of any assets or principal amounts. For example, in a simple crude oil swap a refiner and oil producer enter a five-year swap with monthly payments. The refiner pays the producer a fixed price per barrel. The producer pays a variable price which could, for example, be based on the settlement price of a futures contract on the final trading day of the month. The notional amount of the contract is 10,000 barrels. Payments are netted so that a payment of differences only occurs.
  Consider another example where a large consumer of electricity purchases electricity from a local distribution company at variable market prices. He wishes to hedge against increases in electricity prices and can do so by entering a fixed for floating

swap contract with monthly payments. The notional principal for the contract (the swap contract load) is 10 MWh and the swap fixed price is $50 per MWh. If the average spot market price exceeds (is less than) the agreed strike price, then the counterparty (consumer) will pay the consumer (counterparty) the difference. Suppose that the market clearing price for the month is $60 per MWh, then the counterparty pays the consumer $100, being the swap contract load of 10 MWh multiplied by the price difference ($60 – $50 per MWh).

- *Basis Contracts.* A basis contract helps to hedge locational and product differences between exchange-traded standard contracts and the actual exposure of the user. Suppose that a local distribution company needs to purchase gas and decides to hedge in the futures market. The futures contract allows the company to lock in a future Henry Hub price. The actual price paid for gas in the local market may, however, differ from the Henry Hub price. If the local price increases by more than the Henry Hub price, then the company will incur a loss due to basis risk. A basis swap is an OTC contract that fixes the price gap to give the company complete price certainty.

Today regulated futures exchanges have been slow to react to changing markets and unable to launch many successful energy futures contracts due to the success of the OTC energy markets. The effectiveness of the OTC energy markets is most clearly seen in Asia, which overtook Europe as the second largest oil-consuming region in the world several years ago. However, Asia still does not have a liquid and internationally recognized futures exchange for energy markets. This is because its needs for energy-related derivatives contracts seem to be well served by the established OTC market, for which Singapore is the key trading hub.

In Asia, the vast majority of physical transactions and OTC swaps are priced using the industry-recognized publication Platts, which is a division of McGraw-Hill. Platts publishes a daily assessment of the price of any given crude oil or oil product in any given location, and also publishes an assessment of the forward curve. These daily value assessments are based on the aggregated bids and offers from many brokers and dealers around the world during a specified time window for each geographic region— usually towards the end of each business day in each major time zone: Asia (Singapore), Europe (London), USA (New York, and then the West Coast).

Price swaps are usually priced off the monthly average of these Platts assessments and lead to a monthly financial payment equivalent to the difference between the traded fixed price and the calculated average floating price multiplied by the contractual monthly quantity. Only the difference is paid and there is no exchange of physical energy, hence no delivery risk.

The futures exchanges have reacted to the OTC markets which tend to be longer-term in nature by launching clearing house platforms. By clearing these OTC contracts on an established futures exchange which is government-regulated, the contracts become quasi-futures contracts. OTC clearing for NYMEX through Clearport and the ICE through the London Clearing House have created more liquidity for the exchanges. The structure of the energy derivatives markets has been that futures contracts are very liquid and traded in the front months and the deeper OTC markets are used for longer-term hedging needs. By linking OTC to exchange-traded through clearing, the markets now show many more points of trade and eliminate performance risk since the exchange clears for both buyer and seller, and assumes counterparty risk. Exchange members guarantee performance and are overseen by government regulatory agencies. The effect is that the core OTC energy derivatives are becoming more and more indistinguishable from futures trades, and there has been increasing convergence between OTC and futures contracts.

The Singapore Market

The Singapore market is the trading hub of Asia and is oriented to cargo size shipments, so individual transactions, sometimes referred to as "clips" are quite large compared to an ICE Brent futures contract which is a minimum trade of 1,000 barrels. Almost everything in Singapore market is sold in 50,000 barrel clips and the typical cargo size is 150,000 barrels; high sulfur fuel oil used for ships bunkering is the only exception. To put this into perspective in terms of growth, in 1998 the Singapore swaps market was estimated to be around 150 million barrels per month. There is an active OTC swaps broking community in Singapore (there are around 10 active OTC broking companies there) which adds market liquidity by assisting price discovery in the market and by developing two-way markets for buyers and sellers of oil. Typically most Asian oil products and related crude oils can be traded up to 18 months forward, with most of the liquidity in 1–12 months forward markets. Beyond two years forward, the number of participants quoting prices become more limited (mainly to large bank traders and major international oil companies). The key products traded are:

- Singapore gasoil 0.5%
- Singapore jet fuel (kero)
- Regrade—the spread between Singapore gasoil and Singapore jet fuel
- 180 CST fuel oil
- 380 CST fuel oil
- Naphtha
- Tapis crude oil—Malaysian exported crude oil
- Dubai/Oman crude oil—Middle East marker crude, meaning many Asian refiners are buying crude oil as feedstocks for their refineries on a Dubai/Oman pricing basis

The European Energy Markets

Europe has a very active and well-developed OTC oil market. Unless otherwise specified by traders or brokers, a quote on European-based swaps will normally price against the mean average of Platts high/low assessment of the relevant European physical market. Fixed for floating swaps and caps and collar options will normally be available in the following markets:

- Premium unleaded barge f.o.b. ARA
- Premium unleaded crack swap North West Europe (NWE)
- Naphtha c.i.f. NWE
- Naphtha crack NWE
- Jet diff c.i.f. NWE
- Gasoil crack swap NWE
- Gasoil 0.2% cargo c.i.f. NWE
- Gasoil 0.2% barge f.o.b. ARA
- EN590 cargo c.i.f. NWE
- Gasoil 0.2% cargo f.o.b. Mediterranean (MED)
- Fuel oil 1% cargo f.o.b. NWE
- Fuel oil 3.5% Barge f.o.b. ARA

- Fuel oil 3.5% cargo f.o.b. MED
- LPG propane c.i.f. ARA large
- Brent/Dubai swaps
- West Texas Intermediate (WTI) crude oil versus Brent crude swaps

More exotic one-off derivative structures are normally available, given the higher number of participants in the European oil swaps market and the higher liquidity in the plain vanilla market. Key OTC products include:

- Rotterdam gasoil 0.2% sulfur barges
- Jet fuel, NWE cargoes c.i.f. basis
- Jet fuel, Rotterdam barges f.o.b.
- Gasoil ICE futures look-alike swap
- Fuel oil 1% NWE cargoes c.i.f. basis
- Fuel oil 1% NWE cargoes f.o.b. basis
- Fuel oil 3.5% Rotterdam barges f.o.b. basis
- Fuel oil MED 3.5% cargoes f.o.b. basis
- Dated Brent related swap (dated Brent is spot North Sea oil)
- Brent ICE futures look-alike swap
- Brent bullet swap
- Dubai crude oil swap trade out of London (as well as Singapore)
- EN590 grade gasoil NWE cargoes c.i.f. basis
- EN590 grade gasoil MED cargoes
- Gasoline—Rotterdam Eurograde barges
- Naphtha NWE c.i.f. cargo swap
- European natural gas firm physical, fixed price
- European natural gas firm physical, fixed price, spread Zeebrugge versus National Balancing Point
- UK National Balancing Point indexed OTC Swaps basis NBP97 contract
- LPG Mid East/North Africa/Asia—Saudi CP pricing used as index for OTC swaps
- LNG with Crude related pricing formula—proxy hedging in crude futures/related OTC derivatives markets

The North American Markets

The most developed and liquid OTC energy derivatives market is in North America. Oil futures trading began in 1978 and the price swap was invented by Chase in 1986. The OTC price swaps markets have not been regulated since the July 1989 regulatory ruling by the US Commodity Futures Trading Commission that the commission would not regulate commodity swaps. This action has been reinforced by the Commodity Futures Modernization Act of 2000.

Price swaps are active for crude oil and petroleum products, natural gas, electricity, coal, and emissions. There are very sophisticated OTC options products offered as well. The demise of Enron and merchant energy did not affect the oil markets as much as the gas and power markets in North America, since Enron and other merchant power market makers were substantial financial players in gas and electricity trading on both the futures exchanges and the larger OTC markets. They were not substantial players in world oil markets. Investment banks and hedge funds are increasingly stepping in to make up for the loss of trading liquidity in natural gas and power.

Unless otherwise specified by traders or brokers, a quote on a USA-based price swap will normally price against the mean average of Platts high/low assessment of the relevant American physical market. Fixed for floating swaps and caps and collar options will normally be available in the following markets:

- Nymex light sweet crude oil related 1st line futures look-alike swap
- Nymex light sweet crude oil related bullet swap
- Nymex heating oil futures related bullet swap
- Nymex heating oil futures related 1st line futures look-alike swap
- Nymex gasoline futures related 1st line futures look-alike swap
- Nymex gasoline related bullet swap
- New York Harbor #2 heating oil barges
- 1% fuel oil New York Harbor c.i.f. cargo basis
- 3% US Gulf Coast cargo
- US Gulf Coast gasoline 87
- New York Harbor reformulated RFG gasoline 87 barges
- New York Harbor gasoline 87 barges

- Canadian natural gas firm physical, fixed price
- Canadian natural gas firm physical, Canadian gas price reporter
- Natural gas, fixed for float (inside FERC)
- Natural gas, fixed for float (NGI)

The density of the North American OTC energy derivatives market is illustrated by the fact that there have been over 500 different locations for trading for natural gas and electricity on the North American continent. The oil markets are even more complex as there are hundreds of grades of gasoline, for example. The point is that the OTC markets have customized contracts to manage energy price risk for many more commodities than are listed on exchanges. The exchange response has been to clear OTC contracts through their clearing houses. These efforts have been quite successful since their launch in 2002. Nymex Clearport has grown to be the dominant growth vehicle for NYMEX and now offers over 300 contracts in the OTC markets for clearing.

EMERGING ENERGY MARKETS

There are several new emerging markets in the energy world. These include coal, weather derivatives, and environmental financial or "green trading" markets.

Coal Trading

Most electric power in the world is still coal-fired, but risk management for coal is still beginning. The reason is that most coal was formerly priced on long-term contracts. The development of a spot market for coal in recent years has been a slow process but the recent active buying by China, and US electricity deregulation, have brought it into global commodity markets with greater price volatility. China's position and recent structural changes in its production profile (lots of small mines closures, etc.) have been the key to global supply and demand. The USA has more high-quality coal than any other country, with nearly 30% of the world's bituminous and anthracite coal reserves and 250 years of supply. Australia, Indonesia, and Columbia are other high-quality coal exporters. Only China produces more bituminous coal than the USA, but almost all of its production is consumed domestically. US coal exports, chiefly central Appalachian bituminous, make up 16% of the world export market and are an important factor in world coal prices. The importance of coal can be seen from the fact that coal-fired power stations still account for approximately 55% of total electricity output in the USA. Coal is transported by rail or barge. Railroads carry more than half of the coal mined in the USA, often hauling the coal in unit trains. The US inland waterway system is the other major mode for coal transportation, especially along the Ohio and Mississippi rivers.

The impact on the environment of coal use is a serious issue. Any effort to curtail atmospheric emissions can be expected to involve reduced coal use, even though the amount of air pollution produced by coal burning has been greatly diminished during the past 30 years due to air quality considerations. Therefore, more stringent environmental regulations have created many new arbitrage opportunities between coal and emissions.

Coal is still mainly traded in the OTC market, for both the US coal mining and electric power industries. The NYMEX coal futures contract has, however, been gaining liquidity in recent years. The OTC coal markets trade the NYMEX futures contract specification. Today, many financial houses and commodity traders such as Cargill, EdF, Morgan Stanley, and Goldman Sachs trade coal markets and are making markets in coal derivatives. There are also very well established OTC brokers such as TFS, GFI, Spectron, Evolution Markets, and Natsource. More recently several hedge funds have also become active in coal trading. For the international coal trading or consuming market, the OTC market dominates coal pricing and hedging.

Coal producers can sell future production contracts to lock in a specific sales price for a specific volume of the coal they intend to produce in coming months. Electric utilities can buy coal futures to hedge against rising prices for their baseload fuel. Power marketers, who have exposure on both the generating and delivery sides of the electricity market, can hedge with coal futures to mitigate their generation price risk, and hedge with electricity futures to control their delivery price risk. Non-utility industrial coal users, such as steel mills, can use futures to lock in their own coal supply costs. International coal trading companies can use futures to hedge their export or import prices. Power generating companies that use both coal and natural gas to produce electricity can use coal futures in conjunction with the NYMEX Henry Hub natural gas futures to offset seasonal cost variations and to take advantage of the "spark spread"— the differential between the cost of the two fuels and the relative value of the electricity generated by each of the two fuels.

For the coal derivatives market to develop, it is important that there is a solid critical base of consumers, producers and financial traders. The good news is that new large entrants on both the consumer and trading sides have entered the market. Also, more financial traders have been looking to join the market. The key is that pricing indices are needed for coal derivatives trading due to the lack of viable futures contracts. In Europe, it is the traditional tonnage delivered into the ARA region. While the majority of the coal delivered into ARA is shipped from South Africa, it also includes tonnage (depending on market conditions) from the USA and Columbia.

Price indexes are widely used in energy derivatives trading and typically started with price reporters for trade publications. Later brokers starting offering their quotes based on their deal flow and now many price quotes are on the internet. The key is that for emerging markets price indices provide price transparency which stimulates more trading. It began in oil trading and now is used for gas, power and coal. In coal trading, there have been index deals up to four years forward. The majority of participants actively trade up to two years forward in the cash-settled coal swaps (based on ISDA agreements). The standard documentation used in energy market settlement for the OTC markets is provided by ISDA, the International Swaps Dealers Association.

Weather Derivatives

The market for weather derivatives dates back to 1997. Weather derivatives began as more hype than a successful fungible commodity, but that changed in 2005. In 2005–2006, the total volume of weather trades reached $45.2 billion according to the Weather Risk Management Association (WRMA, see www.wrma.org). There are now many liquid weather futures contracts on the Chicago Mercantile Exchange (CME) where open interest, a good indicator of contract success, exploded 600% in 2005. That success continues as the global weather derivatives markets are expanding and getting some impetus from concerns on climate change risk management. Weather futures contracts on the CME are now very active and, according to the exchange, totalled $19 billion trading for the year ended March 31, 2007. This was a 100-fold increase over the past four years.

While to a great degree weather remains a reinsurance financial product, it has successfully become a commodity trading market since

2005. There are now seven weather hedge funds as well as larger multi-strategy hedge funds such as D.E. Shaw and Tudor Investments participating in the market. While the reinsurance industry created crop reinsurance products for farmers based on weather over two decades ago, weather futures contracts trade for 18 cities in the USA, nine in Europe and two in Asia on the CME. These contracts are correlated to heating and cooling degree days (HDD and CDD).

Weather risk embraces a wide variety of natural phenomena, but if the focus is limited to temperature risk, the marketplace starts to look almost as standardized as any commodity futures market. In fact, the 2002 survey conducted for the WRMA shows that weather derivatives referenced against temperature accounted for over 80% of the total volume. (i.e. heating degree days (HDD)/cooling degree days (CDD)). Temperature-related weather derivatives help people hedge or trade the temperature at certain agreed geographical points around the world. Demand for weather risk derivatives indexed against temperature references is most probably driven by energy producers and users. The link between the two markets arises since energy demand varies with fluctuations in temperature. The most prevalent use of weather derivatives has been to hedge uncertainty in volumetric demand for energy, due to temperature fluctuations. For this purpose, deals are often referenced to the number of heating (or cooling) degree days in a period. This measures the daily deviation from a reference temperature (e.g. 18°C), and sums the negative (for HDDs) or positive (CDDs) deviations over the period. Rainfall and even wind speed are other types of weather derivatives contracts. Rising concerns over managing climate change risk will add more liquidity for weather derivatives trading as players will want to spread the volatility of weather among more financial market players.

Green Trading

The Kyoto Protocol of 1997 called for the trading of emission reductions as a way of leveling out the cost of reducing greenhouse gases. The most important emission for green trading is carbon dioxide, but other emissions include methane and nitrous oxide. Emission reduction credits (of which carbon credits are the most common) can be earned in several ways: upgrading power-generating equipment so that there are fewer emissions per kilowatt-hour generated, planting trees or reducing soil erosion so that more carbon is sequestered or absorbed, and producing electricity using renewable sources such as solar panels and wind turbines. Once carbon credits are earned, they can be sold to other companies. The credit is subtracted from the recipient party's total output of emissions, so that the recipient can meet a voluntary or legislative emissions target. So carbon credits generated in Germany could be used to meet emissions targets in Australia. Some countries/industries are more efficient at producing emission reduction credits and they can exploit their comparative advantage through green trading. Since greenhouse gases released into the atmosphere can wander globally, the source of the emission credits is not important.

Kyoto became effective in February 2005 and it aims to reduce global greenhouse gases to 5.2% below 1990 levels by 2012. 172 countries will be participating in this market. The major exceptions are the United States and Australia which both have voluntary markets, although states in the North-eastern USA and California are implementing their own mandatory emissions reductions in 2009 and 2012 respectively. Under Kyoto, emissions trading is one means to reduce greenhouse gases. Other emissions reductions will be met through Kyoto's Clean Development Mechanism (CDM) and Joint Implementation (JI) plans. Both CDM and JI are project based which means that investment in clean energy projects will generate credits in the developing world that can be sold to the developed world to comply with Kyoto emissions reductions targets. It is estimated that such projects will only produce half of the required Kyoto reductions by 2012.

Simultaneously to the development of the Kyoto Protocol market, the EU Emissions Trading Scheme (ETS) was launched on January 1, 2005, and impacts 12,000 facilities in the EU to reduce its carbon footprint by 2012 as well. EU mandates are more aggressive than Kyoto. In 2008, the second phase of the EU ETS begins.

Green trading encompasses the convergence of the capital markets and the environment. It is the first global market that we have seen since crude oil trading and presents many opportunities for both the energy industry and financial institutions. The energy industry, the world's leading emissions polluter, will be the leading supplier of environmental solutions because it is good business. Today, the industry is at a turning point on global warming as carbon intensity continues to grow whilst time to stabilize carbon dioxide (currently 380 parts per million) and other greenhouse gas emissions is limited. The carbon emissions footprint of the major oil companies is evidenced by their global oil and gas production, refining and transportation, and their involvement in the power industry continues to expand. Environmental issues are becoming corporate financial issues. Greater financial disclosure of corporate environmental risks, including climate change, has raised the issue of environment as a corporate fiduciary responsibility. Increasingly, environmental and financial performance of companies is intertwined, and these new financial risks and liabilities will prompt change and market creation.

Environmental financial markets today are a $40 billion market which pales in insignificance compared to a $3 trillion energy derivatives market, but the growth trajectory suggests that green trading markets today should be compared with the oil markets of 1978. However, this time, maturation will be global and simultaneous as carbon trading regimes take root in the EU, Asia, Australia, and North America. It is estimated that emissions trading will become a $3 trillion market over the next 20 years. The global energy industry will be the primary supplier of liquidity to this market followed by the agricultural industry. Cross-commodity arbitrage opportunities are likely as oil, gas, coal, and power, like weather derivatives, have environmental dimensions.

As almost all environmental financial contracts such as those in sulfur dioxide and carbon dioxide are traded on the OTC markets, there is an opportunity for exchanges such ICE and NYMEX to offer OTC clearing, which would effectively make them quasi-futures contracts with regulatory oversight. This could help to make them more acceptable to risk managers. The ICE recognized this opportunity in April 2004 and has linked its platform to both the Chicago Climate Exchange (www.chicago-climateex.com) and the European Climate Exchange.

The green trading markets will encompass not only emissions trading but renewable energy credit trading. Renewable energy such as wind, solar, hydropower, tidal energy, and biomass each create carbon credits that can be used to reduce pollution. This market is more developed in the USA at the present time. Finally, the low hanging fruit of environmental financial markets is energy efficiency. Since energy prices are now significantly higher than before, there are now more incentives to invest in both clean technology and energy efficiency to reduce pollution. These markets are very immature but developing behind carbon and renewable energy markets, and one day will be fungible commodity markets. Today, we are in the beginning of a market shift to clean energy caused by the emergence of global environmental standards to reduce emissions. These markets are illiquid and full of risk, but offer risk managers incredible opportunities to apply financial engineering techniques to environmental remediation. Going green will be good for business and better for energy trading markets as a facilitator to achieve that goal.

Freight-Rate Swaps

Freight is an integral part of the global energy business, either directly or indirectly, as the cost of shipping oil or gas around the world affects power prices in some way. The biggest and in the past the least hedgeable risk in an international oil transaction, for example, has been the freight-rate movements. Tanker freight swaps are a beneficial risk management tool for the energy industry because, in the past, companies sometimes had unhedgeable freight exposure on both physical and paper positions. The main participants in this market are petroleum products traders and shipping charterers, as well as tanker owners and banks. Trading volume can be tailored to users' needs, and the most commonly traded lot is 10,000 tonnes per contract month. Most frequently talked tenures for these swaps are 2–3 months in the future, while bid/offer quotations are usually available for up to 6 months in the future. Today, there are four shipping hedge funds that participate in the freight derivatives market.

Derivative Forward Price Curves

A very recent development has been the introduction, by a few specialist firms, of independent assessments of the forward curves for an increasing number of global energy derivatives markets. This enables both bankers and end users to have a trusted third-party forward curve for day-to-day valuation and accounting purposes. The Enron scandal of 2001 rocked many shareholders' confidence in companies' use of energy derivatives as well as their pricing and accounting as Enron "tilted" the curve (Enron fraudulently reconfigured their forward price curves to meet quarterly financial targets). Therefore, the opportunity to utilize third-party market assessments of forward curves is a very positive step towards ensuring that a reasonable value is attached to derivatives. Indeed, under the new accounting regimes of FAS133 and international accounting standards, derivatives need to be revalued on a regular basis, even if they are employed by an end user such as a power producer or airline.

THE FUTURE OF ENERGY TRADING

Re-emergence of Speculative Trading?

Enron and the merchant power sector in 2001–2003 depended on highly leveraged trading to boost paper profits. Since their demise much of the energy industry has returned to the relative safety of trading around assets and marketing activities, avoiding more speculative trading. However, energy markets have been characterized by increasing prices and high volatilities across all energy commodities in recent years. That price volatility has been very attractive for speculator traders at investment banks and now hedge funds.

As a result of geopolitical issues, the relative weakness of the US dollar, and other supply/demand factors, higher oil prices are sustainable with high price volatilities set to be the norm. The future for North American natural gas is similar as supply and production declines have also resulted in higher sustainable prices and increased price volatilities. These sustainable higher oil and gas prices are evidenced by the lack of investment in energy infrastructure in both the upstream and downstream segments of the industry, the higher costs of finding and developing new energy resources, lack of conservation effects and the complacency of energy companies to make substantial profits without taking on new financial risks. Meanwhile, robust demand for coal is also apparent with over 90 new coal plants in line for construction in the USA as the attraction of natural gas as a generation fuel recedes. Electric power is also showing price volatility.

It is a combination of this price volatility and available trading talent that is creating the opportunity for hedge funds. With over 580 energy hedge funds already playing or set to play in energy commodities, these funds are primed to bring more risk capital to bear in energy markets. They also bring sophistication, liquidity, the risk culture, and trading acumen to bear on energy markets and have access to readily available experienced trading resources that were let go by the mega-merchants. While new hedge funds are being created specifically for energy trading, existing larger hedge funds are also planning to enter energy markets.

Electronic Energy Trading

The electronic energy solution is upon us. The willingness to embrace the more flexible OTC market at the expense of more efficient exchange mechanisms suggests that an open electronic platform combined with the flexibility of the OTC market is the way forward. The trading platform of the future must be able to match identical bids and offers as well as be flexible enough to negotiate deals that cannot easily be matched. Electronic trading is popular with hedge funds and other market participants who value the anonymity it confers.

While NYMEX has an electronic platform called ACCESS that trades after trading hours on the floor are completed, there is a larger internet platform that is the chief competitor to NYMEX. The ICE was launched in August 2000 and does not take title or any participatory interest in any transactions on the exchange. In a sense, the exchange provides the arena and defines the rules. The actual playing of the game is left entirely to the users of the exchange. It is a level playing field for all, without favouritism or control by a chosen few, open to any user.

In April 2005, ICE closed its trading floor in London which has forced all trading to cyberspace. Today, the exchange lists over 800 unique products covering a variety of commodities, structures, and settlement terms including:

- oil, natural gas, electric power, precious metals, emissions, and weather;
- physical delivery and financial cash settlement;
- forwards, swaps, options, spreads, differentials, complex derivatives.

The ICE is primarily a matching system. It allows credit and risk managers from all registered companies to specify and pre-clear credit for trading with each other. This is done using the Counterparty Credit Facility which can open or close credit with each registered user at any time, set tenor limits and set daily dollar limits for trades with each user. In addition to bilateral credit, the ICE supports clearing services for some major products, supported by the London Clearing House, and is now establishing its own credit support.

NYMEX has responded to this competition by creating a strategic alliance with CME's Globex, the world's largest financial futures trading system. The impact has been huge. NYMEX floor trading is now less than 20% of trading volumes and internet trading has expanded globally.

Trading in Asian Markets

Energy trading and the use of energy risk management tools have been slow to evolve in Asian energy trading. This has been primarily due to the scarcity of natural resources in the region and its focus on security of supply. Asian energy markets are still oriented to security of supply issues over financial risk management and are just beginning their ascendancy into much more mature financial markets; consequently, there are no viable energy futures contracts in Asia as most trade is bilateral and off exchange. Risks in energy markets are pervasive today. This is largely due to deregulation, globalization, and privatization trends in many countries, coupled with robust energy demand growth. Borrowing heavily from the institutional memory of well-developed New York and London capital markets, energy trading and risk management are on an upward trajectory in Asia fuelled by growing oil and gas dependencies and the need for more electric power.

While short-term physical oil trading has always existed in most Asian countries, the energy complex is now broadening to include gas, power, petrochemical, coal, and weather risk management. Lurking on the horizon is emissions trading to reduce plant emissions and reduce greenhouse gas emissions. Asia is now primed to embrace the active use of energy derivatives and much more sophisticated trading techniques and financial engineering.

Today, Asia is ripe for fundamental change in its trading and risk profile, with the region experiencing rapid economic growth fuelling increased needs for crude oil and refined products supply. The largest consumer in the region, China, is currently the world's second largest oil consumer, behind the USA, and has recently surpassed Japan. Chinese oil consumption will reach some 10.9 million barrels per day by 2025, with net imports of 7.5 million barrels per day, in order to support its domestic growth, giving it a major role in the world oil market. This growth in demand is driving rapidly increasing supply chain complexity as new trading patterns develop. Growth in the region, and in China specifically, is leading to the development of new supply markets in both the Middle East and Russia and in new infrastructure construction from the point of supply to the refinery and beyond. Since most shipments are undertaken by water, the new infrastructure includes tankers, terminals, storage facilities, refineries, and overland distribution systems.

While trading remains largely based on term OTC contracts without a standard regional marker for price transparency, it is this supply chain complexity that will drive costs and risk in the medium term, both in China and the Asia Pacific region generally. The risks and costs involved are becoming too great to rely on the in-house developed or spreadsheet-based energy trading. Thus, transaction and risk management systems are used more today by many of the region's major energy companies. The transition in the market from monopoly to competitive markets has funda- mentally changed how utilities and others buy and sell electricity. It is now the beginning of the transition to competitive markets and trading in Asia Pacific. Asia is gradually moving more aggressively into the energy trad- ing world particularly with the new Dubai Mercantile Exchange launch- ing of energy contracts in 2007.

CONCLUSIONS

Twenty-nine years after the first successful oil futures contract we are now seeing the development of a true multi-commodity market that encom- passes oil, gas, power, coal, freight rates, weather, and green trading. Energy commodity trading is evolving into many areas of the energy complex and extending into emerging markets such coal, emissions, and weather trading. Convergence (a term often much overused) is actually now upon us as multi-commodity arbitrage is the watchword of today's energy trader. High price volatility, the extra liquidity provided by finan- cial institutions, and a greater risk appetite are three major factors that make the present time the real dawn of energy trading. Energy risk man- agement has become not only a fiduciary responsibility but also a core competency of energy companies. Broader penetration into the emerging markets of the developing world, and particularly Asia, shows that there are no barriers to entry in trading on the internet. The true financialization of the energy markets is upon us.

The extension of energy trading expertise for natural gas began in North America in the early 1990s and spread to Europe in the late 1990s. A global gas market is now emerging due to the emergence of LNG as a commodity market. Both physical and financial markets for electric power are now established in North America, Europe, and Australia, and are beginning in Asia. Since 1995 there has been an active emissions market for sulfur dioxide in North America, and this environmental financial market has proved to be the template for global trading of carbon dioxide which is now accelerating rapidly. A true financial market for energy trading is emerging globally.

While the oil and gas industry has been gradually using energy risk management tools to manage its financial risk over the past two decades, the consistently high price volatility of the past few years in oil, gas, and power is accelerating industry's adoption of both financial instruments and internet energy trading. While liquidity on the internet today still remains low, it is the vehicle for global commodity trading and will be a tool for establishing trading throughout those areas of the world that have no liquid energy contracts, particularly in Asia. The costs are now lower and the security is more reliable. Internet trading will force the migration of the energy exchanges to the web for the paper trading of oil, gas, and power. Moreover, the other industry trends of market consolidation, market liberalization, globalization, and privatization are creating greater risks to be managed proactively. The medium for that risk management will be the internet.

Commoditization has been accelerating due to the financial wherewithal and risk capital of investment banks, multinational energy companies and now the hedge funds. The good news is that energy markets need more players to provide and develop fungible financial products and provide liquidity. The key message for risk managers is that there is a greater need for proactive energy risk management than ever before. Energy continues to be a risky business!

REFERENCES

Alexander, C and Sheedy, E (2008a) *The Professional Risk Managers' Guide to Finance Theory* (New York: McGraw-Hill).
Alexander, C and Sheedy, E (2008b) *The Professional Risk Managers' Guide to Financial Instruments* (New York: McGraw-Hill).

NOTES

1. Data for 2005, Energy Information Administration
2. The spot market is a commodity market for sale and delivery of energy. Spot markets exist for oil, natural gas, electricity, and coal. "Price discovery" refers to the process of determination of market prices through the interactions of buyers and sellers in the marketplace.
3. Pennsylvania Jersey Maryland Interconnection.
4. New York Independent System Operator.

INDEX

add-on interest, Eurocurrency market, 39
Alternative Investment Market, 100
arbitrage
    commodities markets, 182–4
    covered interest arbitrage, 90–1
    no-arbitrage condition, 182–4
Asian markets, energy markets, 238–9
asset-backed securities, 26
auction process, futures markets, 149–52
automated trading systems, liquidity, 9–10

back office, foreign exchange market, 94
backwardation
    commodities markets, 177–84
    energy markets, 222
    forwards markets, 177–84
    futures markets, 177–84
    reasons for, 180–2
balance of payments, exchange rates, 83–4
bankers' acceptances (BAs), money market
    securities, 43–4
banks
    bond markets, 51–2
    CBs, 85–6
    corporate bond market, 65–6
    credit facilities (lines), 34–5
    exchange rates, 85–6
    foreign exchange market, 76–7,, 78
    interbank market, 76–7
    investment, 51–2
    loans and deposits, 33–5
    retail, 51
    underwriting a new issue, 66
BAs *see* bankers' acceptances
basis contracts, energy markets, 224
best efforts, futures contracts, 137
bid-offer spread, stock markets, 116
bid price, bond markets, 53
bond markets, 49–74
    banks, 51–2
    bid price, 53
    bond types, 53–63
    bonds by issuers, 53–63,, 73

capital market, 63
corporate bond market, 65–6
corporate bonds, 60–2
credit risk, 69–73
dealers, 53
defaults, 69–73
Eurobonds (international bonds), 62–3
Government bond market, 64–5
government bonds, 54–8
IDBs, 53
institutional investors, 52
intermediaries, 51–2,, 73
international bonds (Eurobonds), 62–3
investment banks, 51–2
investors, 73
issuers, 53–63,, 73
long-term institutional investors, 52
market conventions, 69,, 70
market makers, 53
market making, 51–2
market professionals, 52–3
markets, 63–9
mixed horizon institutional investors, 52
money market, 63
municipal bonds, 59–60
offer price, 53
origination, 52
players, 51–3
primary market, 63
private offer, 63
proprietary traders, 53
public offer, 63
regulators, 63–4
retail banks, 51
secondary market, 63
short-term institutional investors, 52
size, 50–1
traders, 53
US agency bonds, 59
brokerage
    commodities markets, 169–70
    and dealing, 24–5
    electronic brokering systems, 79
    foreign exchange, 78–9

brokerage *(continued)*
  retail/wholesale, 23–5
  vs trading, 169–70
businesses
  deposits from, 33–4
  loans to, 34–5
buying on margin, stock markets, 117–19

calendar spreads, speculators, 162
call features, money markets, 33
call options, futures contracts, 144
call provision, corporate bonds, 61–2
capital accounts, common stock characteristics,
  102–3
capital market, bond markets, 63
cash market, energy markets, 208
CBOE *see* Chicago Board Options Exchange
CBs *see* central banks
CDOs *see* collateralized debt obligations
central banks (CBs)
  exchange rates, 85–6
  moral suasion, 85–6
certificates of deposit, money market
  securities, 45
Chicago Board Options Exchange (CBOE),
  stock markets, 121–3
CIF *see* cost, insurance and freight
clearing associations, futures markets, 132,,
  152–3
coal trading, energy markets, 229–31
collateralized debt obligations (CDOs), 26–8
commercial paper, money market securities,
  42–3
commissions, stock markets, 115–17
commodities markets, 167–201
  arbitrage, 182–4
  backwardation, 177–84
  brokerage, 169–70
  characteristics of commodities, 168
  contango, 177–84
  corners, 184–7
  delivery, 170–1
  exchange limits, 187,, 188
  forwards markets, 169–70
  futures markets, 169–70
  gold, 173–7
  gold as reserve asset, 175–7
  grains and oilseeds, 168
  hedging, 173
  historical experience, 184–7

Hunt brothers, 185–7
Hutchingson, Benjamin, 184
liquidity, 171–4
livestock, 168
Lyon, John, 185
metals, 168,, 173–7,, 187–96
no-arbitrage condition, 182–4
price drivers, 197
regulation, 184–7
returns distributions, 196–7
risk decomposition, 187–96
risk management, 187–96
settlement, 170–1
short squeezes, 184–7
silver squeeze, 185–7
softs, 168
spot commodity markets, 169–70
spot-forward pricing relationships,
  177–84
squeezes, 184–7
structure, 167–201
traders, 169–70
types, 169–70
types of commodities, 168
value-at-risk (VaR), 187–96
wheat squeezes, 184,, 185
commodity derivatives, global markets, 8
commodity futures, futures contracts, 125
commodity product spreads,
  speculators, 163
common stock characteristics
  capital accounts, 102–3
  dividends, 103–4
  equity price data, 105
  equity valuation, 107–8
  limited liability, 102–3
  liquidation, 101–2
  market capitalization, 105–6
  preference shares, 104–5
  share premium, 102–3
  shareholders' rights, 103–4
  stock markets, 101–8
comparison/confirmation, post-trade processing,
  21–3
contango
  commodities markets, 177–84
  energy markets, 222
  forwards markets, 177–84
  futures markets, 177–84
'continuous', interbank market, 77
contract features, energy markets, 210–14

convergence
    energy markets, 239
    financial exchanges/OTC markets, 17–21
    technological change, 17–21
corners, commodities markets, 184–7
corporate actions, stock markets, 122
corporate bond market
    banks, 65–6
    bond markets, 65–6
    sectors, 65
    underwriting a new issue, 66
corporate bonds
    bond markets, 60–2
    call provision, 61–2
    credit risk, 69–73
    example, 62
    release-of-property clause, 61
    sinking funds, 60–1
    substitution-of-property clause, 61
cost, insurance and freight (CIF), delivery, 171
counterparty risk, financial exchanges, 16–17
country characteristics, government bonds, 54–8
country yield curves, government bonds, 55–8
covered interest arbitrage, foreign exchange
    market, 90–1
covered interest differential, foreign exchange
    market, 90
credit derivatives market, 28
credit facilities (lines), 34–5
credit risk
    bond markets, 69–73
    corporate bonds, 69–73
    money market securities, 41
    municipal bonds, 72–3
    Treasury bills, 72
cross rates, exchange-rate quotations, 81–2
cross trades, exchange-rate quotations, 81–2
currency derivatives, global markets, 8
currency swap rates, foreign exchange market,
    88–9

daily trading limits, futures markets, 130–2
day traders, speculators, 160–1
dealers, bond markets, 53
dealing, and brokerage, 24–5
'decentralized', interbank market, 76–7
delivery
    CIF, 171
    commodities markets, 170–1
    EFP, 171

energy markets, 220–2
ex store, 170
FAS, 171
FOB, 170–1
futures contracts, 135–7
in store, 170
demand deposits, 33
deposits
    from businesses, 33–4
    demand deposits, 33
    fixed-term deposits, 34
    notice deposits, 33–4
deposits and loans
    banks, 33–5
    Eurocurrency market, 36–40
    Eurodollar market, 36–40
    international markets, 36–40
    money markets, 33–40
derivative forward price curves, energy
    markets, 235
derivatives
    commodity derivatives, 8
    credit derivatives market, 28
    currency derivatives, 8
    energy markets, 222–9,, 231–2
    equity derivatives, 7–8
    fixed-income derivatives, 7–8,, 13
    forward-based derivatives, 126–8
    OTC derivatives, 6,, 222–9
    stock markets, 121–3
    weather derivatives, 231–2
direct dealing, exchange-rate quotations, 78
dividends
    common stock characteristics, 103–4
    stock markets, 122
'double auction', interbank market, 77
drivers, liquidity, 9–13

ECNs *see* electronic communications
    networks
EFP *see* exchange for futures or physicals
electric power, energy markets, 204–5
electronic brokering systems, exchange-rate
    quotations, 79
electronic communications networks (ECNs),
    technological change, 19–21
electronic energy trading, energy markets,
    236–7
emerging energy markets, 229–35
employment level, exchange rates, 83

energy markets, 203–40
  Asian markets, 238–9
  backwardation, 222
  basis contracts, 224
  cash market, 208
  coal trading, 229–31
  contango, 222
  contract features, 210–14
  convergence, 239
  delivery, 220–2
  derivative forward price curves, 235
  derivatives, 222–9,, 231–2
  electric power, 204–5
  electronic energy trading, 236–7
  emerging, 229–35
  Enron, 235
  European markets, 226–7
  financial exchanges, 209–10
  forward contracts, 223
  freight-rate swaps, 235
  future, energy trading, 236–9
  futures markets, 208–9
  green trading, 232–5
  hedging, 214–20
  Kyoto protocol, 232–3
  market overview, 204–22
  option contracts, 223
  options, 212–14
  OTC derivatives, 222–9
  physical delivery, 220–2
  Platts, 224–5
  products, 205–6
  risk, 206–7
  Singapore market, 225–6
  speculative trading, 236
  swaps, 223–4, 235
  US markets, 228–9
  weather derivatives, 231–2
Enron, energy markets, 235
equity derivatives, global markets, 7–8
equity price data, common stock
  characteristics, 105
equity valuation, common stock characteristics,
  107–8
EUREX, 7–8, 21–2, 149
  liquidity, 10
  technological change, 19
euro bonds, vs Eurobonds (international
  bonds), 62
Eurobond market, 66–9
  downside, 67–9

  reasons for, 67
Eurobonds (international bonds), 62–3
  vs euro bonds, 62
Eurocurrency market, 36–40
  LIBOR, 39–40
Eurodollar market, 36–40
European markets, energy markets, 226–7
ex store, delivery, 170
exchange for futures or physicals (EFP),
  delivery, 171
exchange limits, commodities markets, 187, 188
exchange-rate quotations
  brokers, foreign exchange, 78–9
  conventions, 80–1
  cross rates, 81–2
  cross trades, 81–2
  direct dealing, 78
  electronic brokering systems, 79
  foreign exchange market, 77–82
  market conventions, 80–1
  quoting conventions, 80–1
  US dollar role, 79–80
exchange rates
  balance of payments, 83–4
  banks, 85–6
  CBs, 85–6
  defining, 75
  determinants, 82–6
  employment level, 83
  fundamental approach, 82–4
  GDP, 82–3
  interest rate, 83
  liquidity, 84–5
  moral suasion, 85–6
  politics, 85
  productivity, 82–3
  short-term approach, 84–5
exchanges, financial see financial exchanges
exercising futures options, 145–8
exotics, foreign exchange market, 93
expiration dates, stock markets, 122

fair value forward rates, foreign exchange
  market, 91–2
Fannie Mae see Federal National Mortgage
  Association
Farm Credit System (FCS), US agency bonds, 59
FAS see free alongside ship
fast markets, futures contracts, 138–9
FCS see Farm Credit System

Federal Home Loan Bank System (FHLBS),
  US agency bonds, 59
Federal Home Loan Mortgage Corporation
  (Freddie Mac), US agency bonds, 59
Federal National Mortgage Association (Fannie
  Mae), US agency bonds, 59
FHLBS *see* Federal Home Loan Bank System
fill or kill (FOK), futures contracts, 138
financial exchanges
  see also stock markets
  counterparty risk, 16–17
  energy markets, 209–10
  financial markets, 15–17
  futures, 149–52
  global markets, 2–8
  vs OTC markets, 15–17, 113–15
  price information, 16
  services, 15–17
  SETS system, 18, 114
  standards, 15–16
  technological change, 17–21
financial futures, futures contracts, 125
financial markets, 1–30
  financial exchanges, 15–17
  global markets, 2–8
  liquidity drivers, 9–13
  new, 25–8
  new financial markets, 25–8
  OTC markets, 15–17
  post-trade processing, 21–3
  retail/wholesale brokerage, 23–5
  structure, 1–30
  technological change, 17–21
fixed-income derivatives
  global markets, 7–8
  repos, 13
fixed-term deposits, 34
flex options, stock markets, 122
FOB *see* free on board
foreign exchange advisory services, foreign
  exchange market, 93–4
foreign exchange market, 75–97
  back office, 94
  banks, 76–7, 78
  covered interest arbitrage, 90–1
  covered interest differential, 90
  currency swap rates, 88–9
  defining, 76
  exchange rate definition, 75
  exchange rate quotations, 77–82
  exchange rates determinants, 82–6

exotics, 93
fair value forward rates, 91–2
foreign exchange advisory services, 93–4
forward desk, 92–3
forward discount, 88–9
forward premium, 88–9
forwards markets, 87–92
front office, 93–4
interbank market, 76–7
interest-rate parity, 89–90
LVTS, 87
middle office, 94
spot desk, 92–3
spot market, 86–7
structure, foreign exchange operation, 92–5
turnover, 75–6
foreign exchange turnover, global markets, 5–6
forward-based derivatives, history, 126–8
forward contracts, energy markets, 223
forward desk, foreign exchange market, 92–3
forward discount, foreign exchange market,
  88–9
forward premium, foreign exchange market,
  88–9
forwards markets
  see also futures markets
  backwardation, 177–84
  commodities markets, 169–70
  contango, 177–84
  foreign exchange market, 87–92
  hedging, 92
  liquidity, 171–4
  no-arbitrage condition, 182–4
  spot-forward pricing relationships, 177–84
Freddie Mac *see* Federal Home Loan Mortgage
  Corporation
free alongside ship (FAS), delivery, 171
free on board (FOB), delivery, 170–1
freight-rate swaps, energy markets, 235
front office, foreign exchange market, 93–4
FTSE, 100 index contracts, futures contracts,
  142–7
funding, liquidity, 11
future, energy trading, 236–9
futures contracts, 125, 128–42
  see also futures markets
  best efforts, 137
  buying, 133
  call options, 144
  characteristics, 129–32
  commodity futures, 125

futures contracts *(continued)*
  daily trading limits, 130–2
  defining, 125
  delivery, 135–7
  exercising futures options, 145–8
  fast markets, 138–9
  fill or kill (FOK), 138
  financial futures, 125
  FTSE, 100 index contracts, 142–7
  good 'til cancelled (GTC), 137
  hedging, 155–60
  interest rates insurance, 148–9
  leverage, 140
  limit order, 138
  long hedge, 158–60
  maintenance margin, 139, 153–5
  margin, 153–5
  margin requirements, 139
  market if touched (MIT), 138
  market on close (MOC), 137
  market on open (MOO), 137
  market order, 137
  marking-to-market, 139, 153–5
  offsetting transaction, 132, 133–5
  options, 142–9, 212–14
  order types, 137–9
  put options, 144
  settlement, 132–7
  settlement by delivery, 135–7
  short hedge, 155–7
  spread order, 138
  stop order, 138
  types, 125
  worked order, 137
futures markets, 125–66
  see also forwards markets; futures contracts
  auction process, 149–52
  backwardation, 177–84
  characteristics, 129–32
  clearing associations, 132, 152–3
  commodities markets, 169–70
  contango, 177–84
  daily trading limits, 130–2
  energy markets, 208–9
  financial exchanges, 149–52
  futures exchanges, 149–52
  growth, 165–6
  hedging, 155–60
  history, 126–8
  liquidity, 142, 171–4
  managed accounts, 163–4

  managed funds, 163–4
  managed futures investors, 163–4
  no-arbitrage condition, 182–4
  quotations, 140–2
  speculators, 160–3
  spot-forward pricing relationships, 177–84
  top, 15 futures exchanges, 127
  trading costs, 142

GDP *see* gross domestic product
Ginnie Mae *see* Government National Mortgage
  Association futures
global markets, 2–8
  commodity derivatives, 8
  currency derivatives, 8
  equity derivatives, 7–8
  financial exchanges, 2–8
  financial markets, 2–8
  fixed-income derivatives, 7–8
  foreign exchange turnover, 5–6
  global debt markets, 4
  key statistics, 3
  market capitalization of bonds, 4–5
  OTC derivatives, 6
  OTC markets, 2–8
  terminology, 2–8
GNMA *see* Government National Mortgage
  Association futures
gold
  commodities markets, 173–7
  gold lease rates, 176, 182–4
  as reserve asset, 175–7, 182–4
good 'til cancelled (GTC), futures contracts, 137
government bond market, 64–5
  primary market, 64
  repo market, 64
  secondary market, 64
  when-issued market, 64
government bonds
  bond markets, 54–8
  country characteristics, 54–8
  country yield curves, 55–8
  off-the-run securities, 58
  on-the-run securities, 58
Government National Mortgage Association
  futures (GNMA or "Ginnie Mae"), 128
grains and oilseeds, commodities markets, 168
green trading
  energy markets, 232–5
  Kyoto protocol, 232–3

gross domestic product (GDP), exchange rates,
   82–3
GTC *see* good 'til cancelled

hedging
   commodities markets, 173
   energy markets, 214–20
   foreign exchange market, 92
   forwards markets, 92
   futures markets, 155–60
   liquidity, 173
   long hedge, 158–60
   short hedge, 155–7
historical experience, commodities markets,
   184–7
history
   forward-based derivatives, 126–8
   futures markets, 126–8
Hunt brothers, commodities markets, 185–7
Hutchingson, Benjamin, commodities
   markets, 184

IDBs *see* inter-dealer brokers
in store, delivery, 170
index options, stock markets, 121
indices, stock markets, 106–7
initial public offerings (IPOs), stock markets,
   99, 111–12
institutional investors
   bond markets, 52
   long-term, 52
   mixed horizon, 52
   short-term, 52
inter-dealer brokers (IDBs), bond markets, 53
interbank market
   'continuous', 77
   'decentralized', 76–7
   'double auction', 77
   foreign exchange market, 76–7
   LIBOR, 39–40, 77
   'open bid', 77
intercommodity spreads, speculators, 162–3
interest rate
   exchange rates, 83
   money markets, 32–3
interest rate markets, 31
interest rate parity, foreign exchange market,
   89–90
interest rate risk, money market securities, 40–1

interest rate swaps, OTC markets, 17
interest rates insurance, futures contracts, 148–9
intermarket spreads, speculators, 163
intermediaries, bond markets, 51–2, 73
international bonds (Eurobonds), 62–3
   Eurobond market, 66–9
international markets, deposits and loans, 36–40
intramarket spreads, speculators, 162
investment banks, bond markets, 51–2
investors, bond markets, 73
IPOs *see* initial public offerings
issuers, bond markets, 73

key statistics, global markets, 3
Kyoto protocol
   energy markets, 232–3
   green trading, 232–3

Large Value Transfer System (LVTS), foreign
   exchange market, 87
leverage
   futures contracts, 140
   repos, 12
   stock markets, 117–18
LIBOR *see* London Interbank Offered Rate
LIFFE *see* London International Financial
   Futures Exchange
limit order
   futures contracts, 138
   stock markets, 114
limited liability, common stock characteristics,
   102–3
limits, daily trading, futures markets, 130–2
liquidation, common stock characteristics,
   101–2
liquidity
   automated trading systems, 9–10
   collapse, 15
   commodities markets, 171–4
   defining, 13–14, 171
   differences, 10
   drivers, 9–13
   EUREX, 10
   exchange rates, 84–5
   forwards markets, 171–4
   funding, 11
   futures markets, 142, 171–4
   hedging, 173
   LIFFE, 10

liquidity *(continued)*
    repos, 11–13
    risk, 10–13
    risk management, 13–15
    risk, money market securities, 41
    value-at-risk (VaR), 14–15
livestock, commodities markets, 168
loans
    see also deposits and loans
    to businesses, 34–5
locals, speculators, 160
London Interbank Offered Rate (LIBOR),
    39–40
London International Financial Futures
    Exchange (LIFFE)
    liquidity, 10
    stock markets, 121–3
    technological change, 19
long hedge, futures contracts, 158–60
long-term institutional investors, bond markets, 52
LVTS *see* Large Value Transfer System
Lyon, John, commodities markets, 185

maintenance margin
    futures contracts, 139, 153–5
    stock markets, 118–19
managed accounts, futures markets, 163–4
managed funds, futures markets, 163–4
managed futures investors, futures markets,
    163–4
margin, futures contracts, 153–5
margin requirements, futures contracts, 139
market capitalization, common stock
    characteristics, 105–6
market capitalization of bonds, global markets,
    4–5
market conventions
    bond markets, 69, 70
    exchange-rate quotations, 80–1
market if touched (MIT), futures contracts, 138
market impact, stock markets, 117
market maker, secondary market, 109–10
market makers, bond markets, 53
market making, bond markets, 51–2
market mechanics, stock markets, 110
market on close (MOC), futures contracts, 137
market on open (MOO), futures contracts, 137
market order
    futures contracts, 137
    stock markets, 114

market professionals, bond markets, 52–3
marketability, money markets, 33
markets, global *see* global markets
marking-to-market, futures contracts, 139,
    153–5
matched market, secondary market, 109
metals, commodities markets, 168, 173–7,
    187–96
middle office, foreign exchange
    market, 94
MIT *see* market if touched
mixed horizon institutional investors, bond
    markets, 52
MOC *see* market on close
money market, bond markets, 63
money market securities, 40–5
    BAs, 43–4
    certificates of deposit, 45
    commercial paper, 42–3
    credit risk, 41
    interest-rate risk, 40–1
    liquidity risk, 41
    Treasury bills, 41–2
money markets, 31–47
    call features, 33
    characteristics of instruments, 32–3
    deposits and loans, 33–40
    interest rate, 32–3
    loans and deposits, 33–40
    marketability, 33
    money market securities, 40–5
    principal, 32
    put features, 33
    security, 33
    term, 32
MOO *see* market on open
moral suasion, CBs, 85–6
municipal bonds
    bond markets, 59–60
    credit risk, 72–3

NASDAQ, technological change, 19–20
netting, post-trade processing, 21–3
new financial markets, 25–8
    asset-backed securities, 26
    CDOs, 26–8
    credit derivatives market, 28
    secondary loan market, 27–8
    structured notes, 25–6
    syndicated loan market, 27–8

no-arbitrage condition
    commodities markets, 182–4
    forwards markets, 182–4
    futures markets, 182–4
notice deposits, 33–4

off-the-run securities, government bonds, 58
offer price, bond markets, 53
offsetting transaction, futures contracts, 132,
    133–5
on-the-run securities, government bonds, 58
'open bid', interbank market, 77
option contracts, energy markets, 223
options
    energy markets, 212–14
    futures contracts, 142–9, 212–14
order types, futures contracts, 137–9
origination, bond markets, 52
over-the-counter (OTC) markets
    counterparty risk, 16–17
    derivatives, 6, 222–9
    energy markets, 222–9
    vs financial exchanges, 15–17, 113–15
    financial markets, 15–17
    global markets, 2–8
    interest-rate swaps, 17
    Platts, 224–5
    price information, 16
    technological change, 17–21
overnight repos, 35

percentage margin, stock markets, 118
physical delivery, energy markets, 220–2
Platts
    energy markets, 224–5
    OTC markets, 224–5
politics, exchange rates, 85
position limits, stock markets, 122–3
position traders, speculators, 161
post-trade processing, 21–3
    comparison/confirmation, 21–3
    financial markets, 21–3
    netting, 21–3
    settlement, 21–3
preference shares, common stock
    characteristics, 104–5
price drivers, commodities, 197
price information
    financial exchanges, 16

OTC markets, 16
primary market
    bond markets, 63
    Government bond market, 64
    stock markets, 111–13
principal, money markets, 32
private offer, bond markets, 63
private placements, stock markets, 111–13
proprietary traders, bond markets, 53
public offer
    bond markets, 63
    stock markets, 111–12
put features, money markets, 33
put options, futures contracts, 144

quotations, futures markets, 140–2
quoting conventions, exchange-rate quotations,
    80–1

RefCorp *see* Resolution Funding Corporation
regulation, commodities markets, 184–7
regulators, bond markets, 63–4
release-of-property clause, corporate
    bonds, 61
repo cost, stock markets, 119–21
repo market, Government bond market, 64
repos, 35–6
    fixed-income derivatives, 13
    leverage, 12
    liquidity, 11–13
    overnight repos, 35
    reverse repos, 12–13, 35
    'shorting' of securities, 12–13
    uses, 12
repurchase agreements *see* repos
reserve asset, gold as, 175–7, 182–4
Resolution Funding Corporation (RefCorp), US
    agency bonds, 59
retail banks, bond markets, 51
retail/wholesale brokerage, 23–5
    financial markets, 23–5
returns distributions, commodities markets,
    196–7
reverse repos, 12–13
risk
    counterparty risk, 16–17
    credit risk, bond markets, 69–73
    credit risk, corporate bonds, 69–73
    credit risk, money market securities, 41

risk *(continued)*
 energy markets, 206–7
 liquidity, 10–13
risk decomposition, commodities markets, 187–96
risk management
 commodities markets, 187–96
 liquidity, 13–15

Sallie Mae *see* Student Loan Marketing Association
scalpers, speculators, 160
seasoned new issues (SNIs), stock markets, 111
secondary loan market, 27–8
secondary market
 bond markets, 63
 Government bond market, 64
 market maker, 109–10
 matched market, 109
 stock markets, 109–10, 113–15
security, money markets, 33
SETS system, financial exchanges, 18, 114
SETSmm system, 18
settlement
 commodities markets, 170–1
 futures contracts, 132–7
 post-trade processing, 21–3
settlement by delivery, futures contracts, 135–7
share premium, common stock characteristics, 102–3
shareholders' rights, common stock characteristics, 103–4
short hedge, futures contracts, 155–7
short sales, stock markets, 119–21
short squeezes, commodities markets, 184–7
short-term approach, exchange rates, 84–5
short-term institutional investors, bond markets, 52
'shorting' of securities, repos, 12–13
silver squeeze, commodities markets, 185–7
Singapore market, energy markets, 225–6
single stock options, stock markets, 121
sinking funds, corporate bonds, 60–1
SNIs *see* seasoned new issues
softs, commodities markets, 168
speculative trading, energy markets, 236
speculators
 calendar spreads, 162
 commodity product spreads, 163
 day traders, 160–1

futures markets, 160–3
intercommodity spreads, 162–3
intermarket spreads, 163
intramarket spreads, 162
locals, 160
position traders, 161
scalpers, 160
spreaders, 161–3
TED spreads, 162–3
time spreads, 162
spot commodity markets, commodities markets, 169–70
spot desk, foreign exchange market, 92–3
spot-forward pricing relationships
 commodities markets, 177–84
 forwards markets, 177–84
 futures markets, 177–84
spot market, foreign exchange market, 86–7
spread order, futures contracts, 138
spreaders, speculators, 161–3
squeezes, commodities markets, 184–7
standards, financial exchanges, 15–16
stock-borrowing costs, stock markets, 119–21
stock exchanges *see* financial exchanges
stock markets, 99–123
 Alternative Investment Market, 100
 bid-offer spread, 116
 buying on margin, 117–19
 CBOE, 121–3
 characteristics, 99–108
 commissions, 115–17
 common stock characteristics, 101–8
 corporate actions, 122
 derivatives, 121–3
 dividends, 122
 expiration dates, 122
 financial exchanges vs OTC market, 15–17, 113–15
 flex options, 122
 index options, 121
 indices, 106–7
 IPOs, 99, 111–12
 leverage, 117–18
 LIFFE, 121–3
 limit order, 114
 maintenance margin, 118–19
 market impact, 117
 market mechanics, 110
 market order, 114
 participants, 108–10
 percentage margin, 118

stock markets *(continued)*
   position limits, 122–3
   primary market, 111–13
   private placements, 111–13
   public offer, 111–12
   purposes, 99–100
   repo cost, 119–21
   secondary market, 109–10, 113–15
   short sales, 119–21
   single stock options, 121
   SNIs, 111
   stock-borrowing costs, 119–21
   strike prices, 122
   trading, 123
   trading costs, 115
   up-tick rule, 120
stop order, futures contracts, 138
strike prices, stock markets, 122
structure
   commodities markets, 167–201
   financial markets, 1–30
   foreign exchange operation, 92–5
structured notes, 25–6
Student Loan Marketing Association (Sallie
  Mae), US agency bonds, 59
substitution-of-property clause, corporate
  bonds, 61
swaps
   energy markets, 223–4, 235
   freight-rate swaps, 235
syndicated loan market, 27–8

T-bills *see* Treasury bills
tax, structured notes, 25–6
technological change, 17–21
   convergence, 17–21
   ECNs, 19–21
   EUREX, 19
   financial exchanges, 17–21
   financial markets, 17–21
   LIFFE, 19
   NASDAQ, 19–20
   OTC markets, 17–21
TED spreads, speculators, 162–3
Tennessee Valley Authority (TVA), US agency
  bonds, 59

term, money markets, 32
terminology, global markets, 2–8
time spreads, speculators, 162
top, 15 futures exchanges, 127
traders
   bond markets, 53
   commodities markets, 169–70
trading
   vs brokerage, 169–70
   stock markets, 123
trading costs
   futures markets, 142
   stock markets, 115
trading limits, daily, futures markets, 130–2
Treasury bills
   credit risk, 72
   money market securities, 41–2
TVA *see* Tennessee Valley Authority

underwriting a new issue, corporate bond
  market, 66
up-tick rule, stock markets, 120
US agency bonds
   bond markets, 59
   Fannie Mae, 59
   FCS, 59
   FHLBS, 59
   Freddie Mac, 59
   RefCorp, 59
   Sallie Mae, 59
   TVA, 59
US dollar role, exchange-rate quotations, 79–80
US markets, energy markets, 228–9

value-at-risk (VaR)
   commodities markets, 187–96
   liquidity, 14–15

weather derivatives, energy markets, 231–2
wheat squeezes, commodities markets, 184, 185
when-issued market, Government bond
  market, 64
wholesale/retail brokerage, 23–5
worked order, futures contracts, 137